Around the Table

Around the Table

Talking Graciously about God

Jonathan P. Case

CASCADE *Books* · Eugene, Oregon

AROUND THE TABLE
Talking Graciously About God

Cascade Books
An Imprint of Wipf and Stock Publishers
199 W. 8th Ave., Suite 3
Eugene, OR 97401

www.wipfandstock.com

PAPERBACK ISBN: 978-1-5326-1645-7
HARDCOVER ISBN: 978-1-4982-4025-3
EBOOK ISBN: 978-1-4982-4024-6

Cataloguing-in-Publication data:

Names: Case, Jonathan P., author.
Title: Around the table : talking graciously about God. / by Jonathan P. Case.
Description: Eugene, OR: Cascade Books, 2019. | Includes bibliographical references and index.
Identifiers: ISBN 978-1-5326-1645-7 (paperback) | ISBN 978-1-4982-4025-3 (hardcover) | ISBN 978-1-4982-4024-6 (ebook)
Subjects: LCSH: Conversation—Religious aspects—Christianity. | Christianity and other religions. | Christianity and atheism.
Classification: BV601.8 C17 2019 (paperback) | BV601.8 (ebook)

Manufactured in the U.S.A.   06/10/19

For my Dad, who taught me to love good conversation
and storytelling

Contents

Acknowledgments

I suppose every author feels like *I'm glad that's finally over* when a project comes to close. I feel like that now, but of course none of this is really over—I've just stopped writing. The writing has been the easy part; the hard part is learning to live out all the things I pretend to understand.

But I do have heaps of people to thank. Chris Spinks at Cascade Books has been supernaturally patient with my lame excuses for *yet one more* delay. I'm grateful to Steve Dunmire (director of Church Relations at Houghton) for inviting me to present an early version of chapter 2 several years ago at a regional pastors' conference, and to J. Richard Middleton and the organizers of "Evangelical Theology: New Challenges, New Opportunities" at Northeastern Seminary (October 2017) for allowing me to present a shortened version of chapter 4 (on the New and Newer Atheists). Several of my students at Houghton also contributed their valuable time in reading and commenting on the early drafts: Ben Murphy, Lex Dakin, Bethany Kuiken, and the snarkiest and best assistant I've ever had, Holly Chaisson (who I miss dearly). I also must thank my *old* friend Andy Johnson (Nazarene Theological Seminary) for taking the time to read sections of the manuscript and give me candid advice.

And then, above all people on this planet, I have to thank my daughter Carolyn and wife Miriam for putting up with my endless theological rambling and talking through issues aloud in the car and around the dinner table. That didn't start with the writing of this book, of course, but it certainly worsened as the writing continued! Carolyn, a master of the art of verbal jiu-jitsu, knows how to both shut me down and crack me up, while Miriam knows exactly when to leave me alone while I'm working out a theological horn stuck in my gut, when to tackle me, and when to tell me to put down the books, grab my fly rod, and get out on the river before I drive everyone crazy. She helped enormously with proofreading and formatting the manuscript, but in the grand scheme of things, that pales in comparison to all that she does. I don't know how I'd get through this life without her.

My dad never understood what I do for a living; academia was an alien world to him. He was a truck driver, a mechanic, and a machinist, but he read voraciously, loved good conversation, and told the most outrageous (and lavishly embellished) stories you ever heard. Toward the end of his life, he told me that he was learning to love people even if they didn't love him in return. This work is dedicated to the memory of that grand old man.

Pentecost Sunday, 2018

Abbreviations

LW   *Luther's Works*
Works   *The Works of John Wesley*

Introduction

Can We Talk?

What This Book Is About

Several years ago, my wife, daughter, and I decided to stay away from an annual family reunion. This was an extended family reunion: siblings, aunts and uncles, cousins and shirttail relations, in-laws (and outlaws), and even some friends of the family would all be attending. Our work schedules would have allowed us to attend, we were all in good health, and we hadn't made holiday plans over reunion weekend by mistake. We decided to skip out because the previous year's reunion had been racked by tension over a host of culture war issues (all the usual suspects: healthcare reform, climate change, immigration, same-sex relationships). During the previous year's reunion, what should have been a happy, back-slapping time of reconnecting with friends and relatives descended into alternating periods of sharp exchanges and awkward silences around the picnic tables, with some people quietly excusing themselves and others firing off cheap shots toward their favorite political or religious targets.

When people dragged God and the Bible into the discussions, things only got worse. You know the kinds of statements: "Well, *my* Bible says . . ." when the Bible says nothing of the sort. "You can't be a Christian and believe . . ." when thoughtful Christians line up on both sides of an issue. No one cared to listen to me, of course, since I'm a professional theologian. I came home that year frazzled and scratching my head over what it would take for people to talk through contentious issues, especially those issues that concern theology, or simply, God-talk. God-talk makes most of our conversations more difficult.

This book comes out of a sense of pain and bewilderment as I've wrestled with this question: How can we talk graciously about God, especially in view of our disagreements? Through the years I've served as pastor, missionary, and (currently) professor of theology. Much of what I do in the classroom is help students from various positions on the theological spectrum—from Roman Catholics to independent Baptists to nones—gain perspective on their positions, think about what's at stake, and consider carefully how to navigate the disagreements they have with each other. As someone who stands in the Wesleyan-Methodist tradition, my theological DNA is irenic, and in this book I don't pretend to solve actual theological problems. I'm interested in aerial-view or big-picture questions about the kinds of disagreements we have with three different groups of people: other Christians, members of other faiths, and atheists and agnostics. Sometimes we're so caught up in the heat of the moment, with misperceptions and accusations flying about, that we lose perspective on what our disagreements are really about. In a nutshell, this book is about questioning the questions, and questioning our conversational stance when we attempt to offer answers.

Other authors have addressed some of my concerns, of course. Richard Mouw's *Uncommon Decency: Christian Decency in an Uncivil World* emphasizes the importance of maintaining Christian civility and developing conversational skills in a fractured and divisive world. Rob Bell's *What We Talk About When We Talk About God* is a provocative (if a bit fluffy) piece about the oddness of God-talk in an age that seems increasingly dissatisfied with conventional answers given by the church. Francis Spufford's *Unapologetic: Why, Despite Everything, Christianity Can Still Make Surprising Emotional Sense* offers a brilliant and witty rendering of Christianity's legitimacy in public discourse and its capacity to speak to human beings' deepest emotions and needs. Finally, Os Guinness's *Fools Talk: Recovering the Art of Christian Persuasion* attempts to revive the persuasive art of Christian apologetics, although in my view it dismisses too blithely serious questions posed both by members of other religions and our atheist critics, and of course it doesn't address the situation of Christians disagreeing theologically amongst themselves.

What's largely missing from books like these are conceptual tools that help us gain the big-picture view I'm talking about, tools that enable us to see the forest for the trees. So in this book I explore questions such as:

Why and how our conversations over heated theological issues tend to break down.

Why all arguments between Christians about God don't carry the same weight, and why Christian unity has to be based on more than doctrinal unity.

Why our conversations with people of other faiths stall precisely over the question of salvation "through Christ alone," and why we should affirm a providential role for the world's religions.

Why all agnostics and atheists are not the same, and why our apologetics attempts often miss the boat entirely with these people.

Why our aims in these various conversations should be different, given our different conversation partners.

These are the sorts of questions that keep me up at night, and in this book I attempt to piece together an aerial perspective on the issues we argue about in a way that helps reduce the temperature in the room and enables us to talk with each other more thoughtfully and graciously. The importance of being able to do so in these times shouldn't be lost on anyone.

Talk Talk Talk

I can hear it coming already: talk is cheap. We constantly hear the complaint about politicians and clergy that they're all talk. If anything, we're told that we need more action and less talk. When it comes to Christian love, I couldn't agree more. We *blah-blah-blah* way too much about the gospel and fail spectacularly to enact it. But talking is rarely a matter of merely sharing what we think or feel about something. We talk with others and about others and about what those others believe. Our talk can encourage or discourage, heal or wound, bless or curse, calm or incite. Every major political decision to take action has been preceded by talk, and the effects of that action are usually spin-doctored to death by more talk. From international conflicts to discussions amongst family and friends, knowing how to talk to each other remains one of the most important skills we can have. I used to joke that we never talked about three things in my family: religion, politics, and everything else. That was a joke. Sort of.

In a world where caricaturing one's opponents and shouting people down often carries the day (as one politician infamously put it, "Never retreat; instead reload"), some folks would say that reflection on the different types of conversation we have (talking about talking) is an indulgence few people can afford. Real-world problems demand that we ram our agenda through by any means necessary: the fate of the nation, church, or world (or all three) is at stake! But this "real world" argument itself is part of the problem. Anyone with real-world experience knows that settling issues by majority vote never settles issues and that you never convince anyone by sheer volume, misrepresenting their position, or flat-out lying about them. These short-term "solutions" in the end serve only to alienate people. The other problem with this position is that it's not Christian. God doesn't temporarily suspend our commitment to the Golden Rule and give us license to use whatever means necessary because we're convinced we have the truth, or because we're dealing with people we consider enemies because they disagree with us.

In the digital age, the sheer nastiness directed toward anyone who disagrees with us has reached dizzying levels. Digimodern theorist Alan Kirby paints a familiar picture of internet rancor. When I read the following description, I think of the jagged-edged online theological discussions in which I've participated.

> One individual locked in a tiny room sitting at a computer screen typing out their irritation, projecting their bile into the atmosphere; and fifteen miles away a stranger doing the same; and five hundred miles away another, and so on, around the world. All of these streams of rancor and loathing then coalesce in the sky into a thin cloud of black and shallow dislike, and fall gently but dishearteningly to earth. None of the projectors is aware of any other: they spew in a void, and the contents of their irked guts are displayed potentially to everyone forever. I'd argue that this tends to be the pattern of Internet forums in general.[1]

If Kirby is right, then one of the downsides to this new textuality called digimodernism is the proliferation of trolls (people who disrupt conversations with extremist or "hater" comments). I shouldn't be shocked by now, but I'm still amazed by how many online arguments, over issues you ordinarily wouldn't consider all that controversial, end with variations on a common social media benediction: "Fuck you and die." The human race has never been without trolls, but now we possess the technological means at our fingertips to amplify our trollish tendencies. Theological trolls number amongst the worst, and I hope that, at a minimum, this book would help us become a bit less trollish. But that's a bare minimum. Is it possible for us to become more gracious, deliberative conversation partners whilst bringing the full weight of Christian conviction into our conversations? That's what I'm really after.

Before laying out how I mean to break down and tackle my central concerns, I'm going to offer a few reflections on why talking about God in our present national and global contexts is so tricky, and what we might reasonably hope from conversation, given different discussion partners. Following that, I'll try to flesh out the central metaphor that holds this book together: that of sitting around the picnic table and talking at a family

1. Kirby, *Digimodernism*, 107.

reunion. Then I'll wrap things up by explaining where I'm coming from theologically, and what to expect in the following chapters.

Political Rhetoric: It's the Worst!

Given the massive political divide currently afflicting the United States, talking graciously about nearly anything is becoming a lost art. In the world of guns and trumpets, political discourse gears itself toward anything but genuine conversation. We refer to the public form of discussion amongst politicians as debate, which should mean something like principled argumentation designed to convince others of your position (surely a laudable aim of conversation). But, while having the semblance of vigorous and open debate, the majority of political debates are a waste of time in terms of real conversation. No matter how well or poorly a candidate performed during a debate, even a casual political observer can predict with near 100-percent accuracy the blinkered post-debate commentary from the Right and the Left. In other words, public political discussions as a means of learning anything or changing minds are almost worthless, and these United States presently suffer from politicians' inability to engage in anything resembling a genuine conversation. Most of us who have memory stretching back farther than a few decades would be hard-pressed to name a time in which political discourse was so debased. The old ideals of statesmanship (even if they were largely ideals) have gone by the boards.

This book is not about politics; it's about God-talk. However, I bring up the example of political debate for this reason: I'm convinced that the more we come to imitate the rhetorical gamesmanship of our elected officials, the worse shape we'll be in as a church. In this country, where politics and religion often slide seamlessly into one another, theologically liberal and conservative churches can barely talk to each other without lapsing into abusive *ad hominem* arguments, engaging in slander, or dropping the h-bomb (heresy!) on each other. Some churches, of course, unashamedly align themselves wholesale with one side or the other of the culture wars, to the point that they seem like little more than ecclesiastical extensions of the Republican or Democratic parties, all the while forgetting that the one, holy, catholic, and apostolic church possesses its own idiom irreducible to modern political cant.

We're Talking Not Merely Amongst Ourselves

If this were strictly an inbred American conversation, it would be bad enough. But the American church increasingly finds itself a marginalized player within the context of global Christianity. Philip Jenkins noted over a decade ago that, during the last century, the Christian world's center of gravity has shifted southward, to Africa, Asia, and Latin America. "Today the largest Christian communities on the planet are to be found in Africa and Latin America. A 'typical' contemporary Christian may be a woman living in a village in Nigeria or in a Brazilian favela."[2] If we northerners, who share a common history and language, can't talk to each other, how will we ever be able to talk with these southerners (vast numbers of whom are now among us) with whom we share even less culturally?

As if talking to fellow believers isn't difficult enough, the stakes are even higher when you consider talking to members of other religions. American Christians' ignorance of the rudiments of other religious traditions often results in disturbing stereotypes, caricatures, and even violence. Many liberals hold that all religions say the same thing; many conservatives point out the differences, but often don't understand them, and those that do frequently interpret them as a threat. Both perspectives render conversation superfluous or almost impossible. As Stephen Prothero puts it,

> What we need on this furiously religious planet is a realistic view of where religious rivals clash, and where they can cooperate. Approaching this volatile topic from this new angle may be scary. But the world is what it is. And both tolerance and respect are empty virtues until we actually know something about whomever it is we are supposed to be tolerating or respecting.[3]

With religious differences often at the root of violent clashes around the world, many of our fiercest critics see religion and its "totalizing discourse" itself as the real problem. As careful as authors such as Mark Juergensmeyer[4] or William Cavanaugh[5] might be when nuancing the relationship between religion and violence, ham-fisted agnostic and atheist critiques, such as those offered by Christopher Hitchens,[6] Richard Dawkins,[7] and Sam Harris,[8] con-

---

2. Jenkins, *Next Christendom*, 1–2.

3. Prothero, *God is Not One*, 4–5.

4. Juergensmeyer, *Terror in the Mind of God.*

5. Cavanaugh, *Myth of Religious Violence.*

6. Hitchens, *God is Not Great.*

7. Dawkins, *God Delusion.*

8. Harris, *End of Faith.*

tinue to exert considerable influence on the public imagination. Religious people, our critics say, tend to be scientifically and morally arrogant, and perhaps primed for religious violence on account of their unquestioned beliefs in divinely revealed truths about the origin, order, and end of this world. Even if you are religious, it's hard to not see the point. When talking with people shaped by these new atheists and agnostics, we need an orientation toward conversation that's different from our orientation toward other Christians or members of other religions, and we should be honest about our expectations in these conversations.

What Can We Hope from Conversation?

In graduate school, I studied the works of the philosopher Hans-Georg Gadamer, and in my more idealistic moments I'm still drawn to the way he describes, perhaps a bit naively, what genuine conversation looks like:

> A conversation is a process of two people understanding each other. Thus it is a characteristic of every true conversation that each opens himself to the other person, truly accepts his point of view as worthy of consideration and gets inside the other to such an extent that he understands not a particular individual, but what he says.[9]

The to-and-fro movement of *play* emerges as one of the central motifs in Gadamer's analysis. Similar to the experience of playing a game in which you lose all sense of time, the mysterious nature of conversation holds us sway in a reality that seems to overwhelm us. It happens almost effortlessly.[10] Taking Gadamer's description to the extreme, you might picture sitting round the pub with your mates through the wee hours of the morning, losing all sense of time as you surrender to the effortless to-and-fro of the conversation. Passion, wittiness, and sharp jabs abound as you banter about everything from sports to movies to music to office politics, but it's all good fun and carried out in good will. Who doesn't live for these kinds of conversations?

Do most of our conversations proceed like this, however? In the academic, egg-heady world I inhabit, two contemporary philosophers in particular, Juergen Habermas and Jacques Derrida, have kicked the legs out from any rosy understanding of how we actually communicate. While mutual understanding remains the goal, Habermas demonstrates how various levels of power always condition our attempts at communication, and

9. Gadamer, *Truth and Method*, 347.

10. Gadamer, *Truth and Method*, 94, 98.

how the very language we use is frequently systematically distorted so as to marginalize or even silence dialogue partners.[11] Derrida muddies the water even further by revealing how the slipperiness of language itself constantly trips us up as the hard and fast distinctions we rely on dissolve or "deconstruct" themselves.[12]

You might think these discussions are a bit rarefied, but most of us recognize on-the-ground conversations in which the balance of power is anything but equal. We're often expected to say buzzwords or phrase things a certain way, or to avoid particular questions or topics at all costs, since we already know what the other person will say in response to delicate questions. These pressures prevent people from having real conversations. We frequently follow, to varying degrees, scripts in order to maintain order or position, and we've all experienced those times when no matter how hard we tried to explain our position, the meaning we were aiming for slipped further and further away the harder we tried to make ourselves clear. So, while explaining the ins and outs of Habermas or Derrida would fall outside the scope of this book, their core insights throw a little cold water on us and remind us that it's impossible to enter into conversations with others on an absolutely level playing field and/or to predict how things will go. We shouldn't expect all conversations to go or end the same way.

Getting clear about our expectations in conversations can save us loads of frustration. In Paul Varo Martinson's book *Families of Faith*, he describes four levels of dialogue.[13] Low-level dialogue is the basic activity of getting to know something about each other, maybe chatting across the backyard fence or on the footpath or in the supermarket. Mid-level dialogue attempts genuine understanding of each other, perhaps through engaging in cooperative efforts like community projects or local government. This level involves empathy: trying to put yourself in your conversation partner's shoes and seeing what things look like from her perspective. High-level dialogue is where the deepest sharing, out of mutual trust, becomes possible; in other words, friendship. Most of our conversations with people never reach this level, even if many people crave these relationships, and it's uncomfortable when someone tries to jump levels before you're ready, or you've tried to move to this level before your conversation partner is ready. Yet, Martinson says, beyond these forms is the kind of relationship that Jesus had with people. "It is a relationship defined on the Christian side by self-expenditure

11. See Habermas, *Communication and the Evolution of Society*.

12. See Derrida, *Dissemination* and *Margins of Philosophy*.

13. Martinson, *Families of Faith*, 199–201.

for the sake of the other, a self-giving for the other's sake, regardless of how we might agree or disagree."[14]

Martinson's four-level taxonomy provides a good reference point for understanding the various levels of conversation, but I suspect that a question in the back of many people's minds as they read this book is whether I'm in love with an unattainable ideal of conversation (perhaps his third or fourth level). In truth, I don't think absolute transparency and trust is possible (or even desirable) with any human being; we always have to reckon with the fact of finitude and its sundry warts. Given the thorny conversations we find ourselves in, and the angularities of our different conversation partners, I'd be happy if what I'm doing in this book could help us approximate the second level (seeing things from someone else's perspective) and nudge us to the brink of the third level (mutual trust and friendship). That would go a long way toward defusing "fighting talk."

In Search of Models and Metaphors

I've tried to think of a helpful model or metaphor that would integrate the various themes in this book, and, as a theologian, I suppose I should come up with something theological (or at least biblical). Theologians' fondness for models and metaphors sometimes glosses over the difference between these two terms. To rely on a classic distinction by philosopher Monroe Beardsley, a model is a precise description of the properties and interactions of whatever we happen to be investigating, with little room left for ambiguity or interpretation. The more precise a model is the better, to the point that it can exercise a kind of prescriptive or controlling function. A metaphor, on the other hand, redescribes something familiar in different terms so we can approach it in a new light, and leaves room for the listener or hearer to creatively fill in some of the details.[15]

Over the past few decades, many people have employed the doctrine of the Trinity as a model for ecclesial fellowship, and it's tempting to drag the relations between Father, Son, and Holy Spirit into this discussion as a model for conversation. For many theologians, I suspect that the inspiration for this way of thinking comes from books like Yale theologian Miroslav Volf's extraordinary *After Our Likeness: The Church as the Image of the Trinity*.[16] But even Volf admits that, while the way we think about God's triune life shapes the scope of Christian thought, there's no easy one-to-one cor-

14. Martinson, *Families of Faith*, 201.
15. Beardsley, "Metaphor," 284–89.
16. Volf, *After Our Likeness*.

respondence or application from the Trinity to our social reality.[17] Any sort of application you might dream up has to be nuanced carefully before it can address our situation in any meaningful sense. I don't mean to discount the power contained in the idea of the triune persons engaged in dialogue, but the divine persons always carry on in complete agreement (the Holy Spirit never says to Father and Son, "That's a terrible idea! I'm outta here!"). Our conversations rarely proceed so precisely or harmoniously, nor should they.

The other problem with developing a trinitarian model of conversation is more of a generic problem in developing theological models: we tend to think that if we just get our theological models correct, our practice will eventually sort itself out. I no longer believe this. I've read too many theological models of this or that recommended to the church through the years and, at the end of the day, people continue to act pretty much the way they want to. Now, of course, belief does shape (or should shape) practice to some degree, but we generally ignore how our habits and practices shape the beliefs we say we would die for.[18] In this book, I'm more concerned with our actual way of talking when confronted by issues that divide us. So, while I'm a committed trinitarian theologian, I'm not convinced that a trinitarian model of conversation helps us when it comes to thinking about the rough-and-tumble talk with ornery Christians, members of other faiths, or snarky atheists or agnostics.

So, if a trinitarian model doesn't prove to be very helpful, then what about a biblical model using examples of conversation in Holy Scripture? People come to expect that way of using Scripture. The problem is that biblical examples for what I'm talking about aren't exactly forthcoming in Scripture. Old Testament kings and prophets generally aren't the kind of people interested in having conversations with people who think differently than they do. In the New Testament, Peter and Paul seem a bit inept when it comes to dealing with disagreements. Most of us aren't kings, prophets, or apostles (even if we act like it sometimes), and trying to speak and act like we are when talking with people who think differently than we do only contributes to the problem. This sort of hermeneutical problem arises every time we try to derive models or principles from the Bible to address problems we're facing by using the behavior of Bible characters who aren't concerned with those problems or questions. Don't say or do what Jephthah did just because it's in the Bible.

So, if neither a trinitarian model nor biblical examples are helpful, what then? My general point of orientation is Jesus' central strategy in his

---

17. Volf, *After Our Likeness*, 191–200.

18. Miller, *Consuming Religion*.

announcement of God's kingdom: love for our opponents. In *Jesus and the Ethics of the Kingdom*, Bruce Chilton and J. I. H. MacDonald characterize the ethos Jesus attempted to cultivate in his disciples in the following clunky manner: "Though members of a group, you must not react with an absence of love towards those whose group loyalties and interests are divergent or opposed."[19] This kingdom's group dynamics aren't centripetal, winding us up into exclusivity or defensiveness, but centrifugal, spinning us out and opening us up to others in a way that reflects God's hospitality extended to all people. In encountering opposition, Jesus calls his followers to remain true to this vision of the kingdom, so when we butt heads with our opponents, we don't even think about cursing them, but instead try to radiate *shalom*.[20]

If there's a single image from the New Testament where this ethic seems particularly fitting, and one that I'd like to play with and tease out as the central metaphor in this book, it would be Jesus' table fellowship, a right messy affair. Jesus ate dinner with those devoted to him and those who denied and betrayed him, those who enjoyed him and those who were trying to trip him up, and in one of his parables he calls for those people on the margins you would never invite to a banquet to come and have a seat at the table. In Jesus' vision of the kingdom of God in its fullness, people from all four directions in the earth will take their seats at the great feast, while the chosen (those who always excluded the gentiles) will themselves be excluded (Matt 8:10–12; Luke 13:29). Craig Blomberg even calls Jesus' table fellowship "enacted prophecy" of the kingdom's surprising inclusions.[21] (I'm not, by the way, suggesting that we use the sacrament of Lord's Supper as a means for including members of other faiths, or agnostics and atheists, but even the Orthodox share bread with non-Orthodox.)

To be clear, what I have in mind is not a work of hard exegesis, because (exhortations to love and peacefulness aside) the Bible doesn't give us detailed digressions on how to carry out a nuanced theological conversation with those who disagree with us. But I *am* attempting to tease out a biblical image in such a way that I believe to be true to the central theological and ethical trajectory of the gospel. So, if I can play with this metaphor a bit and return to my family reunion failure at the beginning of this chapter, I'm wondering what it would take to morph that nightmare into a vision for the future and then find a way to turn as much of that vision as possible into reality. Even reality-*ish*, as some of my students might say.

19. Chilton and MacDonald, *Jesus and the Ethics of the Kingdom*, 102.
20. Chilton and MacDonald, *Jesus and the Ethics of the Kingdom*, 102.
21. Blomberg, "Jesus, Sinners, and Table Fellowship," 61–62.

I envision an extended family reunion in which four or five picnic tables are pushed together to form one huge table. My mother, daughter of European immigrants, was one of fifteen children, so I have childhood memories of sprawling, boisterous family reunions! Several conversations are going on around the table, some carried out between brothers and sisters who share long histories together, some happening between cousins who haven't seen each other in years, some occurring between blood-relations and new in-laws, and some between family members and outsiders—those odd neighbors who wondered what the commotion was all about and wandered over. Some conversations are heated, others lively but a bit silly, still others awkward between people who don't know each other very well, and someone mentions that old Uncle Angus refuses to come because his nephew Stephen brought his gay friend and Aunt Fiona said she's not coming because there are "too many damned religious fanatics" at this party. (You can bet, however, that she'll want to hear all about what went on at the reunion.)

The complexities people try to navigate in these conversations vary from table to table. Some conversations seem effortless as the beverage of choice flows freely, while other people must navigate generational issues (Uncle Bill holding forth on where the country went wrong), painful personal histories, and lingering mistrust of each other. Still others, no matter how understanding and broad-minded they try to be with family and friends, can't help putting their feet in their mouths and making the situation worse until the conversations go off the rails and they have to try and start again. But what seems to unite everyone is the conviction that these conversations are worth continuing, that staying together and facing whatever comes along together is better than pulling apart, that we might arrive at levels of understanding and empathy (maybe quite by accident!) we hadn't experienced before, and that even some failed attempts have been worth it anyway, given what we've come to learn about each other. This central conviction underscores what I'm trying to do throughout the book.

Granted, this metaphor of a family reunion raises a host of problems when you think about real theological conversations. We all know ingrown families who are suspicious of outsiders. Still less is a metaphor a method, as though conversation could be reduced to a method. But I wager this metaphor still warrants careful reflection. In terms of Christians talking about God, I imagine a series of concentric circles: theological conversations amongst family members include those brothers and sisters in the faith (other Christians), another set of conversations include near and distant cousins (members of other religious traditions) and still other conversations take place with friends and outsiders (agnostics and atheists). As in large family reunions, we should expect messiness and even a bit of chaos. Maybe a good-natured food fight will occasionally break out! Many of these conversations overlap; sometimes a brother or sister finds that they have more in common on a particular issue with a distant cousin or friend than they do with siblings, and sometimes people who disagree radically in terms of their views about God find that their actual practices and lifestyle are hugely similar (which may say something about those views they protect so fiercely).

What I'm describing might sound like an awful lot of work. At several points in writing this book, I kept coming back to swirl around the question, "Why keep talking at all? Especially with difficult people?" The best answer I can come up with is that valuing people lies at the core of the gospel, and at the heart of our relationships with others we find the thrilling, exhausting, and sometimes dangerous roller-coaster ride called conversation. As difficult as it is, in this world of hatred and seemingly endless spirals of revenge, Jesus' call to be peacemakers is a call we ignore, or outright oppose, at our peril. Christ followers should expect to be hated in this world; Jesus said so. But let's be hated for all the right things, and never be the haters.

Where I'm Going and Where I'm Coming From

This metaphor of an extended family reunion structures what I've envisioned for this book. Because conversations about God (with brothers and sisters, in-laws and cousins, and friends and outsiders) often become messy and unstable and go off the rails, I detail the anatomy of a conversational train wreck—or why people desert the table—in chapter 1. Even if you don't agree with my further suggestions in this book, you may recognize elements of what I'm describing as you attempt to talk about God, and then of course it's up to you to find your own way to work through these conversations. In the latter part of the same chapter, I lay out some broad conversational guidelines that can be applied to any of the kinds of conversations amongst those at the table. Chapter 2 deals specifically with conversations between sisters and brothers (other Christians). Why do we find it so difficult to talk to each other about God when we all read the same Bible and worship the same Christ? Chapter 3 looks at conversations with cousins (members of other religions). Do all of these conversations need to have conversion in mind, and if not, then what's the point? What's at stake in these conversations if we admit to a providential role for the world's religions? In chapter 4, I tackle the thorny problem of trying to talk with outsiders (agnostics and atheists) and suggest a few ways that will allow us to talk and live peaceably together. In the concluding chapter, I slip a bit into preacher-mode and ask what it would cost us to take seriously a couple of passages from the Gospels that speak about responding to opposition. But the concluding chapter isn't really my conclusion. Be sure to read the appendix (my Unconcluding Conversational Postscript).

As I've written these chapters, I've tried to maintain an informal tone and minimize specialized theological vocabulary as much as possible. One of my great hopes is that if you have little theological background, you might enjoy the ride to the point where you can take your hands off the handlebars and exclaim, "Look, Mom! I'm doing theology!" At points I'm downright snarky, believing as I do that if you can't occasionally poke fun at religion (especially your own), then you risk becoming an insufferable boor, authoritatively pronouncing judgments on matters finally beyond our feeble grasp of reality. As an academic, much of what I've written in my career amounts to little more than fodder for other academics, but even so I try to adhere to one of the best rules for writing I've ever heard: the more important the issues are, the clearer you need to be. Having said that, sometimes the complexity of an issue can't be reduced beyond a certain point (some things are flat-out complicated) and writers don't render readers any service by offering simplistic solutions to complex questions. Hence, at points I've tried merely to make the complexities clear (if that makes sense), so at least you'll understand why an issue is difficult. As I said, I'm an academic.

Where we end up depends a lot on where we're coming from. My upbringing, and most of my work, has been in conservative evangelical circles in the Wesleyan theological tradition, although in recent years I've been questioning exactly what *evangelical* means anymore. Historically, to be an evangelical has meant a cluster of commitments like having a personal relationship with Jesus Christ, maintaining the authority of the Bible, cultivating discipleship and a holy lifestyle, and carrying out the Great Commission. It's not clear today if most people think that's what being an evangelical means, or if so many cultural and political overtones have been attached to the word that its theological meaning has been lost. In this work, I mean to retain the word in its theological sense, and personally have few qualms about embracing progressive evangelicalism.[22]

My particular strand of the Wesleyan tradition remains heavily influenced by Pietism, and views Christianity as a religion primarily of the heart (as opposed to the head), with an emphasis on practical Christian living over doctrinal correctness. This often leads to anti-intellectualism (and its flip-side, emotionalism) and bloody-minded pragmatism, and in a culture

22. As articulated, for example, in "Confession of Faith."

marked by illiteracy and disinterest in anything that can't be reduced to dollars and cents, my tradition has sometimes mirrored unhelpful cultural trends and tendencies more often than I care to admit. Having gotten that off my chest, Philip Jacob Spener, John Wesley, and other figures in the Pietist tradition realized how disagreements over theological issues led to fractures in the body of Christ, and why it was important to keep doxology and missional concerns central. So, handled with care, I believe that Spener, Wesley, and other Pietist theologians can speak to the conversational problems plaguing the church presently, and along the way, in what follows, I've tried to reinvigorate and incorporate some of their insights.

In this introduction, I've tried to emphasize the aerial-perspective I intend to pursue throughout, but of course no one can avoid giving at least implicit answers to many of the questions we'll look at. And while it's impossible to give definitive answers to theological questions that have puzzled the best minds in history, even the provisional answers we hazard in response to specific questions invariably color the big-picture perspective we construct (so, yes, I do lay my cards on the table occasionally throughout the book). I suspect that my positions will frustrate and perhaps infuriate conservatives and liberals alike, which leads me to believe I'm probably on the right track. One of my favorite authors, John Gierach (who is a fly fisherman and not a theologian) puts it like this: If people don't occasionally walk away from you shaking their heads, you're doing something wrong.[23]

Be Nice, Yes, But Be More Than Nice

This book is more than about being *nice* to each other. Sometimes theologians and philosophers rubbish the term, as though being nice means you're not having a serious conversation or you're compromising on truth in order to get on with someone. In terms of our everyday dealings with people, if nice means something like civility and keeping something as simple as the Golden Rule in mind, then I'm not interested in being the opposite of nice (there's nothing virtuous, after all, about being nasty). But beyond nice, my aim is to explore how we can hold serious, productive conversations and hold to our most cherished convictions and confessions without allowing our talk to turn into an occasion for bitterness and hatred. The alternative of refusing to talk at all seems untenable to me. Silence between people who need to talk about their differences acts as that soil in which suspicions and stereotypes sprout up and flourish, and too often serves as an eerie prelude to violence.

23. Gierach, *Death, Taxes, and Leaky Waders*, 405.

I once heard Spencer Burke at a conference say something to the effect that he looked forward to the day when there's no *us* and *them*, but only *us*. There's a heap of the Holy Spirit and eschatological hope in that comment, but it can be misunderstood in several ways. Certainly in an age in which we've witnessed the terrors of totalitarianisms and collectivisms, only *us* can sound ominously like group-think or, even worse, an attempt to marginalize those who aren't like us. Emphasizing the unity of the body of Christ sometimes results in uniformity, witch hunts, and further fragmenting of the same body! But if only *us* means everyone's invited to join in the fun at the table, then it's a hope worthy of our prayers and hard work.

I

Why People Desert the Table

(And How to Keep Them There)

He stormed into my office unannounced, and didn't bother to introduce himself. I'm guessing late sixties, balding with glasses, brow furrowed—apparently a feral visitor running wild on campus. It's always a risk when you work with your office door open.

"Can I ask you a question?" he growled at me, standing over me as I sat in front of my computer. *Oh boy*, I thought, *my day's about to get weird.* Now here's the thing. I can't imagine a stranger bursting into offices in the accounting or biology or history departments, intent on tangling with professors there. But the "Professor of Theology" plate on my door triggers the strike instinct in some people who consider it their calling in life to sort out people like me.

"Can I ask you a question?"

I resisted the snarky urge to respond, *I think you just have.* Instead, I opted for, "Sure. Go ahead, sir" (hoping that calling him *sir* might hint at my desire to remain polite). He was having none of it.

"Why don't you preach Christ around here?!" He was already breathing hard.

"Sorry, sir, I'm . . . not . . . quite following."

"Over the past couple of years I've talked to a few of your graduates and some of them say they don't even believe in God anymore." He raised his voice a bit more. "So why don't you preach Christ?"

I stayed in my chair, took a deep breath, and tried to remain calm. Through similar encounters I've learned that when people huff that at you usually means, "Why don't you preach Christ like I do?"

"Ok, sir. Look, to begin, you can't force anyone to believe. Some people come to the point where they no longer can—or want to—believe, no matter how much anyone works with them. And secondly, I'm not sure *who* you mean when you say, 'Why don't *you* preach Christ around here?' *I* certainly preach Christ."

"Well, the *other* professors around here must not," he continued, now starting to shout. "You're a Christian college! Don't you care about what the Bible says? This place has really gone to the dogs! How can you let people out of here who don't believe?"

My deep Anglo-Saxon sense of loyalty to kith and kin gets me into trouble from time to time. This was one of those times. Insult me to my face and I'll probably laugh at you or conclude you're a lunatic. But attack my friends and suddenly the red mist descends and something dark leaps out of me. I know how hard my colleagues work and how deeply committed to Christ they are. So now I'm standing up, shoulders squared to his, our noses a few inches apart. Picture a baseball manager and an umpire. The adrenaline rush has commenced.

"Hey, just a minute. Let me ask *you* a few questions. Have you ever attended our college chapel service?" I asked him.

"No."

"How 'bout a service at the college church?"

"No. I don't have the time to get over here for these services."

"So you really don't know if we preach Christ around here or not, do you? *Do you?* And let me ask you this: Do you have children?" Now *I'm* breathing hard.

"Yes." (Turns out, he had a few.)

"Are any of them still in church?"

"Well . . . no."

"Big surprise there. So let me get this straight. You burst into my office, wanting to wring me out for not 'preaching Christ' because you met a few of our former students—out of thousands we've graduated—who don't believe in God, while you raised your own children for *eighteen years* and *they* are no longer in the church? I guess you didn't preach Christ in your family, huh?" At this point, I've entered attack mode. Not only do I want to take the wind out of his sails, I'm out to chop down the mast and set fire to the ship.

As you can imagine, the conversation went downhill from there. We barked at each other for a few minutes, and when I finally backed him out of my office, the last thing he sneered at me was, "You know, a mind's like a parachute—it only works when it's open."

"Right back at ya, pal," I retorted. *That went well*, I thought. I never saw him again.

Why People Desert the Table

This chapter is the most rambling and probably most important in the book. Most of the observations and suggestions in what follows apply to theological conversations in general: how we tend to argue, how our arguments incrementally get off track, and how we might keep people at the table by adhering to some basic conversational ethics and commitments. I'm concerned here with what you might call the form of our conversations, but by form I'm including several less tangible elements (e.g., gauging the emotional intensity of a conversation, learning to recognize who your friends are) that shape the way we talk. In subsequent chapters, I deal more with the content of our conversations: why certain theological questions get us lathered up, and why the positions we hold in relation to these questions produce different outcomes in the way we carry on talking.

Why do theological conversations so often end with people deserting the table? Here's how it happens.

Polite Beginnings?

I'm the first one to admit that I have trust issues, so it shouldn't be surprising that I'm suspicious of excessive politeness at the beginning of conversations, especially between people who hold dramatically different positions. To me, that's a signal that either a real conversation will never take place or that when it happens, it'll be a train wreck. The former scenario typically happens when one or both people don't like conflict and try to avoid it if at all possible. So, instead of talking about differences, someone attempts to change the subject or offers platitudes in hope of heading off any risk. You hear comments like, "Well, people just have different opinions about this" (always enlightening) or "I choose to believe this and you choose to believe that" (as though the act of choosing is what matters) or "You certainly have strong convictions about that" (again, not very helpful, since I have strong convictions on everything from how soccer should be played to how Indian food should be prepared). Some Christians think that this avoidance strategy and these puffball comments count as evidence of one's "Christlikeness" in potentially volatile conversations (because Jesus avoided conflict whenever possible, right?).

Although you might find it hard to believe, Americans on the whole try to avoid open one-on-one conflict (we'd rather hole up in our talk-radio show or Facebook political action group and, amongst our own kind, sledge people we don't like—or simply gossip about them in the hallway or around

the watercooler). Especially with people we barely know, unvarnished disagreement is considered impolite. But while politeness overkill may work
sometimes, things go sideways and often spiral out of control when it
doesn't, which happens when one of the conversation partners won't drop
the subject. This pushes the other person (desperate to avoid conflict) to
adopt either more severe avoidance measures or to "snap," which sometimes
results in over-the-top anger. You may have seen good Christians suddenly
lose it when they felt trapped in a conversation that was becoming too contentious for them. And then, suddenly, the battle's on.

Marshall Your Forces!

Martial and pugilistic metaphors often shape the way we think about conversations. In our "war of words," we "marshal our forces" to make our
case, which usually involves lining up "what the Bible says" (as opposed to
"what man says") or, in the case of a disputed passage, "what the Greek (or
Hebrew) means" or what some celebrated figure (e.g., Calvin) in church history said about a passage. The "gloves come off" and we find ourselves in the
"heat of battle." We may score a "body blow" to our opponent's argument, or
we may believe our partner has taken a "cheap shot" at us. And if we're not
doing particularly well in a debate, we often "beat a hasty retreat."

Believe it or not, many Christians look to the Bible to support this way
of talking to *those* people who hold "unbiblical" views. People sometimes
drag out this passage from 2 Corinthians as justification:

> Indeed, we live as human beings, but we do not wage war ac-
> cording to human standards; for the weapons of our warfare
> are not merely human, but they have divine power to destroy
> strongholds. We destroy arguments and every proud obstacle
> raised up against the knowledge of God, and we take every
> thought captive to obey Christ. (2 Cor 10:3–5)

But let's be clear on a few things about this passage. In 2 Corinthians 9–10,
Paul defends his apostolic authority as he urges the Corinthian believers
to generosity. Given the immediate context, the "strongholds" and "arguments" he's out to demolish are precisely those arguments that suggest we
live by "human standards" (1 Cor 10:2) and therefore remain unconcerned
for "the needs of the saints" (1 Cor 9:12). Ripped out of this context and
taken as general guidelines for how to disagree, however, the passage orients
people toward "demolishing" the other person's viewpoint and "taking captive" their thoughts.

So what are those forces we typically muster? The *forces* are nothing other than the classical *sources* of theology: Scripture, tradition, reason, and experience (not surprising, since so much theology emerged from polemical situations).

Amongst evangelicals and fundamentalists, the "first strike" in a theological conversation is nearly always "what the *Bible* says" as opposed to "what *man* says"—even though this piece of artillery is often rolled out precisely when people are arguing about Bible verses. (So *my* interpretation is what the Bible says, while *yours* is what "man" says.) More nuanced versions might be "what the Greek (or Hebrew) text says" as opposed to the dodgy translation you happen to be using.

"Church tradition" per se is rarely brought forward as a first strike argument (people often juxtapose "man-made tradition" with "what the Bible says"), but code words like "orthodox" or "classical" Christianity are sometimes used to draw lines between who's in and who's out, even though what Protestants and Orthodox (and Roman Catholic) believers mean by these tags may differ wildly. Occasionally someone cites a figure from church history (almost always from the Western Church, and frequently Calvin or Luther) to lend weight behind their punch.

And although many Christians wouldn't admit it, the standard arsenal includes making judgments about the *reasonableness* of someone's position. Over the past few decades in the Christian community, evangelicals tend to tag anyone or anything that smells like "postmodernism" or "progressive" as "irrational." And if irrational, it must be based on someone's experience, which is "subjective" and therefore "relativistic." (People who make this charge often fail to acknowledge their own dependence on their experience—what they see and interpret in the church around them.) However, as some charismatic believers would charge, *too much* reliance on reason in someone's argument probably means that they don't have the Holy Spirit or don't know Jesus personally, which means the experiential dimension of their Christianity is lacking. (Watch a Christian committed to rationalist apologetics shift gears to an experiential basis when arguing with a secular humanist committed to scientific rationalism!)

Frustration Sets In

So I line up all my forces and create an airtight argument to prove my point. And what happens? I fail to make much of an impact on the other person. The way I've constructed my case *doesn't make sense* to him. So I try again, perhaps by employing different words, bringing in more Scripture passages, and attempting to make the connections between ideas clearer. Again, he's not persuaded. Eventually, frustration sets in. More "evidence" hasn't helped, repeating myself hasn't done the trick, trying new ways to make my case seem reasonable hasn't worked. Inside I begin saying to myself, "Why can't he see that what I'm saying makes sense?"

Why something *makes sense* to one person and not another remains one of the most vexing questions in philosophy. Philosophical movements have tried to clarify language and its relationship to both logic and the world, but the ultimate ground of rationality remains a mystery—indeed, some philosophers question whether there is such a thing as a universal rationality. If there is, no criteria for it has gained consensus; in fact, some Eastern systems of thought have developed in ways contrary to Western standards of rationality.

But people disagree over *what makes sense* for more than lack of rationality. Words are loaded differently for people from different cultural backgrounds, and we each carry around in our heads our personal idiolect that reflects our own psychology and interests. Sometimes people reject what someone says not on account of the soundness of the argument but for fear of where it might lead. Personal, mystical religious experience ("the Holy Spirit revealed to me") generally trumps all viewpoints to the contrary, and while we might be skeptical of some of these claims, all of us are subject to deep, subconscious forces that we don't understand and over which we have little control. In sum, *what makes sense* can rarely be read off the surface of any but the most mundane conversations, and even then there's no guarantee.

In the online world, where conversations increasingly take place, we experience and express this frustration in a variety of ways. So many informal verbal and nonverbal cues go missing from our online exchanges, and frequently we converse anonymously, which tends to bring out the worst in people. Disembodied letters and words flickering on a screen erase and replace the web of trust within which almost any living conversation happens. And when frustration begins to peak, what do many of us resort to? The "convince font"—caps lock!—as though taller characters and the emotional intensity behind them have a better chance of convincing someone.

A Shadow Grows: Suspicious Minds

The frustration I've been describing arises in large measure by our inability to come to terms with the simple fact of our *situatedness*, our being limited by both space and time.[1] Surely reason should be able to lift us both out of our limitations until we can see matters the same way. But that aerial viewpoint resulting in complete agreement is never reached. And so a shadow, a suspicion, begins to grow in my mind. I begin to suspect that the problem doesn't lie in the limits of sheer creatureliness, but in my conversation partner's ability or willingness to see my point.

Most benignly, I might begin to suspect that my conversation partner is unable to follow an argument, perhaps due to a lack of raw intellectual horsepower, his level of education, or his knowledge of the larger subject area. But beyond intelligence quotient or education, I might begin to suspect more insidious things of him. I imagine all the "wrong" people and books that he's been listening to and reading. "His mind is already made up." "He's committed to [ideology X]." "He doesn't really believe the Bible" (like I do!) "He's out to destroy the church and lead people astray!" And perhaps worst of all: "Satan has blinded him to the truth." He doesn't agree with me despite my best efforts to convince him—therefore, something must be wrong with him.

Well, That Escalated Quickly

Because "God's truth" and people's "eternal destiny" is at stake, after this point the emotional temperature and charged rhetoric quickly nears the red line. Eventually I express my suspicions as accusations: "You don't believe the Bible" or "You're leading people astray" or "You're only saying that because you're [a liberal, a fundamentalist, a sexist, a bigot]," or, sometimes, the h-bomb is dropped: "You're a *heretic*." In the next chapter, I'll examine in detail how many Christians use the term *heretic*, but here I note only that, historically speaking, the term *heresy* hasn't meant what many today think it means (in some ways its reference is both wider and narrower, but more on that later).

At this point in the conversation, I've observed one of two things taking place: one of us (inclined more toward flight than fight) will beat a hasty retreat and excuse ourselves from the conversation, or (if both of us incline more toward fight than flight) the emotional intensity of each exchange rises degree by degree. When this happens, the conversation has effectively ended, as now we're mainly responding to the emotional intensity of the moment rather than anything the other is saying. Winning at any cost has become paramount.

1. See Smith, *Fall of Interpretation*.

One of the most difficult lessons to learn, however, is this: this way of "winning" an argument is never really winning. In fact, the effects that normally follow from this point amount to exactly the opposite. The Buddhist classic *The Dhammapada* reminds us, "Victory breeds hatred, for the conquered is unhappy. He who has given up both victory and defeat, he, the contented, is happy."[2]

From this point, when further conversation is pointless, the exchange often takes darker and darker interpersonal turns in the forms of insults and *ad hominem* attacks. The irony hardly could be more delicious. We began by talking about God, putatively the source of love, and yet in the course of our conversation about God—indeed on account of it—we end by acting at cross-purposes with the very subject we're talking about.

I've witnessed this irony in my own tradition (Wesleyan), when people argue about one of our distinctives: the doctrine of "entire sanctification." In a nutshell, John Wesley (the founder of Methodism) taught that the Holy Spirit could "sanctify" or set apart believers for God's purposes by removing from them the desire to willfully disobey God and enabling them to more fully love God and neighbor as oneself. Wesley called this the doctrine of "Christian perfection," a phrase that's occasioned enormous misunderstanding amongst non-Wesleyans ("You Wesleyans think you're perfect?"), but by *perfect,* all Wesley meant was that love was the *telos* or aim of Christian life.[3] "Be perfect, therefore, as your heavenly Father is perfect" (Matt 5:48).

You might think that if there was one doctrine less susceptible to arguments resulting in rancor amongst its proponents, this would be it. But jagged-edged disagreements have taken place amongst Wesleyan theologians over how the Holy Spirit effects this change in the lives of the believer, when it can occur, the extent of it, whether it can be "lost," the metaphors we use to describe it, etc., to the point that factionalism infects even the Wesleyan theological tradition—over the nature of what it means to be perfected in love! Something's gotten lost, that's for sure. "Those who say, 'I love God,' and hate their brothers or sisters, are liars; for those who do not love a brother or sister whom they have seen, cannot love God whom they have not seen" (1 John 4:20).

Historically, of course, different church bodies have mutually condemned each other (more about this in the next chapter) over doctrinal issues, but we frequently see it play out between individuals. In my upbringing, it was common for Roman Catholics and evangelicals to end any discussion they might be having by claiming that God was going to send the

---

2. *The Dhammapada* 15.201.

3. Wesley, "On Perfection," §1.4 (*Works* 3:74).

other to hell. And too many times I've witnessed these arguments finally brought to a shuddering halt by expletives being hurled back and forth.

You might think this would be the end of it. Both of us wash our hands of each other, walk away and never have anything to do with each other again. Sometimes it ends this way; too often it doesn't. Because God's truth and people's eternal destiny are at stake, *something must be done* about that person teaching falsehood and leading people astray. And so I'm going to report you to a church administrator or pastor. Some of these authorities may be so concerned about how things appear to their constituencies that, rather than doing the right thing, they take the path of least resistance and get rid of a troublemaker like you. Failing that, I'll use my website, my blog, my voice in the church, my influence at your school to have you blackballed, destroy your reputation, and put an end to your career. I'll mock and even come within a hair's breadth of slandering you, because I'm sure that you probably hold a host of other dangerous views I could uncover if I had the time and patience. In other words, once I'm convinced that you're spreading falsehood like a cancer, all standards of Christian conduct go out the windows—for I must defend the truth at all costs and by any means necessary. I'm now justified in spreading my venom. And so what started out as an attempt to understand each other and forge the beginnings of a friendship has spiraled and crashed into condemnations and revenge. Because I'm committed to God's truth and you're not, *I must hate you in Jesus' name.*

I'd never use that language, of course, because it's too difficult to reconcile a bald-faced statement like that with Jesus' talk about love. But it wouldn't be the loving thing to do to leave you in your present state (and therefore to leave others under your influence). So what looks like hatred is in fact a "tough love." I actually have your best interest at heart, even if I come close to destroying all you hold dear, for that's what it might take for you to change and come to the truth. The ends do justify the means, even if those means turn upside-down any conventional notions of what looking after your well-being might mean. And so we've come well and truly through the looking glass now, in a topsy-turvy world where *love* means *hatred* in the defense of God's truth. Not only have people deserted the picnic table, the table's been flipped over, soaked in kerosene, and set on fire.

Keeping People at the Table: A Few Steps in the Right Direction

I've personally witnessed—and unfortunately experienced—what I've been describing more times than I care to admit. To say that the Spirit is "grieved" over situations like this would be genteel understatement. (Can you make the Spirit angry?) And of course every time this happens, we confirm to outsiders that, when push comes to shove, Christians act like everyone else. So is there anything we might do to avert disasters like this, anything we might do that would help keep people talking at the table?

I'm far from having all this worked out, on both the theoretical level and in terms of my own temperament. Part of my problem is that if it's ever a choice between *fight* or *flight*, I find it difficult to resist *fight*. But what follows are a few lessons I'm learning, mostly by the hard way.

Be a Person of the Truth, Even if It Costs You

Being a person of the truth demands strenuous intellectual and emotional commitment, especially if we are interested in the *whole* truth. Sometimes, when we're talking with a person who holds radically different views (perhaps even views we consider "non-biblical"), we're really listening selectively instead of fairly, stockpiling those phrases and references we can later use as "ammunition." (I was approached once to take part in an impartial "survey" of theological views that was little more than a fundamentalist litmus test that could be used against me.) But we can't accuse others of "hearing only what *you* want to hear" if we practice this way of listening ourselves. Listening fairly means we may have to adjust or discard some ideas we have about our conversation partner and what they believe. It means that we don't intentionally misrepresent those with whom we disagree; we tell the truth about them, even if it makes our position weaker. It means admitting that issues we thought were black and white are more nuanced and complex than that. It means, in other words, that we may have to learn and change precisely on account of this other who is proving to be so troublesome to what I *thought* I knew (and who wants to do that?).

Listening fairly means continually learning about others and their beliefs. So many of our accusations and judgments stem from silly misunderstandings that could be cleared up with a few minutes on Google. Evangelicals who pride themselves on being people of the truth too often indulge in half-truths or distortions when presenting others' views. For example, I remember reading an article a few years ago in a denominational magazine on the "Buddha's bones," a self-congratulatory, quasi-apologetics piece designed to compare the dead Buddha with the risen and living Christ. (I say "quasi-apologetic" because I can't imagine anyone besides Christians reading that particular magazine). Yet the writer of the piece failed to appreciate that, for the Buddhist, recognizing the historical Buddha's bones actually confirms central Buddhist beliefs in the truth of impermanence and the importance of non-attachment. So, the article would cut no ice whatsoever with Buddhists, and gave a potentially misleading picture of Buddhists to Christians (as though Buddhists were sitting around moping over the fact that the historical Gautama Siddartha is dead). I also remember seeing a well-known television preacher railing on about Hindus worshiping the god *Hindu*. Being humble and ignorant is one thing; puffing out your chest, strutting across the platform and announcing your ignorance to a television audience is another. Ignorance *never* helps your case when having a conversation with someone, and intentional ignorance of the other is one of the worst things in which we can indulge ourselves.

Being a person of the truth involves recognizing that you're not the only one interested in truth. This means giving the other person the benefit of the doubt regarding their pursuit of truth. Don't automatically assume that, because they disagree with you or your theological tradition, they're your intellectual or spiritual inferior, or that they're up to no good. John Wesley once advised to never assume anyone sins because he disagrees with *you*.[4] If I want to be taken seriously, as someone who pursues the truth in good conscience, I must grant my conversation partners the same courtesy, even if, despite my best efforts, I fail to convince them.

So many theological disagreements emerge from interpretive commitments that remain invisible to us and that, as I mentioned above, verge on the nature of rationality itself—why something makes sense to one person, church, or culture, and not another. When one Christian, for example, accuses another Christian of not believing the Bible, usually all this means is "You don't believe the Bible like I do," but that "like I do" contains a heap of interpretive decisions of which the person making the statement is probably unaware. Many of those decisions have little or nothing to do with the text of the Bible itself, but rather stem from the psychological, cultural, and theological biases that form our interpretive lens. When the light sometimes comes on and we realize those commitments in a conversation, we often don't know how to proceed. We can't argue from the text, so the argument then shifts to accusations about the other person's moral character, upbringing, or political leanings. But this much is sure: abusive *ad hominem* attacks never help someone make sense of your approach. Maintain respect throughout.

With some issues, the most difficult and interesting question often boils down to this: what do we do when both sides believe they have exclusive possession of the truth, and no agreement, compromise or even further

4. Wesley, "Farther Thoughts Upon Christian Perfection," Q37 (*Works* 13:121).

civil conversations seems possible? When all the best available exegetical and theological arguments have been laid on the table, and we look each other in the eye and realize that there's nothing more to be said, how then do we then treat each other? Sometimes the best we can do is settle for a "do-no-harm" policy. I may not agree with you, but I will not engage in libel or slander against you, incite ill-will toward you, or demonize you.

Someone once asked me, "But if you adopt a 'do-no-harm' policy, aren't you allowing wrong and dangerous ideas about God to influence people? Shouldn't we aggressively expose error and attempt to shut down those people promoting it whenever we can?" To begin, I try to distinguish between ideas that I think are wrong and ideas that are both wrong and dangerous. I think many of my close friends have wrong ideas, but I'm on no crusade to rid the world of them. I teach systematic theology as part of my regular teaching load, but as a Wesleyan theologian I've never believed that I have to "expose the dangers" of Roman Catholics, Southern Baptists, or Presbyterians, even if I do think they're wrong about important theological issues. I try to point out what I take to be the strengths and weaknesses of different theological positions and make a case for my position. Besides, with internet in the classroom, if I try to pronounce authoritatively on a theological debate that's been going on for centuries, my students are savvy enough to realize that I've settled nothing (and most likely they're googling ten different theological perspectives on the issue as I'm talking about it).

With members of other faiths, the issues (as we'll see in chapter 3) are a bit more complex, but for the most part I've found that I don't have to "denounce" anything. I give talks on a regular basis about the differences between Christianity and the world religions, and usually all I need to do is, without rancor, lay out those differences and trust the Spirit! People will draw their own conclusions about content; what they usually need help with is how to treat Muslims or Mormons now that they understand what they believe—that is, how to practically negotiate difference with real human beings.

More often than not, I find that amongst Christians I have to act as a kind of advocate for other religious groups. By that, I mean that Christians by and large are ignorant of even the rudiments of other faiths, and all kinds of ridiculous ideas grow in that soil of ignorance. Vigorous, honest, and loving conversation about religious ideas that matter is desperately needed, but we'll never have those kinds of conversations by trading in caricatures, straw man arguments, and outright slander.

Of course there are times when you need to actively challenge and attempt to shut down someone's theology, such as when that theology promotes hatred or violence. But in the area of less-crazy interpretive disagreements, many Christians haven't thought very carefully about the different levels of importance in Christian belief (which I'll treat in the next chapter), with the result that they can't distinguish between simple differences of theological opinion and "dangerous" teaching.

Humanize the Encounter

In contentious conversations, we tend to dehumanize our conversation partners by reducing them to a bundle of beliefs and propositions. Years ago, I used to start conversations with members of New Religious Movements (e.g. Jehovah's Witnesses, Mormons, etc.) by coming out point-blank and asking them what they wanted to argue about. But of course, once you frame the conversation in adversarial terms, the point becomes winning, not understanding. It's common for apologists to justify such an approach by saying that they're planting seeds of doubt or questions in the minds of their opponents, which may lead them to do their own research and eventually leave their cult or church (the lines are frequently blurry). That may happen in some cases; why people leave religious groups is a complex question. But as a strategy, this approach blinds us to the personal character of our conversations: we're talking to *people*.

By contrast, I've learned that one of the most important elements of having a genuine conversation is learning to humanize (or rehumanize) the encounter, and you can't do this without actually getting to know someone. You might think that is self-evident; unfortunately, it's not. In my classes, for example, on a fairly regular basis I hear critical remarks about Democrats or Republicans, fundamentalists or liberals, Roman Catholics or Muslims, members of the LGBT community, yet often I find out that the person making the comment has never had a substantial conversation with one of "those" people and almost never has had a friendship with them. The problem is, it's impossible to have a productive conversation without respect for each other's identity, and perhaps the best way we come to gain this is by taking the time to share our *stories*.[5]

Storytelling works in a couple of important ways. To begin, narratives shape and express what it means to have an identity, either through telling our own story or by imaginatively entering another's story. Furthermore, through paying close attention to each other's stories, we come to develop *empathy* for each other, a capacity critical for mutual understanding. You sometimes hear people who are intent on "telling it like it is" claim that they don't care about empathizing with others. My response to these truth

5. See Falcon et al., *Getting to the Heart of Interfaith*, 27–50.

warriors has always been, "Then I guess you don't care if people aren't listening to you."

The Confucian tradition places a high value on developing empathy
for our fellow human beings. One of the cardinal Confucian virtues is
known as *ren*, usually translated "benevolence" or "human-heartedness."
This quality, which is close to the heart of what it means to be a human
being, needs to be cultivated carefully, or else it degrades to the point that a
person becomes uncaring and hateful, a "petty person." The person who exemplifies *ren* is, by contrast, a "noble" person, one who embodies what a human being is supposed to be because she empathizes with others. "Now the
ren man, wishing himself to be established, sees that others are established,
and, wishing himself to be successful, sees that others are successful. To be
able to take one's own feelings as a guide may be called the art of *ren*."[6] From
the Confucian perspective, trying to relate to others purely on the basis of
logic or argument reveals a shortcoming in one's moral development. Are
you *human-hearted*? That's the question.

From listening to people's stories, you can find out about their upbringing, where they went to school, triumphs and struggles they've experienced, and what drew them to a particular church or religious group.
I'm not encouraging anyone to play armchair psychologist or sociologist
on the basis of listening to someone's story; still less am I suggesting that
their viewpoint on a particular subject is, in the final analysis, true merely
on account of their story (that *would* be relativism). I *am* saying that if we
want to know what a person holds dear, what they hope for and what they
fear (all of which are ingredient to any genuine conversation), then we have
to learn to listen out of this sense of human-heartedness. This process of
listening lowers our fear of the other, as we come to view them as more than
a bundle of opinions and beliefs, and as a person with a story all their own.
But be prepared. To do this well, remember that you're in it for the long
haul. One of the most difficult conversational goals is to develop and maintain a long-term friendship with someone who holds dramatically different
views to your own, and to listen carefully to their developing narrative. But
this is crucial, because it's a rare individual who can come to grapple with,
and perhaps change, their own deeply held convictions without personally
getting to know anyone on the other side.

At the root of humanizing our encounters lies the basic question,
"What do we do with otherness?" This is a question we had better consider
carefully as the world becomes smaller, more interconnected, and more
dangerous. Typically we adopt one of two strategies in the face of otherness:

6. Confucius, *Analects of Confucius*, 6.30 (80).

We don't know what to do with it, so we effectively despair before it, wall ourselves off from those people, and then, in that space of self-imposed isolation, suspicion, and lies begin to grow. Or, because we can't stand the thought that someone really *is* different from us, we seek to subjugate or conquer the other. Those people must conform or assimilate until they are like us; or, if the otherness becomes too disgusting to us, we may silence and perhaps liquidate them.

The Jewish philosopher Emmanuel Levinas offers striking insight into humanizing our encounters with the other. In view of these strategies for dealing with otherness just mentioned (despair or subjugate), Levinas would say that we've been hornswoggled by the legacy of western metaphysics, with its pipedream of the totality of knowledge. Through the rhetorical violence of philosophical discourse (or actual, physical violence), we attempt to reduce the otherness of the other to something that can be absorbed into a grand theory about how progress requires your sacrifice or obedience, or what it may take to keep *my* people pure. "Philosophy itself is identified with the substitution of ideas for persons."[7] But any true knowing, Levinas argues, occurs when we encounter the vulnerability and irreducibility of the "face" of the other—and by "face" Levinas means literally a person's face and the vulnerability that strikes us when we really look at each another (which we lack in most online communication). Levinas further insists that "*face* and *discourse* are tied. The face speaks. It speaks, it is in this that it renders possible and begins all discourse . . . It is discourse, and more exactly, response or responsibility which is this authentic relationship."[8] Our responsibility arises when we realize that through the other we encounter the Infinite, and that no knowledge of God exists apart from our relationships with others.[9]

Gauge the Escalation and Know When to "Cool Out"

Once you put a human face on a theological disagreement and take the time to know someone holding a radically different position to your own, the emotional temperature surrounding "the problem" usually goes down a few degrees and the conversation can proceed in more productive directions. If you (or your conversational partner) can't or won't do this, then at least have the good sense to recognize that after a certain emotional temperature has been reached in a vigorous "discussion," further attempts to convince

7. Levinas, *Totality and Infinity*, 88.
8. Levinas, *Ethics and Infinity*, 87–88.
9. Levinas, *Totality and Infinity*, 78.

actually become counter-productive. Once your conversation partner is "in the zone," the chances of changing their mind in the heat of battle are pretty remote. I've observed that most people change their minds on important issues over a lengthy and painful period of study, reflection, and conversation, until they reach a tipping point in their thinking, and almost never through a silver-bullet conversation with someone holding an opposing viewpoint. But before that point, even clear evidence to the contrary will cause many people to dig their heels in deeper.[10] There's generally too much at stake, especially for professionals, to stop in the middle of a heated argument, slap the forehead, and say, "Yup, you've convinced me! I've held this position for all these years but now I see I'm wrong about it."

Recognizing when conversations reach the red zone takes practice, because when you're caught up in arguing with someone, your perspective on the tenor and overall direction of the conversation becomes lost to you. I've learned to pay attention to physiological indicators, some of which I mentioned in the conversation snippet at the beginning of this chapter: Am I feeling flushed, or has my heartbeat quickened? Have I raised my voice, or are my words coming out in a rush (or gasps)? Have I "squared off" in the way I'm standing or sitting in relation to my conversation partner? These all indicate that I might be taking conversation in unproductive or downright dangerous directions. If the person you're talking to has learned to recognize these signs, he may even use what he sees in you to further "wind you up" or "push your buttons" until you lose your cool. (And you *really* don't want to throw a punch at someone because they disagree with you about Jesus.)

If you're able to remain aware of these factors, then (before things get out of control) sometimes injecting humor into the conversation can prevent things from going off the rails. But this can be hugely misinterpreted by the other person if they think you're not as serious about the issue as they are (or if your jokes suck or your timing is off). So I try to describe what's happening ("Look, we don't seem to be getting anywhere on this" or "I think things might be getting out of hand here") and suggest that we drop the conversation and cool off. If the person you're talking to responds with derision or scorn ("What's the matter? Can't take it? Can't stand the heat? No answer, huh?"), don't take the bait (this is, I fear, preeminently a case of "do-as-I-say" and not "do-as-I-do"). That kind of a response to your suggestion that you both cool off is a surefire indicator that *they*, at least, need to cool off. At that point, I'm learning to say something like, "I could respond, but I think

10. See Shermer on the "backfire effect" in "How to Convince Someone When Facts Fail."

we're close to losing civility, and I'm not going to get into a shouting match with you. That would be pointless."

If you both agree to drop the conversation at that point, each of you eventually will have to ask yourselves if it's worth revisiting the subject at a later date. From my experience, I'd say that if the subject matter is one conversation amongst many with a family member or close friend, it may not be worth revisiting for a while (surviving relationships with the in-laws goes a long way toward domestic tranquility!). Long-term relationships can be difficult enough to maintain, and we probably all recognize certain red zones even with people we're close to.

Recognize That You Won't Keep Everyone in the Conversation

Despite your best efforts, not everyone will want to come to or stay at the table, because not everyone wants to have a conversation, even if they initially appear so. Some people want a platform to preach their convictions (rhetorically marking their ideological territory, as if to say, "Warning! This is my turf!"), others want to air their anxieties or complaints (Surprise! You've become their therapist or confessor), and some—speaking from personal experience—want to lecture a professor on their ideas about God so I can affirm their brilliance (lucky me!). Occasionally I've had to say to people trying to bowl me over with intensity or volume (or both), "As long as the arrows in this conversation flow only one way, it's probably not going to work."

As I've thought about why people won't come to the table or leave shortly after coming, three intertwined factors come to mind: Sociologically, some people don't believe it's possible to keep a friendly conversation going with an ideological "enemy" and maintain their position in the church, college, community, or family, let alone change their mind on a significant theological issue. Some people build their entire careers around defending a set of views about God and attacking others who hold different views. The longer someone has championed a position (especially professionally), the less likely they'll alter their views. Too much is at stake. Your professional reputation and career, as well as networks of family and friends, frequently depend upon holding the "right" views. Happy exceptions exist, of course, but the pressures to keep promoting and defending particular perspectives can be enormous.

Philosophically, many people don't care to remain at the table because talking about a serious theological issue and facing the risk it brings (I may have to change my mind) may be only the tip of an iceberg. These conversations sometimes precipitate a paradigm shift in one's worldview, which takes an extraordinary amount of time and energy to process (who has time for something like that?). Along the way, I've had more than one student tell me that, even though they were challenged and disturbed by questions we tackle in class, they were too busy to deal with the shifting theological plate tectonics and the practical consequences they knew would follow if they seriously thought things through. Much easier to stay with a worldview that works for me, even if I secretly entertain doubts about it.

And then, psychologically, some people don't deal well with open-ended conversations and potentially disturbing questions of any kind. You can find your way through this dangerous and inhospitable world only if the issues are black and white and the corresponding answers are simple. Fortunately, the Bible (or the Qur'an, or the Watchtower Society, etc.) gives us the necessary clarity and simplicity. For many of these folks I suspect that, at bottom, specific theological positions don't drive their commitment as much as a deep, underlying need for clarity and simplicity, and their church, synagogue, mosque, or temple furnishes that level of comfort for them. I *need* simple answers to important questions and closure to important conversations; therefore I *will* have them.

Once, when talking about inviting people to the table and reflecting on who would probably come and who most likely would leave, a friend said something like, "Given what you're saying about the nature of conversation, aren't you going to get only those people who already want to talk? Aren't those people who don't want to talk really the ones you need to be talking to?"

That's a fair question, and one that still troubles me. In response, I'd say first of all that no one should be coerced to talk. But just because some people don't initially want to come to the table, or leave after a short while, doesn't mean they never will come to the table (or return). Changing your mind to want to talk, or to revisit a risky conversation, is less a crisis moment and more a painful process, and much of this process happens in the tacit dimension of our minds (when we're not explicitly thinking about it) and in the inarticulate speech of our hearts. Also, this metaphor of the table, which I've been using throughout, can be misleading if we think of only one conversation to which people are invited. In reality, we're all involved in multiple conversations, and just because some folks may not want to risk conversation at one place at the table doesn't mean they won't find someplace else to sit and talk. Finally, there are plenty of people who belong to local religious communities and who have questions, but feel like they have no place to take their questions—they might even be afraid to be honest about their questions for fear of repercussions.

Because deciding to converse involves this risk, those in the conversation zones should commit themselves to creating a safe, "betrayal-free" zone. We need to be able to communicate to people, perhaps more in the way we talk with them rather than using these specific words: "We welcome all honest questions here. No matter what you say here, we will never use your words against you."

Be Aware of Power and Privilege

Talk about privilege usually elicits groans and eye-rolling from people who disparage anything that smells of "political correctness." I grew up in a working-class family and know by heart the common responses to anyone who suggests that white, lower-middle-class families are privileged. "Privileged? I've worked my ass off my whole life and no one's given me anything for free. Everyone in this country has the same opportunities; you just need to work hard and apply yourself."

But the point is this: as a white, educated American male I'm privileged not in the sense that I get free money in the mail every week or can jump in line in front of women and people of color (although a generation or so ago the latter was close to reality). Rather, to put the matter bluntly, I've benefitted from political, economic, and cultural arrangements that (intentionally or not) make my profile the referent. Look at the CEOs of most major corporations, top military commanders, members of Congress, etc.—is the fact that most of these fields are dominated by white males the result of sheer merit on an equal playing field? Really? I *have* experienced what it's like to be in a minority position at various times in short-term work overseas, but even there, again, *as* a white, educated, American male, which places me near the top of the food chain no matter where I go.

Now I personally buck against the way that identity politics sucks all the air out of the room when issues like this come up, and why it's always the same issues. In commenting on what she calls the "holy trinity" of race, class, and gender dominating higher education in America, eminent historian Gertrude Himmelfarb comments that few people have even noticed that religion is missing from this trinity, as if it's no longer a defining principle of one's identity.[11] Indeed, in academic circles, religious and theological issues are almost always reduced to one of those three markers, and I'm deeply suspicious of all forms of reductionisms. In my more cynical moments, I've asked myself why I should even bother writing anything at all, if it's going to

11. Himmelfarb, "Christian University," 17.

be taken as merely a reflection of my privileged position. Can't an idea stand on its own merits, regardless of who wrote it?

That being said, I have to gird up my idealistic loins, take a deep breath, and look squarely at some uncomfortable realities in the world of theology and religion. Who's written most of the biblical commentaries, church histories, and theologies? Who've been the most influential religious leaders? I'm aware that, in so many circles in which I speak, my voice carries more weight than others as a matter of course, because of the way our theological and religious traditions have been normed in the West. Yes, of course, there have been times when my voice hasn't counted for much—even in theological issues that affect church practice—because someone else in the conversation made *gobs* more money than I do, and in this culture we listen to the powerful and wealthy over the educated. But any of my whining would be silly; the fact remains that a person in my position doesn't know what it's like to be consistently and systemically placed on the periphery. All ideas may not be reducible to one of the three markers of privilege, but it's clear that, at times, certain classes of people *have been* reduced and forced to sit on the margins.[12]

So, with these concerns in mind, I'm learning to do two basic things that don't come naturally to me in a conversation. First, consider how much privilege I bring to the table, in order to make room for other voices and take them seriously, and second, be careful about rushing to dismiss people's opinions because I think they're being merely "politically correct." "Politically correct" is too often thrown about by people who've never been on the other side of the line, who've never been the marginal voice. The most insidious perspectives are the ones we never seem to notice, and hardly ever question, because we're submerged in them. As Marshall McLuhan once observed, "I'm not sure who first discovered water, but I'm pretty sure it wasn't a fish."[13]

Learn to Recognize Who Your Friends Are

Over the past several years, "progressive" Christian thinkers have taken heaps of unfair criticism by more conservative evangelicals. Consider Brian McLaren, one of the poster boys for progressives. Through the years, Brian has been called about every nasty name imaginable, perhaps the least nasty of which is "heretic." Yet you can't hear Brian speak, or read one of his books

12. For a clear and accessible introduction to how systems of privilege operate, see Johnson, *Privilege, Power, and Difference.*

13. The exact origin of the saying is uncertain.

like his *Naked Spirituality*, without realizing that he's a person of deep Christian faith, both personally and intellectually (he writes unapologetically of being "transparently Trinitarian"[14]). Whatever other disagreements one may have with "progressive" theologians on the whole, I'm constantly reminding my evangelical colleagues that, given everything else we have to face in the world today, people like this are our friends.

Recognizing who your friends are isn't always easy. Sometimes we don't understand the issues well enough and haven't thought through where a particular position leads. Sometimes we're expecting too much of each other in a specific area. Sometimes we find that, given a particular topic or issue, we're closer to cousins or people we might consider "outsiders" than members of our own family. (I'm closer to some Buddhist friends on environmental issues, for example, than some members of the church.) In the next chapter I'll argue that, although friendship should remain one of the central goals of conversation, it can and should be based on more than a raft of issues on which we happen to unanimously agree.

If recognizing unlikely conversation partners as our friends requires reflection and patience, then acknowledging them publicly and inviting them to our table involves trust and a bit of *chutzpah* on our part. People might talk about us hanging with all the wrong people. "And the Pharisees and the scribes were grumbling and saying, 'This fellow welcomes sinners and eats with them'" (Luke 15:2). Offering hospitality to people you're not entirely sure of always involves risk; there's always something slightly mad about it, as Jack Caputo puts it, or else it isn't really hospitality.[15] Can I trust this new friend to not "turn ugly" on me or my family? Can I trust my family and friends or my church to also be as welcoming? So many times, my family and I have experienced this kind of welcome from unlikely people. Greek and Coptic Orthodox believers have welcomed us into their conversations and lunch tables (although not the Lord's Table). Muslims have welcomed us to share the evening meal during Ramadan. Evangelicals don't have a monopoly on hospitality.

Pose the Eschatological Scenario

When push comes to shove and you have to make a theological decision, ask yourself what position you'd be willing to defend on that great gettin' up morning. If it turns out I *am* wrong about a position at which I've arrived in good faith and out of consideration for another's well-being, do I need to

14. McLaren, *Naked Spirituality*, 183.
15. Caputo, *What Would Jesus Deconstruct?* 77.

fear being drop-kicked into perdition by the Christ I've worshiped as Lord and God? I suspect that Jesus is going to ask me more questions about my commitment to follow him and love the people around me than he is my determination to defend a doctrinal statement. Am I willing to say before Christ that, *yes*, it was worth disagreeing with someone to the point of ruining their reputation (or resorting to violence), all in your name, Lord? I've become far more willing to err on the side of love and mercy than judgment and condemnation, and more willing to commend others who see things differently than I do to the mercy of Christ. And let's not kid ourselves about love. When the practical effects of our "tough love" are the same as the effects of hatred, we're engaging in self-deception.

Insights from Philip Jakob Spener

In his *Pia Desideria* ("Pious Wishes"), published in 1675, Philip Jacob Spener lays out his perspective on successfully navigating religious disputes.[16] Spener, one of the founders of the University of Halle, is no seventeenth-century idealist who thinks we all merely need to sit around the campfire singing "Kumbaya." Through most of his adult life, he was the target of heated abuse by good orthodox Lutheran theologians, and the theological faculty at the University of Wittenberg finally charged him with 264 errors.

Spener is no relativist; he opens his work by saying that we must know the truth ourselves before attempting to dispute with others, and no disputation will ever be productive if we don't pray for those whom we believe to be in error or set a good example for them. A bad moral example on our part will only succeed in giving others a "bad impression of our true teaching," since people always watch what we do more than what we say. When arguing, Spener says, we can forcefully disagree, but we have to do everything out of "heartfelt love" for our conversation partner, taking care to avoid "invective and personal insinuations."[17]

If, however, in the course of the conversation it becomes clear that we're getting nowhere, then we should at least encourage our conversation partner to not slander us, but to continue to think about the issue and live out those godly principles that all Christians have in common.[18] Spener says that, despite deeply-rooted disagreements we may have with such people, we should always bear in mind that these people are our neighbors, and remember the command to love them as we love ourselves. "To insult or

16. Spener, *Pia Desideria*, 98.

17. Spener, *Pia Desideria*, 98.

18. Spener, *Pia Desideria*, 98.

wrong an unbeliever or heretic on account of his religion would not only be a carnal zeal but also a zeal that is calculated to hinder his conversion. A proper hatred of false religion should neither suspend nor weaken the love that is due the other person."[19]

Spener is writing during a time in which he's already witnessing the fragmentation of the Protestant world. If there's any hope at all for Christian unity, he says, it certainly won't come about solely through argumentation.[20] Too often, theological disputation is carried out by people bereft of the Spirit and faith, but who are filled with "carnal wisdom" directed toward elevating one' status. "How often is the principle of such disputation not investigation and discovery of truth, but rather obstinate assertion of what has once been proposed, reputation for a shrewd intellect and for ingeniousness, and conquest of an opponent, no matter how this is achieved?"[21] Even if we were to add strict boundaries and aims to theological arguments (such as clarifying a particular position), Spener warns that "God may not add his blessing, nor will he always allow the truth to prevail." And then Spener immediately adds this:

> This is the case with those whose thoughts hardly extend beyond making many people Lutheran and do not deem it important that with this profession such people become genuine Christians to the very core. They therefore regard true confession of faith merely as a means of strengthening their own ecclesiastical party and not as an entrance upon a life of zealous future service of God.[22]

Replace "Lutheran" with any denominational identifier today and you can appreciate the relevance of this treatise.

The bottom line is that arguing isn't enough to impart truth to the erring or even maintain it among ourselves. "The holy love of God is necessary."[23] If only we would conduct ourselves in a manner worthy of our calling, and show this in the way we love *even those whom we call heretics*, and if only they too could make an effort to love, based on what they do confess—*then*, Spener says, God would allow us to grow in our knowledge of the truth and we would see people persuaded to the truth. And so "holiness of life contributes much to conversion."[24]

19. Spener, *Pia Desideria*, 99.
20. Spener, *Pia Desideria*, 99.
21. Spener, *Pia Desideria*, 100
22. Spener, *Pia Desideria*, 101.
23. Spener, *Pia Desideria*, 102.
24. Spener, *Pia Desideria*, 102.

Keeping Them at the Table

"The holy love of God is necessary," Spener says, to animate Christian conversation. To sum up the full import of this statement, I'd put it this way: *conversation is a spiritual exercise.* We feel this exercise deeply in our *flesh,* and by that I mean both in our inclined tendency toward egocentricity (our "carnal nature") and literally in our bodies: the effects of inculcating patient habits of listening, restraining ourselves when we feel anger rising, paying attention and asking good questions, being willing to take a deep breath and examine deeply-held convictions and—possibly— change our minds. The way we talk about our opponents behind their backs, what we say about them on social media—all of this should be subject to the sanctifying work of the Holy Spirit and the scrutiny of others in the body of Christ. If we refuse, that says something about us, too.

It's hard to convince even yourself that you love someone if you refuse to talk with them. To the degree that love involves vulnerability, the willingness to stay in difficult conversations is a litmus test of our love. Yes, there are times in which you have to walk away or limit the time and scope of your conversation with someone, and of course no one should ever try to manipulate victims of abuse to stay in conversation with their abusers, although some victims testify to the healing power of forgiveness.[25] But, apart from these exceptions, many conversations reach a dead end or never happen because we so often treat people as positions to be defeated or as potential converts to our cause. Indeed, "the holy love of God is necessary" to keep us at the table.

25. See Cantacuzino's extraordinary book, *Forgiveness Project.*

2

Talking with Sisters and Brothers

Those Contentious Christians!

In the early nineties, I was asked to serve as a discussion moderator at an ecumenical conference held at a small university in the Midwest. Just finishing my dissertation, I was honored to do so. *I'm starting to get noticed,* I thought, and felt a tinge of pride (never an admirable quality in a theologian). I had, of course, entirely misread the situation. Sometimes there's a good reason why young people get asked to do things that more seasoned people shy away from. The older folks know better.

The conference was fairly well-attended (a couple hundred people, perhaps). The organizers divided us into smallish groups and gave us questions for discussions. Everyone in my group was older than me (some by a considerable margin of years). The first question we were supposed to discuss was something like, "Despite our differences, what holds us together as Christians?" Moderating the discussion was a cakewalk. People were friendly and polite, and most of the contributions were ambiguous and saccharine: "our common humanity," "our need to be loved," and so on. Nothing theological.

After everyone had a chance to speak, I dipped my toe in the conversation. "Everything you've said is insightful and interesting," I lied, "but I would add that, *as Christians,* what holds us together is our common confession—and worship—of God as Father, Son and Holy Spirit." Dead silence.

Then an older woman in the group—who had rolled her eyes as I spoke—blurted out,

"Head trip!"

"Excuse me?" I asked, not sure if I had heard her correctly.

"Head trip! Head trip!" she chirped. My answer, she said, was "too intellectual." I protested that no one in our group had actually said anything about God, and surely our basic confession of God as triune—which Christians have made for centuries—wasn't excessively abstract. I mean, after all, weren't we all baptized in the name of the Father, Son and Holy Spirit? Big mistake. She proceeded to tell me that my comment didn't take into account Christians who didn't understand God in those terms.

In my naiveté, I was shocked. Wasn't this supposed to be a *Christian* ecumenical conference? My shock deepened when I learned that she was a former high-ranking representative of one of the largest ecumenical organizations in the country. The rest of the conference did nothing to allay my growing suspicions. The last day of the conference was supposed to be capped off with an ecumenical worship service. Several of the participants said they wouldn't attend if it was held in the university chapel, since their mere attendance in that venue would have "symbolic significance" (meaning, agreement with the host church's tradition). So we decided to hold the event in the gymnasium, but we couldn't agree on a liturgy—and Holy Eucharist, of course, was right out of the question. Someone actually suggested that *this* church could meet in *this* corner of the gym for the Lord's Supper, while *that* group could meet in *that* corner of the gym, but most of us immediately realized that, *no*, that was a really *really* bad idea. We couldn't even agree on a speaker to deliver a homily, so our ecumenical worship service finally amounted to a few readings from Scripture and a few carefully vetted hymns.

I remember thinking, "Well, we're one in the bond of . . . something or other."

Family Feud

The worst spats happen between family members. We share histories, but remember things differently. We have expectations of each other, but rarely live up to them. Family favorites, ex-spouses, and black sheep all show up at the same reunions. Skeletons sometimes come rattling out of closets, disturbing our illusions of family order, but the truly destructive skeletons may never see the light of day. When conversations amongst family members explode and everyone deserts the table, we all remember it for years to come, and the memory takes on legendary proportions.

Similarly, Christians experience some of the worst spats with other Christians. We tend to make allowances for people of other faiths, atheists, or agnostics. They "don't know Jesus," so we have to be patient with them. It seems easier, in some respects, to love them. But fellow Christians should know better. "We all worship the same Lord," we often say (if a bit hollowly). So if you *say* you're a Christian and you *say* you have the Holy Spirit and you *say* you believe the Bible, then, when we disagree over important matters, clearly one of us must be wrong and that must be because one of us is *in* the wrong. If someone doesn't "repent," then (as we saw in the previous chapter) in the heated discussions that follow, things often escalate until someone drops the h-bomb, destroying the conversation.

Not every serious theological disagreement leads to someone being called a heretic. But my observation is that the longer and more heated a conversation becomes, the closer people come to dropping the h-bomb. Even if the actual term is never voiced, the conversation often disintegrates along the lines I described in the previous chapter. Thousands of Christian groups (meaning churches and sects) exist in the world today, and scores of those groups emerged because Christians disagreed over biblical interpretation and theological issues, to the point where someone decided the stakes were so high that it was impossible for *us* to have fellowship with *them*, so the body of Christ must be divided (once again) for the sake of truth. So much for Jesus' high priestly prayer in John 17:22–23 that his disciples would be one, even as he is one with the Father.

In the face of this continuing fragmentation, in this chapter I suggest how we might evaluate the importance of different kinds of theological disagreement—why not every serious theological disagreement should end in someone being called a heretic—and explain why vigorous theological debate may actually be a sign of vitality. But to do that, we first need to understand how the term heresy has been used and abused, and something about divisions within Christianity (within Protestantism in particular).

Everyone's a Heretic!

About the worst thing (theologically-speaking, at any rate) you can call a Christian is a heretic, but the evangelical blogosphere, at any rate, is riddled with theologians lobbing the h-bomb at everyone or every church they disagree with. I even once stumbled onto a website that decried "the heresy of instrumental music in public worship." But what does the word "heresy" actually mean? The term comes from the Greek word *haeresis*, which simply means "choice." The word in itself doesn't refer to the content of any particular belief, only the fact that such choices divide believers. The false teachers mentioned in 2 Peter 2:1 who introduce "heresies" (*haireseis*) amongst believers, are, in effect, introducing *sects* or *divisions* amongst believers. The author of Titus tells his readers to avoid stupid controversies, genealogies, and arguments about the law, as they are "unprofitable" and "useless," and to warn an *haeretikos* (someone who causes divisions) once, then twice, and after that, have nothing to do with them (see Titus 3:9–10). Conversation ended!

In these passages, heresies are primarily a sin against the unity of the body of Christ. "You're out to break up the table with your ridiculous arguments about the fine points of the law or who is descended from whom? No thanks. Go talk to someone else. We're hangin' together." Breaking up a new, fragile community over silly questions was one of the worst (and stupidest) things you could do in the early stages of the church's existence. Unity was critical to the church's survival in a hostile culture; hence, Paul's exhortation: "Make every effort to maintain the unity of the Spirit in the bond of peace" (Eph 4:3). Theologically, Paul grounds this unity in the oneness of God, and universal church practice is supposed to reflect that oneness: "There is one body and one Spirit, just as you were called to the one hope of your calling, one Lord, one faith, one baptism, one God and Father of all, who is above all and through all and in all" (Eph 4:4–6).

Obviously, at this stage in the primitive church, heresy couldn't mean anything like denying the doctrines of the Trinity or the "hypostatic union" (divine and human natures coexisting in the one person of Christ). It couldn't even be distorting "what the New Testament says," since the limits of the canon hadn't established yet. The most 2 Peter 2 says about the false teachers in question is that "They will even deny the Master who bought them—bringing swift destruction on themselves" (2 Pet 2:1b) which sounds like they refused to confess Jesus as Lord, the earliest recognizable Christian confession.

In effect, these earliest heretics departed from that first bundle of tradition (*paradosis*, literally, that which is *passed on*) circulating amongst the primitive Christian community. As an example of those first traditions, consider what Paul says to the Corinthians: "For I handed on to you as of first importance what I in turn had received: that Christ died for our sins in accordance with the scriptures, and that he was buried, and that he was raised on the third day in accordance with the scriptures, and that he appeared to Cephas, then to the twelve" (1 Cor 15:3–5). Short and sweet.

The most important of those early traditions eventually took shape in the earliest form of the Apostles' Creed (called the "Roman Symbol"), which came to be used in examining catechumens before they were baptized. In the years to follow, *heretics* would be those who "chose" what they wanted to believe by distorting or departing from developing church tradition, and in doing so fragmented the body by taking other Christians with them. So the earliest heretics in the church were *schismatics*, those who caused schisms in the church because they insisted others agree with them on some issue pertaining to genealogy or some fine point of the law. Heresy is a deal breaker because it's a church breaker. If you're a heretic, you've cut yourself off from the body of Christ because you've fragmented its unity, with all of the consequences that follow from that.

As Protestants, we're skilled at throwing the h-bomb; it seems to be in our DNA. Consider, for a moment, Martin Luther and the chain of events he set in motion. Most Protestants lionize Luther whenever we talk about pitting the word of God against mere church tradition. In Luther's 1539 incendiary treatise "On the Councils and the Church,"[1] for example, he champions the supremacy of the Bible over the pope and councils, as he does in so many of his writings. Protestants, especially those evangelicals who have an ax to grind against Roman Catholics, love Luther's rhetoric. "Well done, Luther, for pitting the Bible against the false teaching of Rome!"

But Luther contended with more than one opponent in his attempt to reform the church. He inveighs just as strongly against Ulrich Zwingli and his Anabaptist followers, who teach the doctrine of what has come to be called "memorialism" (the view that Christ isn't actually present in the Lord's Supper; rather, the Supper is a remembrance or memorial of the Jesus' death). In his "Confession Concerning Christ's Supper," Luther calls such people "fanatics," "devils," "knaves," and "heretics" for not adhering to Jesus' clear words: "This is my body" (Luke 22:19). Luther writes, "I testify on my part that I regard Zwingli as un-Christian, with all his teaching, for he holds and teaches no part of the Christian faith rightly. He is seven times worse than when he was a papist."[2] What most evangelicals today (who usually hold to a spiritual presence or memorialist view) don't realize is that their champion of God's word, Martin Luther, would certainly rail against *them*, call them "devils," and charge them with heresy for the same reason.

Like it or not, the Reformation opened the door for the fragmentation of western Christendom and for the h-bomb to be dropped more and more indiscriminately. Luther, the heretical boar in the Lord's vineyard, would castigate Anabaptist and Roman Catholic teachings. The Formula of Concord (part of the Lutheran Book of Confessions) condemns not only Roman Catholic and Anabaptist teaching, but also would be used to condemn Calvinist teaching on election as proceeding from the instigation of the devil.[3]

1. See "On the Councils and the Church" in *LW* 41:9–178.
2. See "Confession Concerning Christ's Supper" in *LW* 37:231.
3. See, e.g., "Formula of Concord—Solid Declaration," 632.

The Council of Trent (1545–1563) would reiterate the Roman Church's pronouncement of heresy against the various reformation factions, thoroughly enumerating and condemning their many errors.[4] And peace-loving Menno Simons (founder of the Mennonites), whilst appreciating the many changes brought about by Luther and the Reformers, called the way the Lord's Supper was celebrated by the new Reformation Church "idolatrous."[5] In surveying the theological spats of the sixteenth century, church historians speak of "mutual condemnations" made by Roman Catholics and Protestants, which in many cases lasted up until the twentieth century.

In the period of what's called "Protestant Orthodoxy" (basically the late sixteenth and early seventeenth centuries), the battle lines between the new church bodies emerging from the Reformation became hardened, as new Protestant churches (especially those in the Reformed tradition) began to draw up their distinctive confessions and faith statements. This trend continued and intensified as Protestantism spread and grew increasingly fragmented, all the way until our present splintered Christian world. "One, holy catholic apostolic church" may be the most hypocritical confession we Protestants make in the Creed. And while there have been recent institutional gestures toward ecumenism, such as the *Joint Declaration on the Doctrine of Justification*[6] (signed by Roman Catholics, Lutherans, and Methodists) and *Called to Common Mission*[7] (signed by Lutherans and Episcopalians), the fragmentation and increasing declension of Protestantism continues.

In our contemporary digital world, where more and more people spend their time, the internet has only intensified the problem (as it does to so many disagreements), as now anyone can capslock his or her (frequently ill-informed) theological venom worldwide, which in turn incites others to do the same. Examples are far too easy to come by. Googling will turn up lunatic essays that charge virtually every Christian communion under the sun with heresy. Surveying the present state of affairs, people are likely to call *any* person with whom they happen to disagree theologically a heretic, which means the word is basically worthless.

4. See *Canons and Decrees of the Council of Trent.*

5. Horsch, *Menno Simons,* 120.

6. Lutheran World Federation and the Catholic Church, "Joint Declaration on the Doctrine of Justification."

7. Episcopal Church of America, "Agreement of Full Communion."

Why the Nicene Creed Is Important

Is there a way we can begin to think about theological disagreements we have with members of our own family without resorting to "heretic!" every time we have a serious, "knock-down, drag-out" disagreement with someone? As we approach this question, I'm convinced that we have to consider the interrelationship of theology, worship, and mission, but since most people who fling the word *heresy* around think primarily in terms of theology, I'll start here and then begin to patch together the separation.

To get started, let me suggest that if you examine the history and development of Christian thought, you can discern a few levels or layers of belief that have emerged, and you'll discover that Christians haven't attached the same weight to each level. Roger Olson, in his book *The Mosaic of Christian Belief*, distinguishes these levels by referring to them as dogma, doctrine, and what the theological tradition calls *adiaphora*.[8] Dogma refers to those core beliefs that all Christians have historically agreed upon; typically, this level of belief is found in the great ecumenical creeds of the church: the Apostle's Creed, the Nicene Creed, the Athanasian Creed, etc. Doctrine refers to particular interpretations of dogma held by various Christian groups, as well as a set of "distinctives" that may or may not be related to classic dogmatic formulations (every church has its doctrinal statement or "what we believe") and *adiaphora* refers to those matters in which there are almost as many opinions as there are Christians (generally, things like worship style, dress, etc.). Perhaps intuitively, some Christians would place beliefs like the doctrines of the Trinity, the saving death and resurrection of Jesus, and final judgment in the level of dogma; particular beliefs and practices (like eschatological positions and speaking in tongues) in the level of doctrine; and personal preferences (like choice of music) in the level of *adiaphora*.

And, intuitively, many Christians would get it right. Quite apart from formal theological training, Christians sensitive to the leading of the Holy Spirit can develop an intuitive grasp for what's genuinely important to hang on to, as opposed to things of lesser importance (if they didn't, then the church would be at the mercy of professional theologians—yikes!). But many Christians get it wrong, and that makes theological disagreement so difficult, arguing about doctrine or adiaphora as though you're arguing about dogma.

The modern ecumenical movement, which began in the late nineteenth century, has been grappling with this question for several generations now. How is it possible to call for Christian unity in confession while

8. Olson, *Mosaic of Christian Belief*, 43–45.

still allowing for disagreement in matters of church doctrine and practice? What could serve as such a standard or criterion? Through several discussions at the highest levels between various Christian communions over the past century, the Nicene Creed has remained—or reemerged, depending on your perspective—as the best candidate for dogmatic unity between Christians.[9] The Creed was accepted in AD 325, but the original version ended in anathematizing (i.e., placing a curse on) those who didn't pledge full subscription—not the best tone to set for ecumenism (even though plenty of other creeds and confessions contain similar threats). So a slightly revised version was accepted by the Council of Constantinople in AD 381, and that's the version that the church recites today (so what we call the Nicene Creed is, technically speaking, the Nicene-Constantinopolitan Creed). It's accepted by all three branches of Christianity, and was put forward as "the *sufficient* statement of the Christian faith"[10] by the historic Lambeth conference of 1888, one of the earliest attempts (by the Anglican communion) in the emerging ecumenical movement to suggest a theological basis for Christian unity. It is represented here in its entirety.[11]

> We believe in one God, the Father, the Almighty, maker of heaven and earth, of all that is, seen and unseen.

> We believe in one Lord, Jesus Christ, the only Son of God, eternally begotten of the Father, God from God, Light from Light, true God from true God, begotten, not made, of one Being with the Father. Through him all things were made. For us men and for our salvation, he came down from heaven: by the power of the Holy Spirit he was born of the Virgin Mary, and became man. For our sake he was crucified under Pontius Pilate; he suffered, died, and was buried. On the third day he rose again in fulfillment of the Scriptures; he ascended into heaven and is seated at the right hand of the Father. He will come again in glory to judge the living and the dead, and his kingdom will have no end.

> We believe in the Holy Spirit, the Lord, the giver of life, who proceeds from the Father and the Son. With the Father and the Son he is worshipped and glorified. He has spoken through the Prophets. We believe in one holy catholic and apostolic Church. We acknowledge one baptism for the forgiveness of sins. We

9. See, e.g., World Council of Churches, *Confessing the One Faith.*

10. Davidson, *Lambeth Conferences,* 280. Emphasis mine.

11. *Catechism of the Catholic Church,* 56–57.

look for the resurrection of the dead, and the life of the world
to come. Amen.

The initial theological reason for the Creed's importance in the history of
the church lies in its confession that the Son is "of one Being" (*homoousion*)
with the Father. In recent years, it's become trendy for historians to bash
Nicaea and this formulation, by saying that the council was a political stunt
by Constantine to forge unity between East and West. Well, what decision
by the church or state is ever without any ulterior motives? But the charge
completely misses the legitimate theological concerns at work, and therefore
ignores why the *homoousion* formulation has functioned as the benchmark
of Christian orthodoxy for almost 1700 hundred years.

  If, as Arius argued, Jesus is *not* of one substance with the Father, if he is
merely "of similar substance" or *homoiousion* (God-ish), then his ability to
reveal the heart of the Father is compromised, as is the saving effectiveness
of his death on the cross. As T. F. Torrance puts it, if the *homoousion* formulation were not true, then the bottom would fall out of the gospel.[12] Notice
that the Creed also affirms the personhood and deity of the Holy Spirit,
against factions in the church that argued that the Spirit was merely the
impersonal, immanent force of God (similar to what Jehovah's Witnesses
teach today). As I've always said, the gospel is not "all about" Jesus, as a
popular worship chorus would have it, because Jesus wasn't that egotistical
and didn't think it was all about him. The Creed directs us to Jesus in his
relationship to the God he called Father and the Holy Spirit whom Jesus
sent upon the Church. So far, none of this should be news to anyone who
has taken an introductory course on Christianity.

  The Nicene Creed has functioned as the basic articulation of Christian *dogma* for centuries, recited by Eastern Orthodox, Roman Catholics,
Anglicans, Lutherans, Presbyterian, Reformed, Methodist, and many other
church bodies. As a theologian, the academic bits of me would quiver with
delight if all the Christian bodies in the world would subscribe to it explicitly
as our pledge of allegiance. Especially in an age of religious pluralism, being
able to articulate the identity of the God revealed in the gospel seems to me
to be a crucial responsibility—and this Creed condenses the three persons
or agents of God's identity as seen in Scripture into a short confession.

---

12. Torrance, *Trinitarian Faith*, 138.

But Let's Get Real

As someone who teaches world religions and new religious movements, every religious community I can think of has *some sort* of fundamental confession that its members agree on. If not, then you belong to a discussion group or book club, and maybe you're okay with that. That being said, there are obvious problems in fantasizing that all Christian groups in the world would somehow magically adopt this Creed as *the* precise articulation of Christian dogma. Historically, this hasn't even happened between Eastern Orthodoxy and Roman Catholicism on account of the fact that the Eastern or Greek version of the Creed confesses that the Spirit proceeds only *from the Father* while the Western or Latin version confesses that the Spirit proceeds from the Father *and the Son (filioque)*. (Thank God we divide the body over all the right issues!) The other reason it hasn't happened, of course, is that we live in the real world, and an enormous part of the Christian world is composed of explicitly non-creedal churches—many of them charismatic and Anabaptist bodies.

But no one, I suspect, would say to these churches, "You can't be considered Christian on the dogmatic level because the Nicene Creed isn't printed in the back of your *Book of Worship* or in the 'What We Believe' dropdown box on your website," because many of these churches would affirm the triune orientation of the Creed in both practice and principle, even if they don't recite it—and to that degree, they are what the church historically would refer to as *orthodox*.

To this point I haven't addressed the relationship between the idea of *dogma* and what we mean by *orthodoxy*. Usually when people talk about orthodoxy, they immediately think of it in theological terms: having right statements lined up about God, so that if you don't affirm the correct set of propositions your salvation is at risk (for example, the preface to the Athanasian Creed menacingly reads that anyone who doesn't keep the whole Creed will perish eternally). But what if I have honest doubts or questions about some of the Creedal formulations or language? How much can I screw up on my theology test before my soul is endangered? Is 90 percent a passing grade? Does God grade on the curve? Will there be a makeup test in purgatory? Not to mention the question of hundreds of millions of Christians who confess the Nicene Creed word for word every Sunday, yet have no interest in what it even means.

We can avoid such ridiculous scenarios, I think, if we keep in mind the basic meaning of *orthodox*, which is not right teaching or right doctrine, but right *doxa* or "glory." To be orthodox is to be one who rightly glorifies, which is the central concern of worship (dox-ology) and mission. Doxology

and mission are fundamental because *the* question for the identity of any
religious community is simply this: to whom do you render worship? (That
was an important issue in contending with Arius, by the way—the *doxological* outcome if he was right.) And the way we orient our lives together
in the world, our mission, is the acid test of what *we say* we believe about
this God. As the philosopher Ludwig Wittgenstein observed: if you want to
know what people believe, *don't ask them*. Rather, observe how they lead
their lives.

At this point, I'm reminded of how Lutheran theologian George
Lindbeck said religion and codified theological teaching actually functions.
Most traditional believers have viewed religion from a "cognitive-proposi-
tional" perspective in which religious beliefs are understood as informative propositions about objective realities (similar to science or traditional
metaphysics).[13] This perspective has been most vulnerable to modern scientific and philosophical criticism. Other people hold an "experiential-
expressivist" position, understanding religions and their beliefs as symbolic
expressions (or *objectifications* or *products*) of deep and common experiences of the divine (or the self or world).[14]

But, Lindbeck says, if we look at how religions actually function, we
find something different than both of these perspectives. Religions are
all-encompassing interpretive schemes, cultural-linguistic mediums that
shape how people live and think.[15] This perspective reverses our usual way
of understanding the relationship between concepts and experience to
language and culture. Both "cognitive-propositionalists" and "experiential-
expressivists" understand language and culture to be the *means* by which
we express our concepts or experiences. Lindbeck, however, following the
lead of what is called the "linguistic turn" in contemporary philosophy, says
that language and culture are the ever-present filters that enable us to think
and have meaningful experiences at all. He employs the idea of a "language-
game" (a phrase taken from Wittgenstein) to emphasize the fact that each
religion has its own "grammar" or *communal* rules[16] (there is no such thing
as a private language, Wittgenstein said) for understanding what beliefs
mean, so those beliefs can't be understood apart from a set of rituals and
behaviors prescribed within communities.[17]

---

13. Lindbeck, *Nature of Doctrine*, 16–17.

14. Lindbeck, *Nature of Doctrine*, 31–32.

15. Lindbeck, *Nature of Doctrine*, 32–41.

16. Lindbeck, *Nature of Doctrine*, 33.

17. See Knitter's fine explication of Lindbeck in *Introducing Theologies of Religion*,
173–91.

Religion, therefore, is primarily neither a bundle of propositions that refer to supernatural states of affairs "out there"—which we are trying to convince people are true—nor an array of symbols that express religious feelings about an encounter with the Absolute (the default position of most pluralists). Rather, religion is a cultural and communal phenomenon that *makes possible* those attitudes or feelings, and codified theological teachings function as rules for talking about God in particular ways that are consonant with a religion's sacred texts and communal practices. If you think about it, this cultural-linguistic model harmonizes rather well with Lindbeck's Lutheran theology and its high priority on the word of God, both preached and written. The word alone comes to the hearer and creates faith, and the biblical text, with its interpretations normed by the Christian community, functions as an interpretive lens for viewing the world and ordering church life and practice.

If we take Lindbeck's insights and apply them to our discussion of the Creed, then I would say that the Creed's real point is to interrogate and direct our worship and practice. To what degree has the church's self-identity and understanding of her mission been shaped by the narrative of the triune God? Do we worship the Father, Son, and Holy Spirit? Do we follow the Father's sending of the Son into the world, bearing the cross, in the wake of the Holy Spirit? If I can put it in a sort of Zen-like way, the Creed is not about the Creed. Its importance doesn't lie in believing that the language (e.g., male pronouns) or the form of the propositions themselves (e.g., "of one being with the Father") are sacred and irreformable. Its importance lies in the way it directs us toward a living encounter with God and a way of living together in this world consistent with the story of Jesus and his relation to the Father and the Spirit. So some churches may be "officially" creedal (in the sense that the Nicene Creed is part of their foundational documents), even while practically ignoring it, while other churches may be "officially" non-creedal but "operationally" creedal (that is, Trinitarian in their life and practice).[18]

So, I'd like to say to well-intentioned apologists who want to argue for the truth of those creedal propositions, "You may *think* you know what those 'truth claims' are saying, but if you remain on the level of abstraction you never do, because those truth claims are embedded in an entire way of life and a matrix of communal practices." People were worshiping the Father, Son, and the Holy Spirit and trying to live out the missionary mandate of Jesus long before Nicaea; if they hadn't been, they never would have bought into this way of articulating things theologically. If we keep these

18. Lindbeck, *Nature of Doctrine*, 74–75.

questions of doxology and mission central in considering what the Creed is about, then the triune orthodoxy articulated in the Creed is fulfilled in every congregation, whether it recites it or not.

Evangelicals love to say, "Christianity isn't a religion; it's a relationship," and in a sense all I'm trying to do is think through that often-misunderstood—but essentially correct—insight in relation to questions of heresy and orthodoxy. If someone testifies to that relationship with the triune God and lives in that community of relationships formed around following the way of Jesus, I think we should *never, ever* refer to them as heretics, or claim that they're cut off from Christ's body because they disagree with us on some issue on the doctrinal or explanatory level. Coming back to my early comments, that would be acting like a schismatic, saying to people who worship the triune God, "You have no part in Christ's body, the grace of God cannot reach you, because you disagree with us on this specific issue."

Imagine the scenario in which you come to a person who has recently come to faith in Christ—who has been baptized, who receives the holy sacrament, who testifies to being filled with the Holy Spirit, and whose life is now anchored in the body of Christ—and saying to her, "Oh and by the way, you can't truly be a member of Christ's body unless you believe that justification or sanctification or the sacraments work *like this*. Unless you agree that the invisible metaphysical mechanisms behind these things work *like this*, you are cut off from Christ."

In sum, Christian worship and practice flesh out or embody what those creedal statements *mean* and in so doing form the basis for our unity. Truth be told, we've never "solved" any theological problem in the abstract, because God is not something you solve in the pages of a book or at a conference. My mentor in grad school, the great Lutheran theologian Gerhard Forde, was fond of saying that descriptive, explanatory teaching was sometimes the enemy of the first-person, present-tense character of the gospel (as though sin can be solved in a book or lecture). Christians around the world have always disagreed, for example, on some of the details about the relations between the triune persons or the divine and human natures in Christ, or how atonement actually works.

We'll never fully solve such issues, but that's never been the reason why we work on these things anyway, as though the faith is a kind of theological Rubik's Cube. Rather, the best minds of the church have always understood that the point of these theological discussions is to intellectually work on the conceptual difficulties, but also to inhabit the theological reality in doxology and ecclesiology. We don't solve the "problem" of the Trinity, the hypostatic union, or different atonement theories; we're grasped by these realities as the word is preached, at the baptismal font or Lord's Table, and live them out daily as Christ followers. Apart from a living context, those basic confessions we defend so vigorously can be shaped into rhetorical mortars we use to blast the very picnic table where our own family is sitting.

If I could pull another metaphor into my vision of the picnic table, Robert Jenson (one of the great luminaries of contemporary theology) describes the relations between Father, Son, and Holy Spirit as three singers who take their part in a "great fugue," and closes the first volume of his *Systematic Theology* by saying, "God is a great fugue. There is nothing so capacious as a fugue."[19] As those who have come to inhabit the capacious music that is God, dogma may help us think about the structure of the fugue; however, the point is to sing. If I could translate Jenson's metaphor into an Appalachian idiom, arguing around the picnic table inevitably happens and should happen, but the real fun starts when Aunt Teresa takes out her harmonica, Uncle Ted breaks out his ukulele, and the nephews and grandkids all join in with Nanna Helen in a rendition of "In the Sweet Bye-and-Bye."

So What About Our Disagreements?

If I've articulated the goal of dogma correctly—to be orthodox in the fullest, living, doxological sense of the term—then our theological disagreements appear in a rather different light. To begin, we clearly never recite and pass down a dogmatic statement like the Creed as though it were written in the heavens. On the interpretive level, we have to reckon with the slippage in meaning that occurs whenever we translate words (especially philosophical and theological words) into different languages and different cultural contexts. "Of one being with the Father" doesn't mean *exactly* the same thing as the Latin *con substantialem Patri*, which didn't mean *exactly* the same thing as the Greek *homoousion toi Patri*. Augustine himself (a Latin theologian) admitted that he didn't understand the Greeks and their distinction between the one *ousia* of God and the three *hypostaseis* of God.

The very terms of the Creed and the doctrinal questions that dogma generates have been the subject of extraordinary discussion and refinement over the history of the church. If this didn't occur, it would probably mean that the Nicene Creed was an interesting museum piece but not a living confession. Faithfulness to the dogma enunciated in the Creed involves neither merely repeating it nor jettisoning it, but critically engaging it. So *we* must continue to hammer out, as much as any other Christians in history have done, questions like what in the world we mean by speaking of the *being*

19. Jenson, *Systematic Theology*, 236.

that Father and Son share or what *person* means when you apply it to the triune identity.

In connection with this, I can't help but observe that in the history of Christian thought, some points of dogma were so fiercely guarded that if you deviated from them you were considered a heretic, but now they don't even appear on the radar screen of most churches today. Most people would be bored even thinking about them. Semi-Pelagianism, condemned as a heresy in the Council of Orange in AD 589, is pretty much inscribed as an article of belief in various free church traditions, and I don't think many Eastern Orthodox Christians even *care* that the Coptic Church is Monophysite.

To return to my main point, much of our work on the doctrinal level simply involves trying to unpack the depth and nuances of dogma, trying to figure out how things work and how to meaningfully communicate these realities to different times and audiences. Christians have done so continuously for nearly two millennia. What does it mean to confess "Maker of heaven and earth" in view of contemporary cosmology and evolutionary biology? What can "one, holy, catholic, and apostolic church" mean in face of the ongoing fragmentation of Christianity? In fact, to *not* take up this challenge, to use books or formulations from only the 1750s or 1950s would be a sign of stagnation. There's a reason I don't use Athanasius's *Against the Arians* or Calvin's *Institutes* or Barth's *Dogmatics* as my textbook for systematic theology (besides the fact that my students would rise up and slay me): We don't live in the fourth or sixteenth or twentieth centuries with all their particularities anymore. One of my mentors used to say that Christian theology is best done in a loose leaf notebook, and while that infuriated some students in the classroom, it's an accurate description of what's been the case for two thousand years. Each generation is trying to work it out, trying to get it right, but we have to remember that "it" is finally a living, personal reality with whom we are in a relationship. As we'll see at the end of this chapter, this insight was central to John Wesley and the emerging Methodist movement. So Geoffrey Wainwright, a Methodist theologian who taught at Duke University, tellingly titled his systematic theology *Doxology: The Praise of God in Worship, Doctrine and Life.*[20]

So, you may be a young-earth creationist and I may be a theistic evolutionist. We both worship and confess our trust in and testify to our relationship with the Maker of heaven and earth, of all things visible and invisible. We may disagree over atonement theories or some of the finer points of what it means to be justified by faith, but we both confess that we have been grasped graciously by the One who "came down for us and our

20. Wainwright, *Doxology*.

salvation" and that he was crucified "for us" and raised on the third day. We may disagree on how sanctification takes place and its extent in the life of the believer, but we both have received the Holy Spirit who has been given to the church, making it one, holy, catholic and apostolic. We may disagree on what the end of the age may look like, and the order in which events may occur, but together we look forward to the resurrection of the dead and the life of the world to come. "I'm not a heretic because I have different explanations of *how it works* in any of these areas; I just happen to disagree with you on that level." Worshiping and praying and living these confessions is essential; our doctrinal explanations that attempt to specify how it all happens are ancillary and constantly shifting.

So Why Do We Need Denominations? And Why Should I Join One?

Despite everything I've said, the reality is that denominations make full affirmation of their doctrines and distinctives a condition for membership. So you embark on an awkward series of negotiations when you say to someone, "Of course you don't have to buy into our denominational *Big Best Book of Correct Doctrine and Practice* to be a Christian; in fact, you can worship with us, take the sacrament with us, and probably even teach Christian education classes eventually. But if you want to be a member of Big Best Church Inc. and take on by public declaration the privilege of financially supporting us and adopting our host of elliptical lifestyle commitments, *then* we require your full subscription to what we believe about distinctive X and so on" (which most members probably don't understand anyway). That doesn't incentivize people to become members.

Let's circle back to the bewildering reality mentioned early in this chapter: nearly forty thousand Christian groups exist in the world today. Given the history of theological squabbles between churches and highly publicized cases of corruption and abuse, it's understandable why many people (younger people, especially) are asking why we need denominations at all, and why they should join one. (The questions are not the same, and they're both potentially misleading.) We've heard lots of talk in recent years about "post-denominationalism." Phyllis Tickle dubbed the present transitional period of the church in the West the "Great Emergence," in which people have grown skittish of hierarchies and institutions, while at the same time becoming more invested in community and social justice issues.[21] While many of these folks continue to recognize the denominations that

21. Tickle, *Great Emergence*. See also Faith & Leadership, "Phyllis Tickle."

nurtured them, we're seeing the rise of what Tickle called the "hyphenateds" ("Presby-mergents," "Metho-mergents," "Bapti-mergents" and so on). These groups of people cling to any denominational affiliations lightly, if at all—a fact that keeps denominational leaders up at night.

Roger Olson reminds us that the word *denomination*, as scholars use it, merely refers to any group of congregations that have fellowship with each other, however informal and voluntary that connection may be.[22] In the present climate of the church, with so much emphasis placed on relationships and networks, you'd think that something like a denomination would be a good thing. I suspect that much of the griping is trendy, and mirrors a larger cultural mistrust of institutions and bureaucracies in general (a good deal of the mistrust has been earned, of course). A bit ironically, in the midst of this post-denominationalism palaver, we've seen the proliferation of nondenominational megachurches and parachurch organizations that end up structuring themselves precisely like those denominations they publicly eschew. Scratch one of the so-called nondenominational or post-denominational churches, and despite claims to "just follow the Bible" or replicate the primitive church you'll find out that *de facto* it's merely a variant of some existing group. Given perennial and universal concerns about doctrine and lifestyle commitments, leadership credentialing and accountability, legalities surrounding property and finance, etc., no church can avoid making decisions in these areas that leads to the formation of a "denomination." In fact, when you dig through a relatively nondescript "community" church's website, you often find out they're really a Methodist or Presbyterian or Pentecostal church in disguise. They simply don't like the word "denomination" or recognized denomination monikers because of negative connotations.[23]

In addition to a general distrust of institutions and hierarchies, there's also a sense shared by many people that so many long-standing squabbles between Christians simply aren't worth continuing anymore. Protestants in particular have argued over various points of doctrine for centuries and we've gotten no closer to finding "solutions," so, the thinking goes, shouldn't we find a way to live together with our differences when there's so much practical work to be done? Theologically speaking, evangelicalism (in the West, at any rate) has drifted toward a kind of generic "Bapticostalism" made up of dollops of pragmatism, experiential religion (distrust of too much intellectualism), and a ringing endorsement of free will that would make Pelagius blush. For example, I frequently see people join the Wesleyan

---

22. Olson, "Reflections and Questions," para. 4.

23. Olson, "Why I Like Denominations."

church after being members of Baptist churches for years, without any apparent doctrinal indigestion. Indeed, many of them couldn't articulate the doctrinal differences between the two churches, in part because they don't care enough about the subject and in part because many Wesleyan churches themselves couldn't articulate the differences.

So when people say things like "Why do we need denominations?! We all should *just be Christians*" (meaning, sans denominational labels), they might mean a couple of different things. A person might be using inflated rhetoric to say that traditional denominational differences don't matter in the sense that Christians are *always* going to disagree about something—and we should have the freedom to come to our own conclusions—but we should never let our distinctives become the occasion to exclude or drive other Christians from the table (which happens all the time). Or someone might mean that, since we're all (supposedly) Spirit-filled believers, we all should believe the same thing (which is never going to happen).

Olson (who admits that he likes denominations) asks us to attempt a thought experiment. Imagine a single worldwide Christian "denomination," he says. What would it look like? Whose voices would be muted? Which Christians would be left out because they didn't fit the worldwide church's standards for unity? Which tradition's distinctives would win? "In my opinion," Olson says, "this one world church ideal is not ideal at all—except for Catholics and closet Catholics."[24] Olson says there's no reason why denominations can't worship and work together, let alone harbor or express hostility toward each other. But visible and institutional unity isn't needed, or even desirable, for that. Indeed, he says that his vision is an "ecumenism of the Spirit."[25] (Olson is a Baptist, but if you're really serious about wagering on an ecumenism of the Spirit, the worldwide charismatic renewal movement is all too willing to say, "challenge accepted."[26]) At the end of the day, denominations *are* going to exist—whether you call them denominations or not—on account of Christian liberty of conscience and theological honesty, but acknowledging our differences doesn't need to be an impediment to our cooperation.

"So why *should I* join a denomination?" The question is trickier than it looks, because it's generally folded into the question of becoming a member of a local church, with all the responsibilities a commitment of that kind entails. I mean that you can't "join a denomination" in the abstract. Some churches' "solution" to this hesitancy surrounding formal membership has

24. Olson, "Why I Like Denominations," para. 17.

25. Olson, "Why I Like Denominations," para. 12.

26. See Yong, *Renewing Christian Theology*, 170.

been to make it a non-issue by saying things like, "If you attend our church and consider it your home, then consider yourself a member." Adopting this position poses a new set of challenges for shared decision-making, of course. You generally have to create another rubric or set of criteria for including (and excluding) certain church "members" for (and from) participation in the decision-making process. Now, if the question about joining a denomination is *really* more about joining a local congregation, then the answer seems clear enough: the New Testament knows nothing of a privatized faith. To be a Christian means to be member of Christ's body, locally and concretely so.[27] In this respect, we probably talk way too glibly about "the church" in abstract or spiritualized terms. Refusing to commit yourself to an actual body of fellow believers gives the lie to all that blather about the importance of relationships and community, and probably reflects our obsession with the great temptation of consumer culture, that of "keeping my options open." Of course, I can imagine a person saying, "Well, I can be committed to a local body without formal membership." But I'd say in response, "That's really commitment-*lite*. What you're talking about is more like a promise to yourself than to a local body." When we make public promises (think about marriage or citizenship vows) we become more focused and less likely to bail when the going gets tough or when disagreements arise. And let's face it—we're also more likely to follow through on financial commitments to a local body when we've made a public promise to be part of a congregation.

So, in important respects, this question about local church membership goes a long way toward answering the larger question about whether I can or should be a member of one of those big, bad denominations. The local church of which you are a member is either related to other like-minded churches (in which case you are part of a denomination in Olson's sense of the word) or it functions as a denomination unto itself (some "nondenominational," independent megachurches have more members than entire denominations). But no church, whether it likes the word "denomination" or not, can avoid making decisions that led to some of the existing divisions in Protestantism in the first place. No church can avoid drafting "What We Believe" or a statement of faith. Even if only implicitly, we make doctrinal decisions every time we engage in exegesis, prepare sermons, select Christian education material, and share the gospel with someone. Shall we baptize infants? Commune believers who aren't members of our church? Ordain women? You may not like to make hard and fast decisions about

27. See Stetzer, "Membership Matters."

many doctrinal issues, but we have to make decisions in these and many other areas.

Why and how we hold those positions involves another series of questions, especially for leadership: On what basis have we made our decisions? How much weight have we placed on particular doctrinal positions? What would it take for us to change our minds? What would be the consequences if we did? Have we maintained certain positions at all costs, not because they're theologically worth fighting for, but because we'd look just like denomination X if we let these positions go by the board? L. Gregory Jones points out that one of the most important questions a denomination can ask itself is this: What is the mission for which we exist? "And are we willing for our existence to come to an end for the sake of greater faithfulness to gospel?"[28] Given that question, let's face it: some denominations probably have outlived their usefulness. I suspect that many church leaders across the theological spectrum know that in a generation or two, the names of their floundering denominations will mean little more than a subheading in a chapter of a church history textbook.

So why be part of a denomination at all? Brian McLaren points out that, for all their liabilities, denominations actually do a number of things well: they embody an ethos (something like our brand identity); conserve institutional treasures like communal memories and doctrinal formulations; support relationships on the local, regional, and global levels; protect physical and human assets; see and solve problems; and create policies—all important things.[29] Yet in my experience, individuals take the plunge and become members of a denomination for a variety of less sophisticated reasons: friendships they've developed in local churches, family heritage, or simple geographic convenience, with institutional and theological questions playing little substantive roles in their decision.

Now, to the theologically-sensitive person who says, "I don't agree with the doctrine of *any* of the denominations I've seen out there; therefore, I'm not going to become a member of *any* church," I think we should say, "Yes, you may never agree completely with *any* established church out there, but a local body trying to be faithful to its mission needs you, so make a decision as best as you're able, take a seat at the picnic table where you experience the least amount of theological indigestion, and commit yourself not to 'the church' in an abstract sense, but to an actual body of believers."

28. Jones, "Future of Denominations," para. 9.
29. McLaren, "Denominations Do Invaluable Things."

Insights from John Wesley

The Pietist tradition, with its emphases on worship and practical Christian living, has reflected carefully on issues of unity and disagreements amongst Christians. John Wesley, in his "Farther Thoughts upon Christian Perfection" (1763), found it necessary to give careful advice to the emerging Methodists, who were keen to promote their distinctive teaching of Christian perfection. His first bit of advice was to constantly be on guard against pride; if you think that, since God is so obviously teaching you, you no longer need to be taught by mere humans, "pride lieth at the door."[30] Rather, Wesley says, "you have need to be taught, not only by Mr. Morgan, by one another, by Mr. Maxfield, or me, but by the weakest Preacher in London; yea, by all men."[31] Don't say to anyone, Wesley urges, who would dare challenge or reprove you, "You are blind; you cannot teach me," but rather consider carefully what they say.[32] And let modesty and self-diffidence characterize your bearing throughout.[33]

Related to pride is what the eighteenth century called "enthusiasm," which we might think of as "spirituality on speed," that kind of turbocharged spiritual sensitivity in which nearly *everything* you experience is a direct communication from God. "Give no place," Wesley says, "to a heated imagination. Do not hastily ascribe things to God. Do not easily suppose dreams, voices, impressions, visions, or revelations to be from God. They may be from him. They may be from nature. They may be from the devil."[34] Careful exegesis, in particular, can help prevent our turbocharged spiritual imaginations from running away with us, as can merely taking the time to carefully think through things. "You are in danger of enthusiasm every hour," Wesley says, "if you depart ever so little from Scripture" or if "you despise or lightly esteem reason, knowledge, or human learning; every one of which is an excellent gift of God, and may serve the noblest purposes."[35] Therefore, Wesley advises readers to never, in your super spiritual state, mock the notions of wisdom, reason, or knowledge—as if you have a direct line to the Holy Spirit and your conversation partner doesn't—because you actually need more of these things than you realize. So "If you mean worldly

---

30. Wesley, "Farther Thoughts Upon Christian Perfection," Q32 (*Works* 13:111).
31. Wesley, "Farther Thoughts Upon Christian Perfection," Q32 (*Works* 13:111).
32. Wesley, "Farther Thoughts Upon Christian Perfection," Q32 (*Works* 13:112).
33. Wesley, "Farther Thoughts Upon Christian Perfection," Q32 (*Works* 13:112).
34. Wesley, "Farther Thoughts Upon Christian Perfection," Q33 (*Works* 13:112–13).
35. Wesley, "Farther Thoughts Upon Christian Perfection," Q33 (*Works* 13:113).

wisdom, useless knowledge, false reasoning, say so; and throw away the chaff, but not the wheat."[36]

Besides, Wesley says, all those visions, revelations, and manifestations you might claim as evidence of your spiritual superiority pale in comparison to love, which is God's highest gift. "There is nothing higher in religion; there is, in effect, nothing else; if you look for anything but more love, you are looking wide of the mark, you are getting out of the royal way."[37] So when you try to persuade people of the doctrine or spiritual gift emphasized by your church, and you ask them, "'Have you received this or that blessing?' *if you mean anything but more love, you mean wrong*; you are leading them out of the way, and putting them upon a false scent."[38]

As many people have pointed out, Wesley never originally intended the Methodist societies to break off from the Church of England and become a new denomination. In fact, he counseled the early Methodists against this very thing:

> Beware of schism, of making a rent in the Church of Christ. That inward disunion, the members ceasing to have a reciprocal love "one for another," (1 Cor. 12:25,) is the very root of all contention, and every outward separation . . . Beware of a dividing spirit; shun whatever has the least aspect that way. Therefore, say not, "I am of Paul or of Apollos;" the very thing which occasioned the schism at Corinth.[39]

Practically speaking, this means not "exalting" or "despising" this or that preacher or teacher. In our context, we might say to beware of turning your favorite preachers or teachers into celebrities and demonizing those with whom you disagree (two of our culture's favorite pastimes). Celebrity culture amongst the church can only breed division, and hurts both the people in the spotlight and the cause of God. On the other hand, Wesley says, when you're listening to someone you disagree with, don't nitpick and try to find things you can use against them later. "Do not bear hard upon any by reason of some incoherency or inaccuracy of expression; no, nor for some mistakes, were they really such."[40]

Wesley understood that theological differences were bound to emerge amongst the early Methodists, but his advice to them is perhaps even more

36. Wesley, "Farther Thoughts Upon Christian Perfection," Q33 (*Works* 13:113).

37. Wesley, "Farther Thoughts Upon Christian Perfection," Q33 (*Works* 13:114).

38. Wesley, "Farther Thoughts Upon Christian Perfection," Q33 (*Works* 13:114); my emphasis.

39. Wesley, "Farther Thoughts Upon Christian Perfection," Q37 (*Works* 13:120).

40. Wesley, "Farther Thoughts Upon Christian Perfection," Q37 (*Works* 13:120).

pertinent to our time: whatever you're arguing about with fellow believers, don't let it become the occasion over which you desert the table.

> Suffer not one thought of separating from your brethren, whether their opinions agree with yours or not. Do not dream that any man sins in not believing you, in not taking your word; just as you see, or who judge it their duty to contradict you, or that this or that opinion is essential to the work, and both must stand or fall together. *Beware of impatience of contradiction.* Do not condemn or think hardly of those who cannot see as just as you see, or who judge it their duty to contradict you . . . I fear some of us have thought hardly of others, merely because they contradicted what we affirmed. All this tends to division; and, by everything of this kind, we are teaching them an evil lesson against ourselves.[41]

In "Father Thoughts," Wesley doesn't lay out the actual dogmatic layer of belief that he believed should function as the basis of theological unity amongst Christians; he's more concerned with suggesting what I would call a Wesleyan conversational ethos. We get Wesley's own take on the *content* of the dogmatic minimum he thought all Christians should share in his 1739 letter "To a Roman Catholic." Given the anti-Roman Catholicism that leaps out at various points in his writing, it's astonishing that Wesley penned a letter like this at all, and for that reason it bears close attention. Wesley begins the letter (most likely a treatise for wider readership, since he probably didn't have a particular person in mind) by acknowledging that, with so many representations of Protestants and Roman Catholics floating around, both sides had come to view each other as "monsters," and were always poised to hurt each other. But, he asks, aren't "malice, hatred, revenge, bitterness, whether in us or you" an abomination to the Lord? Our theological opinions may in fact be right or wrong, but these "tempers are undeniably wrong"—so how is it possible to restore at least "some small degree of love" for each other?[42]

He begins by dismantling some of his conversation partner's misapprehensions of what Protestants believe by giving what amounts to a brief exposition (in nine short paragraphs) of the Nicene Creed (even including "true God from true God" in his explanation).[43] His most significant elaborations include adding the triple office of prophet, priest, and king in his explanation of the second article, a one-line summation of Chalcedonian

---

41. Wesley, "Farther Thoughts Upon Christian Perfection," Q37 (*Works* 13:121); emphasis original.

42. Wesley, "To a Roman Catholic" (*Letters* 3:7).

43. Wesley, "To a Roman Catholic" (*Letters* 3:8–10).

Christology ("he was made man, joining the human nature with the divine in one person") and an explanation of the Holy Spirit as the "immediate cause" of all holiness in us. After laying out this summation of Christian belief, he then puts the question to his Roman Catholic interlocutor: "Now, is there anything wrong in this? Is there any point which you do not believe as well?"[44] Wesley realizes that Roman Catholics think Protestants should believe *more* than this, but asks his conversation partner that, if a Protestant "sincerely believes this much and practices accordingly," do you really think that person will "perish everlastingly"?[45]

"Practicing accordingly" was a big deal for Wesley. Apart from this, Wesley insists, your faith will not save you,[46] a position that Calvinists and Lutherans are all too quick to tag as "works righteousness" or "legalism." But Wesley's point is that the very nature of genuine faith is grounded in practice; faith means *faithful living*. Those who live in "open sin" are "open heathens. They are the curse of the nation, the bane of society, the shame of mankind, the scum of the earth."[47] (Wesley isn't shy about sharing his opinions!) You misunderstand the Creed if you think it can be merely recited like a list of correct metaphysical opinions or sacred incantations apart from actual practice. A true Protestant, by contrast,

> has a full confidence in [God's] mercy, fears him with a filial fear, and loves him with all his soul. He worships God in spirit and in truth, in everything gives him thanks; calls upon him with his heart as well as his lips at all times and in all places; honours his holy name and his Word, and serves him truly all the days of his life . . . Now, do not you yourself approve of this? Is there any one point you can condemn? Do not you practise as well as approve of it?[48]

In the course of the treatise, it becomes clear that Wesley isn't out to convert his conversation partner, but to get him to see that the dogmatic minimum we share in common must be rooted in worship and our mission to love others as Christ loved us.

> I am not persuading you to leave or change your religion, but to follow after that fear and love of God without which all religion is vain. I say not a word to you about your opinions or outward

44. Wesley, "To a Roman Catholic" (*Letters* 3:10).
45. Wesley, "To a Roman Catholic" (*Letters* 3:10).
46. Wesley, "To a Roman Catholic" (*Letters* 3:10).
47. Wesley, "To a Roman Catholic" (*Letters* 3:10).
48. Wesley, "To a Roman Catholic" (*Letters* 3:10).

manner of worship. But I say, all worship is an abomination to the Lord, unless you worship him in spirit and in truth, with your heart as well as your lips, with your spirit and with your understanding also.[49]

If we're serious about loving others, then how can we—who share a common confession—refuse to love one another? We *can* put the points of our disagreements aside, Wesley urges. After all, Wesley says, he hopes to see his Roman Catholic friend in heaven, and his friend cannot possibly believe that Wesley, given his confession and practice, will go to hell. So then, "if we cannot as yet think alike in all things, at least we may love alike. Herein we cannot possibly do amiss"—and "loving alike" means, negatively, resolving not to hurt each other, to say nothing unkind of each other, and to harbor in our hearts no "unfriendly temper" toward each other, which is the root of those destructive words and actions.[50] Positively, it means looking for ways to build up each other in love and help each other in what we agree leads to the work of the kingdom.

Around the Table with Our Sisters and Brothers

At the conclusion of this chapter, there are a couple of lessons to keep in mind about Christian dogma and the denominational drive to articulate doctrinal distinctives. The first is this: keep your church's doctrinal spins and distinctives in perspective. Beware of allowing the theological "distinctives" of your tradition to grow in your own mind, Godzilla-like, until they cause you to look down on and trample other believers. Inerrancy, the historic episcopate, justification by faith, double predestination, entire sanctification, speaking in tongues, believer's baptism—most groups have distinctives crucial to their understanding of the Bible, salvation, or the Christian life. Denominational identities rest on those distinctives. But if your tradition alone in all of Christendom holds *this* particular belief, could it be all that important in God's great economy or the key that unlocks the secrets to the Bible or Christian life? Some popular theological watchdogs (self-styled "heresy hunters") roaming the internet, foaming at the mouth over protecting their distinctive, seem to me to be what the ancient church would have called *schismatics*. Brian McLaren is spot on when he says that the future of the church is ecumenical, and that means two things: "It means having a tradition, but it means not being limited by your tradition."[51]

49. Wesley, "To a Roman Catholic" (*Letters* 3:10–11).
50. Wesley, "To a Roman Catholic" (*Letters* 3:13).
51. McLaren, "Denominations Do Invaluable Things," para. 29.

The second lesson is this: keep doxology and mission central. Remember that at the heart of the gospel stands the personal reality of God in Christ, which is a fancy way of saying that Jesus is alive. Because he is alive, our common commitment to doxology (how we respond to this living Jesus) and mission remains our best theological defense against schism. In other words, there's a close relationship between doxology and identity, between the God whom we worship and who we are as a particular community with a mission. Yes, there *are* theological boundaries to our doxology, even if those boundaries are wide indeed. If some church were to finally alight on the position that we shouldn't worship Jesus or be filled with the Holy Spirit, or that we should worship Vishnu or Angelina Jolie in addition to Father, Son, and Holy Spirit, then that would be a deal-breaker, at least as far as table fellowship amongst believers is concerned. But as far as I can determine, worshiping and following the living Christ in the fellowship of the Father and Holy Spirit provides the best basis for family members to lovingly disagree amongst ourselves and remain at the table.

3

Talking with Cousins

Members of Other Faiths

I do some of my best work in coffee shops. There's something about the aroma of coffee, the buzz of people milling about and music in the background that relaxes me and helps me get in the zone. I'm too old to be a hipster, but I appreciate the vibe. No matter where we've lived, I've always managed to find a coffee hangout and set up camp there on a regular basis, spreading my books out on a table and going up to the barista for *yet another* espresso. When we lived in the Twin Cities, I found a little café that became a favorite afternoon haunt. The owner was a Muslim, an immigrant from Pakistan, and we saw each other enough to exchange pleasantries when I'd enter his shop. He once told me that he only knew about two things: tobacco and coffee. I'm not a smoker, but I could vouch for his knowledge of coffee. He served a cappuccino so smooth you could hear the angels sing.

So one afternoon I'm holed up in my favorite corner, books covering the table as usual. I'm the only person in the shop because most people have real jobs. My friend wanders over to the table, glances at my books, and asks what I'm doing.

"Some research for a paper I'm writing," I said.

"What do you study?" he asked.

"Theology."

"That's God, right?"

"Right."

Now I'm beginning to wonder where this is going to go. We chat amiably enough for a few minutes, then he says this:

"I must tell you this, my friend. As a Muslim, of course, I have nothing to do with the Jews politically. But when it comes to God, we Muslims have more in common with Jews than with you Christians, because you say that God has a son, right?"

"Right."

"But how can God have a son?" he asked, voice rising. I noticed a vein in his forehead beginning to bulge out. "God is one, and if God is one, then how can God have a son? That's nonsense! That's blasphemy! That's . . . that's . . . *bullshit!*" By this point, his voice was raising the roof off the shop. I was glad other patrons weren't around.

I was tempted to respond with the same level of intensity—but mentally I held it together, trying to give him the benefit of the doubt that he was a true believer trying to defend the unity of God, even if I didn't think he understood much about divine unity. So I did my best to explain what Christians mean when we say that God is *three-in-one* and that, whatever else we might mean, we didn't intend blasphemy. But I could tell by the look on his face he wasn't buying any of it. I was guilty of what Muslims refer to as *shirk*, meaning "associating partners" with Allah.

And if I didn't change my ways, there'd be hell to pay.

Religious Pluralism—The New Black

The title alone of this chapter will be enough to shock some Christians. How can we possibly speak of Muslims, Buddhists, and heaps of other "pagans" as our cousins? According to the theological tradition in which I grew up, *all* members of *all* other religions were going to hell (and Roman Catholics were not considered Christians). Verses that insist "no other name" than Jesus' can save and that no one comes to the God the Father except by him buttressed this position. With this attitude, in "Christian" America, members of other faiths were held in suspicion at best, and regarded as enemies at worst. There wasn't much point in having serious conversations with people of other faiths—even if you could find them!—except for their possible conversion.

Fast-forward to the twenty-first century. Religious pluralism is the new black. Whereas thirty or forty years ago you might grow up in small town North America and never meet a person of another faith (except maybe for Jews), chances are today your physician will be Hindu, your lab partner a Wiccan, and your child's classmate a Muslim. Religious others are literally seated next to us at our lunch table.

In this chapter, one of my goals is to lay out what's at stake in these conversations: why we should want to have them, how to think about the claims made by other religions in light of the gospel, and how to think about the differences that emerge if we're going to live together on this planet. So I'm going to wrestle with questions like these: How are Christians related to members of other faiths? What's the point of having conversations with these people? Aren't members of other religions rivals, if not outright enemies? Aren't members of other religions going to hell? What's the point of all those warnings in the Bible about hell, and why even engage in missions, if you're going to start making exceptions for people?

Through the years, Christians have developed a number of responses to questions like these as they've grappled with religious pluralism—responses that sometimes raise more problems than they solve. For example: Yes, God is just and has left general revelation (in nature and conscience) so everyone can know about the existence of God in principle, but this general revelation serves only to confirm God's condemnation of humanity (tricky, God, tricky). So in order to defend God's justice, some Christians have come up with the idea that children who can't understand and respond responsibly to the gospel (those under the "age of accountability") will escape divine judgment, while someone who has never even had the opportunity to hear the gospel is bound for perdition. I'll try to show why responses like this don't make a lot of sense, even as I try to explain the determining factor in thinking about the eternal destiny of people, and why we continue to engage in missions.

Cousins? How Are We Related to Other Religions?

I've been warned repeatedly through the years by well-intentioned Christians that other religions are demonically inspired, so studying them even in an academic context is risky business. Someone once asked me if, given the various Scriptures from the world's religions in my office, I was concerned about demonic oppression. I responded by saying that I kept the Muslim Qur'an, Hindu *Bhagavad-Gita*, and Confucian *Analects* touching each other on the shelf, so the devils were so busy fighting amongst themselves they didn't notice me. My conversation partner wasn't amused.

How can I possibly claim that we're cousins to members of other faiths? Some connections in our family genealogies can be historically documented: Judaism and Islam, for example. But we're also related to groups like the Latter-Day Saints church, regardless of the Mormon eschewal of the church for most of its history. Some people try to argue that we're related to other faiths on a deeper level, that of a common mystical "religious experi-ence" that lies at the heart of all religions, to which individual religions give their distinctive twist through doctrines and practices. A growing number of religion scholars today, however, doubt that there's anything like a generic religious experience, which is then expressed and defined by particular re-ligions' symbols and rituals. I won't take up that argument here, but I think that, strictly on the level of what we actually say, the case can be made that we're related to most religious faiths by kind of a minimalist, perhaps even universalist, confession: that, for example, creation is not the product of mere chance, that morality and the meaning of our lives have a transcendent source, and that our present, earthly experience does not exhaust our exis-tence. Furthermore, most major religions would agree that human beings are worthy of respect and that love is the highest expression of the divine or ultimate reality.

That's a bare-bones confession of what most religious believers share. It sets off the kinds of conversations we have around the table from the con-versations we might have with many (all though not all) kinds of agnostics and atheists. This minimalist confession remains abstract, however. We haven't said anything about the character of God or the gods (if they exist), the value of creation, the content of morality, the fundamental problem or crisis confronting human beings, the solution to this problem or crisis, the specific end for which human life is designed, or what the afterlife looks like. Many religions do share similarities in terms of basic morality (comparisons to the Ten Commandments can be made with many religions), but many nonreligious moral philosophies espouse similar tenets. The substantive differences emerge, however, when we try to answer these questions. Some of my students go into shock when they realize that the commonplace state-ment that "all religions basically teach the same thing" disintegrates when you see how the world religions answer these questions in detail. That's when you realize we're cousins to members of other faiths, not brothers and sisters.

We're closer to some cousins than others. Scholars lump religions into categories like Western religions (the so-called monotheisms of Judaism, Christianity and Islam), Eastern religions (Hinduism, Buddhism, Con-fucianism, Taoism) and Indigenous religions (e.g., African or Australian animisms) on account of similarities in how they attempt to answer the big questions. But those similarities don't withstand serious scrutiny. For exam-ple, what Christians and Muslims believe about monotheism breaks down quickly, and "Hinduism" is a convenient but misleading umbrella term for a myriad of religious expressions on the Indian subcontinent. Classification schemes for new religious movements are even more questionable (e.g., are

Jehovah's Witnesses Christians?). Some groups may seem so far out to us that perhaps we should not think of them as cousins, but as nephews, nieces, or even distant shirttail relations.

What's the Point of Talking?

I suspect that, if asked, the average person would say that the point of talking to people of other faiths is to understand them. But what exactly are we supposed to understand? At the top of the list would be the fact of religious diversity itself. How many Christians can tell the differences between Sunni and Shia Muslims? Between Conservative and Reform Jews? Let alone the differences between Nyabinghi and Twelve Tribes Rastafari or Dianic and Gardnerian Wiccans. Yet knowing and respecting these differences is just as important to these believers as knowing the differences between Roman Catholics and Mennonites or between Pentecostals and Lutherans. (If you're a Southern Baptist, how would you like to be lumped together with the Episcopalians?) This isn't merely a matter of beliefs about metaphysical trivia; it has to do with how people view and live their lives in the world. Most Christians don't realize that Nation of Islam and Shia Islam have dramatically different views of eschatology, that not all Buddhists are vegetarians, and not all Muslims are teetotalers. In a religiously pluralistic world growing ever smaller, Stephen Prothero makes a convincing case for improving our level of religious literacy.[1]

Most people would give lip service to the idea that you shouldn't criticize something if you don't understand it, but it's not a stretch to say that most people don't understand what understanding something entails. A ninety-second news soundbite or a Wikipedia article hardly counts. (The digital age makes information instantly available and at once massively unreliable.) At a bare minimum, understanding another religious tradition involves things like having conversations with members of that faith, observing some of their practices, and reading primary sources from that tradition.

Popular Christian apologetic treatments generally aren't the best way to become informed about other religions. These treatments tend to be one-sided when it comes to handling other faiths (pointing out their many shortcomings), and most former members of any religion have shocking anecdotes to tell—that's why they left. (Most Christians avoid reading stories about Christians converting *to* other faiths.) But forming a sound perspective on another faith can't be done by collecting the very worst anecdotes

1. Prothero, *Religious Literacy.*

about that religion. In every religion, a gap exists between the official beliefs "on the books" and how that faith is lived out by its practitioners in various contexts and cultures. Every religion has its share of syncretistic folk varieties, nominal adherents, and straight-up crazies. It's as ridiculous, for example, to judge Buddhism based on a short-term mission trip to a remote city in southeast Asia as it would be to judge Christianity based on snake-handling fundamentalist camp meeting in the back woods of Appalachia.

Developing a well-informed and nuanced view of another's religion helps to minimize fear and foster good relationships everywhere from across backyard fences to international relations. But minimizing fear is only one part of the puzzle. Christians who take time to talk with their Buddhist or Muslim neighbors about their faith often find that they come to understand their own faith on a deeper level. This can happen through discovering areas of agreement, for example, in how Buddhists and Christians talk about the nature of desire or peace-making. My faith is also deepened when we wade into those areas of sharp *disagreement* (I always appreciate the importance of the Nicene definition whilst talking to Jehovah's Witnesses).

But there are other practical areas in which we can learn. If you're a Christian, talk to your Sikh neighbors. You'll learn what it's like to being mistaken for a member of another religion, and you'll learn how people unlike yourself view issues related to immigration, multiculturalism, and religious freedom. If you live in small-town America, especially, you'll find out how others are treated on the street, in the shops, and in school. As a Christian, you'll find out how privileged you are, in ways you never imagined.

In his book *Between Allah and Jesus: What Christians Can Learn from Muslims*, apologist Peter Kreeft observes that, while there are plenty of things we should not learn from Muslims (e.g., subjugating women) and some things we should learn from them (e.g., submitting to God's will), there's something more indefinable (but perhaps more important) that we should learn. Kreeft comes close to calling it the "spirit" of Islam, meaning their spiritual toughness or moral conviction.[2] I'd call it the *sensibility* of a religion. It can't be reduced to bullet points, but what we learn from Hinduism is a sense of eternity, from Buddhism a sense of the interrelationship of wisdom (*prajna*) and compassion (*karuna*), from Daoism a sense of reverence for and harmony of all things, and from Confucianism a sense for moral rectitude and human-heartedness.

My Christian faith, as a religion scholar, is most often deepened when my engagement with other religious traditions pose (perhaps unanswerable)

---

2. Kreeft, *Between Allah and Jesus*, 11–12.

questions that keep me up at night: Is the Buddhist notion of emptiness (*sunyata*) related to the nature of Christ's self-emptying (*kenosis*), and what might divine emptiness mean for how we experience God's presence in moments of God-abandonment?[3] In what sense can you speak of the cosmic Christ ("in whom all things hold together") as the *Dao* of God?[4] Does Christian faith contain an implicit theology of the religions capacious enough to treat these questions? According to the biblical witness, God providentially moves throughout human history and culture, directing not only Israel, but also the Philistines and the Arameans (Amos 9:7); Christ the light of God indeed lightens every person coming into the world (John 1); and the Spirit animates all creatures so intimately (Ps 113) that the ancient Greek poets recognized that we inhabit God's presence (Acts 17).

When I talk like this, my conservative and fundamentalist friends (yes, I still have them) generally say that I'm forgetting about sin and the idolatrous world of religions. As far as forgetting about sin is concerned, *of course* this world is broken and fallen, but it's still God's world, and God's still at work at it in ways that we can hardly imagine. And while the question of idolatry must be squarely faced, it's hardly the exclusive province of non-Christian religions (it's difficult to accuse Jews and Buddhists, for example, of idolatry). You want to talk about idolatry? You can step into any number of American Protestant churches that pay lip service to "Christ alone" but *de facto* worship the gods of celebrity, success, racism, or militarism.

Not Everyone Wants to Talk

Not everyone wants to have a conversation as I've described it. Anyone who has taken the risk of talking to people from other religious traditions knows what I'm talking about. Even after I told a Mormon missionary that I was a Wesleyan minister who taught courses in new religious movements and was interested in talking with her strictly for research purposes, she couldn't rein in her evangelical fervor and proceeded to remind me in no uncertain terms that God revealed to Joseph Smith that all other Christian churches were wrong. (Talk about an awkward conversation starter.) When I encounter individuals like this, I try to remember that every tradition has its share of in-your-face zealots. Even as we would want people to meet the best representatives of a hospitable and loving Christianity, and not judge us on the basis of crazies, so I try to regard any practitioner of another tradition as a friend (or potential friend) until they declare themselves an enemy.

3. See Cobb, *Emptying God.*
4. See Damascene, *Christ the Eternal Tao.*

I'm not a mega-fan of megachurches, but I like the way Rick Warren of Saddleback once answered a question about whether he compromised his beliefs by building bridges to people of other faiths. Pastor Warren, in one of those "Aha!" moments, said that we can't win our enemies to Christ, but only our friends.[5]

Aren't Other Religions Our Enemies?

Even if we don't regard individual members of other faiths as our enemies, a more difficult question to answer is whether a religion is intrinsically antagonistic toward Christianity. Clearly, some New Religious movements (such as the Creativity movement and Satanism) are hostile to Christianity as a religion, and some NRMs that fancy themselves "restorationist" Christian movements (such as Jehovah's Witnesses) are antagonistic toward orthodox and institutional Christianity. (It seems to me that the LDS church, after decades of being antipathetic toward orthodox Christians, has softened its stance in recent years as it has sought to be more accepted by the mainstream.) Islam and Baha'i present more problems, as both of these religions affirm Jesus as one of their prophets, while insisting that the revelation to Muhammad and the Baha'ullah fulfill what Jesus was really on about (contrary to what the Christian church says) and supersedes it.

Islam in particular presents the most complex challenge in thinking about whether other faiths are our enemies. Kreeft says that he can't see how a Christian can deny there's much in Islam that's from God and also things directly contrary to God.[6] Given what I've said about the Nicene (Trinitarian) structure of Christian belief and spirituality, and the centrality of doxology, what do we do with passages from the Qur'an that condemn belief in the Trinity as blasphemy (e.g., 5:73) and refute worship of Jesus (e.g., 5:116)?

Yale theologian Miroslav Volf has argued that enough similarity exists between what Christians and Muslims believe about God for us to say that we *worship* the same God, even though we Christians believe that Muslims misunderstand the *nature* of this God.[7] That's a helpful distinction, but I think that asking whether we worship the "same" God is a confusing question to begin with and gets us off on the wrong foot. Look at it this way: the God who the Bible reveals tells us to worship Jesus; without such worship, there is no Christian faith. The God revealed in the Qur'an expressly

5. Murashko, "EXCLUSIVE Rick Warren," para. 26.

6. Kreeft, *Between Allah and Jesus*, 18.

7. Volf, *Allah*, 109, 145.

forbids this; such worship constitutes *shirk* (associating partners with Allah), the worst blasphemy you can commit. So if you answer, "Yes, we both worship the same God," neither side can really believe that this same God commanded contradictory things (unless God is just being a jerk). The only way around this is to say that *your* inspired book is corrupt, inaccurate, or (at worst) demonically-inspired, but here are a few table scraps for you: somehow God hears your blasphemous prayers anyway, a concession that is neither unique to the Christian-Muslim encounter nor particularly helpful, given the fact that worship is always embedded within communal practices and attitudes that believers on the *other* side of the divide find ungodly.

So even if Muslims and Christians agree that one God exists (a basic philosophical question), the more interesting question swirls around which tradition is correctly *identifying* God,[8] and clearly the Bible and the Qur'an disagree in their claims to identify this one God. Lutheran theologian Robert Jenson is surely right that Christians don't intend trinitarian dogma as *shirk*, that "we are as insistent as Muhammad that God is one and only"[9] with the understanding that God is so precisely by being the Father of Jesus.[10] I'm not going to solve this problem here, but perhaps the best way of explaining to Muslims what we believe about divine unity is to compare Jesus as the eternal Word (*logos*) of the Father to the Qur'an as the eternal speech (*kalam*) of Allah. As Christians believe that the eternal Word became *incarnate*, so Muslims believe that the eternal Speech became *inlibriate*.[11] This explanation may not turn the light bulb on for many Muslims, but it's a start.

Given the rash of problems in the Middle East and Islamist terrorism worldwide, Islam presents the biggest challenge in thinking about our relation to other faiths. On the other hand, it's difficult to know how religions such as Hinduism, Buddhism, and Confucianism, which developed with no Christian contact, can be considered our enemies. Let me shoot off a few examples in rapid-fire order to make my point. In the opening chapter of the Buddhist classic *The Dhammapada*, we read that hatred is never ended by hatred, but by love.[12] And in the *Kakacupama Sutta*, the Buddha instructs his disciple Phagguna that even if someone were to strike him, he shouldn't give in to hatred, but should remain full of love and concern for the other.[13] United Methodist John Cobb, Roman Catholic Paul Knitter,

8. See Tennent's discussion in *Theology*, 31–39.

9. Jenson, "Risen Prophet," 61.

10. Jenson, "Risen Prophet," 63.

11. See Smith, *World's Religions*, 232.

12. *Dhammapada* 1.5.

13. *Kakacupama Sutta* (*Majjhima Nikaya* 21).

and Episcopalian John P. Keenan are some of the more well-known theologians in recent decades who have seen not only similarities between Buddhism and Christianity, but possibilities for "mutual transformation" (to use Cobbs's phrase).[14]

In one of Hinduism's most popular devotional epics, the *Ramayana*, Rama (one of the avatars of Vishnu) sets out to rescue his wife Sita, who has been kidnapped by the demon king Ravanna. After Sita's rescue, the monkey god Hanuman (Rama's great friend) is contemplating revenge on her behalf, but Sita responds by saying that it's appropriate to show compassion even upon criminals who are worthy of death, since there is no one who does not commit a crime.[15]

Christians have claimed Confucianism as a friend almost since Jesuit missionary Matteo Ricci (one of my heroes) encountered it in the sixteenth-century. Indeed, it's hard to not intuit a certain moral compatibility when you read in the *Analects* how Confucius responded to Tze-Kung's question of whether there is one word that could serve as the guiding principle throughout one's life. Confucius's answer? Reciprocity (*shu*). Don't do to others what you don't want done to yourself—the so-called Silver Rule.[16] While Confucius himself was reluctant to speak about explicitly theological matters,[17] Ricci believed that the Lord-on-High (*Shangdi*) of original Confucianism was the same God referred to as *Deus* by Christians back in the West.[18]

I'm not suggesting that all these religions teach the same thing as Christianity; rather, that in these examples you can see traces of what the Christian theological tradition has called "prevenient grace" that God has given to humanity. This common grace enables a moral order to take root in human cultures and preserves us from sheer lawlessness and chaos. Obviously, not all religions are helpful or of equal value when you examine them closely, and plenty of adherents want nothing to do with having a conversation with members of other faiths. But a close reading of these traditions gives us ample reason to confess a providential role for the world's religions.

14. Cobb, *Beyond Dialogue*; Keenan, *Meaning of Christ*; Knitter, *Without Buddha*.

15. Debroy, *Valmiki Ramayana*, 271.

16. Confucius, *Analects* 15.23.

17. Confucius, *Analects* 7.21.

18. Ricci, *True Meaning of the Lord of Heaven*.

They're Still Going to Hell! Conversion, not Conversation, Right?

In the little church in which I grew up, we might sing about the "wideness in God's mercy" and in the same service be assured that all members of other religions were going to hell ("wideness" or something like it, I suppose). That was our main motivation for engaging in apologetics and sending missionaries to convert Buddhists, Muslims, and scores of other religious adherents: to provide a way to keep people from going to hell. Why else would we take the trouble to develop mission organizations, raise funds, and send people around the world if God's ultimately going to sign off on a stack of exceptions on the Day of Judgment? But I suspect that many people were grappling with the same question that was growing in the back of my mind: Will God *really* send to hell all those people who don't believe correctly—like we do?

In recent decades, even though Christians tend to emphasize the present-tense relevance of a relationship with God and this-worldly concerns, avoiding hell is still a big deal. Now, if those who don't repent and confess their faith in Jesus would be reshuffled *samsara*-like into the next life for another go at it, or even annihilated without remainder, missions wouldn't be so urgent, or at least people wouldn't be so morally outraged over the apparent unfairness of eternal punishment. I mean that, at least for many people (Christians included), *eternal* torment as a punishment for seventy years of not believing correctly seems like a hugely disproportionate response. After a million years of torment, the guilty soul, surely convinced of the truth of the gospel by now, cries out: "Please, merciful God, put me out of my misery!" After a billion years? After a trillion years? Begging for a death that will never come? Lin Yutang, in the modern classic *The Importance of Living*, said that if God loved him half as much as his mother did, he wouldn't send him to hell.[19] Many people would appreciate the sentiment.

In recent years, many popular objections to hell and attempts to flirt with universalism are based on this sense of moral outrage. But there's nothing illogical in saying that one way is correct or that choosing the wrong way in matters as weighty as religion has eternal consequences. Most of the world's largest religious traditions paint grim consequences for rejecting their messages: whether remaining stuck on the wheel of *samsara* for thousands of lifetimes (and perhaps coming back as a guinea pig or television evangelist), facing annihilation, or being drop-kicked to eternal torment (Islam and certain schools of Buddhism describe tortures in hell far

---

19. Yutang, *Importance of Living*, 407.

more vividly than Christianity). In fact, about the only religious traditions that have gone soft on hell and eternal torments are a few religious subcultures like Wicca, Mormonism, and the Protestant mainline. (Interestingly enough, most schools of Satanism don't believe in a literal hell, since most of them don't believe in an afterlife. Go figure.)

Given the overwhelming amount of Scriptural warnings about hell, I can't see how the universalism (in various forms) that frequently follows in the wake of moral objections to hell could ever stand as church dogma. Clearly, moral objections to one doctrine don't by themselves furnish positive grounds for holding to another doctrine that you feel okay about, and we get off to a bad start by orienting the conversation about hell from those moral objections. If hell exists, and Scripture seems to think it does, then no amount of moral outrage will make it go away.

Paradigms for Thinking About the Salvation of Our Cousins

Posing the question the way I have ("avoiding hell") is merely the flip side of the question that has for centuries consumed Christians interested in interreligious dialogue: is Jesus the only way to salvation? Over the years, three competing models have emerged for thinking about the salvation of members of other faiths in light of the claims of the gospel: pluralism, exclusivism, and inclusivism. Although each of these models has been roundly criticized as inadequate, the categories have become stock-in-trade nomenclature for theologians working in the area of world religions.[20] In order to give the reader a big-picture view, I'm first going to offer a short description of each model, then go into criticisms of each in considerable detail. My point is not to make a rock-hard case for any of the paradigms, but to help the reader understand what's at stake in each of them.

In brief, pluralism holds that the various religions are all faltering attempts to articulate a common experience of the divine or the Absolute, which in and of itself is beyond human knowing and description. Exclusivism holds that only one religion is true and that the religious devotee must affirm and follow it explicitly. Inclusivism holds that one religion is objectively true, but the grace and power of this path is so great that it can encompass and save even those who've never heard of it explicitly. Understanding these models is important, because adopting one of these positions

20. The pluralist-exclusivist-inclusivist paradigm has been criticized, but I still think it's a good place for people new to this discussion to start thinking about the issues. See Muck's criticism in his "Theology of Religions After Knitter and Hick."

influences what you think is at stake in conversations with members of other faiths. How does being a pluralist or exclusivist or inclusivist shape what we bring to the table?

Theologians generally fall back on these models whenever the question of salvation in other religions comes up, but many of the disagreements have always seemed a bit out of focus to me, since it seems like these models operate with different understandings of what religion and doctrine are about in the first place. To clarify some of these basic issues, once again I'm going to dip into George Lindbeck's analysis before looking at a couple of attempts to break out of the three competing models and finally putting my own two cents into the discussion.

Pluralism

Pluralists hold that Christianity is one of many possible paths up the mountain to an experience of the God, the Absolute, or the Ultimate Concern. Some religions operate with a fuzzy or undefined sense of highest reality, and there are a host of vague descriptors from which to choose. Christianity, Islam, Hinduism, etc., will all get you up the mountain, but the transcendent reality lying at the heart of all religious experience is by its nature beyond all our attempts to describe it. This is what Lindbeck called "experiential-expressivism,"[21] and it's probably the most popular way of dealing with the sheer variety of religions. The religions are objectifications or products of deep and common experiences of the divine (or the self or world).

The late John Hick (philosopher of religion at the University of Birmingham) was the best known exponent of theological pluralism in the previous century.[22] Hick observed that most religious people follow the religion they're born into, and argued that, given the limits of our knowledge, it's not plausible that one single religion has the definitive message of salvation. As far as Christianity is concerned, Hick insisted that critical study of the New Testament revealed that its claims to the deity of Jesus were later distortions of Jesus' own message (turns out, Hick was wrong about this).[23] And even if Christians did have the definitive message of salvation, wouldn't you expect that our Spirit-filled lives would manifest the truth and superiority of our religion? But we all know this is hardly the case.

21. Lindbeck, *Nature of Doctrine*, 31–32.

22. For what follows, see Hick, "Only True Religion."

23. Pannenberg demonstrates how claims to Jesus' divinity are grounded in the latter's proclamation of the kingdom of God. See *Systematic Theology*, 1:308–19; 2:325–62.

Hick said that the problem lies in Christians' trying to settle the question of "salvation" by unfairly defining it for all people as being accepted by God on account of the work of Christ. If we start instead by looking at how religion operates in people's lives, however, we'd come to describe salvation as the gradual transformation of people from natural self-centeredness to a life centered on God (variously defined), a transformation which frees us for love and compassion for others. In this view, those who love their neighbors are on the road to salvation. Different truth-claims people make about the divine reality behind this experience are merely claims about how "the Ultimate" has been expressed within different cultures and different periods in history. We can talk with our cousins because, at the end of the day, we're all struggling to talk about the same Reality behind our feeble attempts at articulation. We're all experiential-expressivists, to use Lindbeck's jargon. Now for those of us who are Christians, Christianity is the only true religion, Hick says, "for we have been formed by it,"[24] but I think it's hard to refrain from putting *true* in quotation marks once you see the emperor's new clothes.

As an ideology, pluralism drips with theological humility and capaciousness. But when you examine it closely, serious problems begin to emerge. For example, maybe the most common device for explaining pluralism is the parable of the blind men and the elephant, with each man describing a portion of the animal. But here's the elephant-sized question that you can't avoid stepping into: who knows that the beast in question is in fact an elephant? How does Hick know so much about this unknowable transcendent reality that he can proclaim what lies behind the staggering variety of religious experience? How does he know that transformation away from self-centeredness to love is a manifestation of the Real? Gavin D'Costa, a critic of the pluralist position, says it turns out that Hick's "transcendental agnosticism" implicitly makes exclusive truth claims![25]

If you look at the practical implications of religion in people's lives, similar kinds of questions arise. Talk all you like about "love," "justice," and the "good" as evidence of the divine; the problem is that different religions define these ideas in different ways. What looks like justice to me might look like malpractice to you![26] So whence the pluralists' criteria for love, justice, and so on? Tibetan Buddhist master Geshe Kelsang Gyatso (head of the New Kadampa tradition) puts to rest the popular misconception of Buddhism as a religious tofu that can be mixed with, and take on the flavor of,

---

24. Hick, "Only True Religion," para. 26.
25. D'Costa, "Impossibilty of a Pluralist View," 229.
26. D'Costa, "Impossibilty of a Pluralist View," 231.

any other religion, when he insists that while beginning students can learn from both Christianity and Buddhism, finally they must cut bait or fish.[27] The messages are different; you have to make a choice.

It's easy to understand the appeal of the pluralist position. In the popular imagination, exclusive claims to religious truth of any kind lead to arrogance and even violence. Far better to adopt, if not outright agnosticism, a position that says all religions are merely external expressions of a common but indefinable experience of the divine or the Absolute. So a pluralist will look at the gospel story and say "Well, that's *your* take on the divine life. But *we know* you can't truly know what God is like deep down. Jesus may be *a* revelation of God as much as any other sacred religious figure, but you're overstepping what's humanly knowable if you try to read too much from this life of this one man into the vast mystery of God's own life." In more precise terms, the pluralist admits that maybe Christians *have* discerned a movement of God in history they can justifiably label as "Father, Son, and Holy Spirit," or what theologians call the "economic" Trinity. (Theological geek-speak alert: Don't think dollars and cents here. "Economic" in this sense comes from the Greek word *oikonomia* or "household." The "economic" Trinity is how God orders the affairs of his household in history.) But it's a huge and speculative jump, pluralists say, to claim that this story in history reveals what God is actually like in the depths of the divine life, internally and eternally (what theologians call the "immanent" Trinity).

The problem is, Scripture makes precisely the claim to know what God is like "deep down." Nowhere in Scripture do we find any notion that Jesus, Diana, and Osiris are all penultimate manifestations of a higher Unknown. You have to ignore way too much to hold that position. That may not bother you; but if you believe that the Scripture is the most important source for Christian faith and practice, it should. I'm not thinking abstractly about individual verses that speak about Jesus being the only way to God or "no other name." Rather, I have in mind the sheer outrageousness of the gospel story and how you must learn to talk about God if you think through this outrageousness. If you do dare to do that, then you'll find that what Christians mean by "God" can't be compared to conventional descriptions of what God is supposed to be like, because what the cross means for God's life makes all the difference. I'd better explain.

Religions since the dawn of time have agreed that God's life or Ultimate Reality (in other words, eternity, variously understood) is utterly Other and untouched by transience, mortality, or suffering; in other words, all the things that afflict us and make life wretched. In Islam, Allah is far too

27. Gyatso, "How Do Buddhists View Other Religions?"

lofty to be dragged down into the muck of mortal life. In Buddhism, the state of enlightenment (*Nirvana*) cannot be turned into an object of desire affected by the web of finite existence; the highest "experience" of no-self is condition-less (words begin to fail). In Hinduism, yes, a god may take on human form in order to visit our reality as an *avatar*, but ultimately this experience is a fleeting and relatively inconsequential bubble in the life of God. *Avatar* doesn't mean the same thing as *incarnation*.

By contrast, Jesus in John's revelation says plainly and bewilderingly in the same breath that he was the first and the last, *and* that he was dead, but now alive forever (Rev 1:18). And astonishingly, John's revelation places the crucified Jesus directly in the life of God (Rev 5:6). This same Jesus, in his resurrected flesh, continues to bear the marks of his torture and death (John 20:24–29). Only in this way does God redeem all of creation in Christ. Here I attempt the impossible, to compress Trinity, incarnation, and atonement in one sentence: Through the Holy Spirit we are enveloped in the incarnation of Jesus, but the incarnation and all it entails (suffering, passion, cross, resurrection) are events in God's own triune life. That's why Jesus can save. It's as though the New Testament were telling us, "Here's a story that turns your conventional notion of God on its head, because what happens in the earthly life of Jesus really does affect what we mean by God."

In theological jargon, the way Father, Son, and Holy Spirit act with us in the rough-and-tumble of history (economic Trinity) affects the way they relate eternally as the one God (immanent Trinity). The gospel story matters to God, and because it matters, *we* matter to God eternally. To back down on the centrality and uniqueness of Christ is to miss the whole point of this revolutionary message. If this relationship between economic and immanent Trinity is not true, then neither is the gospel. If ever we were to agree with the pluralists, the outcomes in our understanding of God and our worship would be enormous: we would no longer worship Jesus as the eternal Son of God, but perhaps only venerate him as a penultimate avatar of the ultimately Unknowable.

Exclusivism

Exclusivists occupy the other end of the spectrum from pluralists. They maintain not only that Jesus is (objectively) the exclusive way to salvation ("no other name"), but that people must name the name of Jesus and put their faith in him (subjectively) explicitly.[28] As a couple of popular proponents of exclusivism put it, salvation has to be done correctly in order to be suc-

28. See Kramer, *Christian Message*, 101–14.

cessful.[29] Most exclusivists would fall under the "cognitive-propositionalist" category in Lindbeck's taxonomy.[30] Religious doctrines function as informative propositions or truth claims about objective realities (similar to science or traditional metaphysics). The exclusivist perspective has been the dominant position of the church throughout the centuries.[31]

Obviously, the Christian mission is an urgent task; the salvation of countless millions lost in the darkness of other religions is at risk if it is "done" incorrectly! Now some exclusivists admit to a provisional revelation of God in other religions, but (don't get excited) this provisional revelation is not saving knowledge. Many exclusivists, in fact, cite Romans 1:18–23 to support the idea that any knowledge of God apart from Christ invariably has been twisted into idolatry and therefore serves as the grounds for God's just condemnation of the religions.[32] John Calvin gives the classic exclusivist perspective when he says that, although God sows the seed of religion in every heart, it never grows to fruition in anyone, so that genuine godliness can't be found anywhere in the world.[33] At the end of the day, general revelation, Calvin says, doesn't do anything else than render us without excuse.[34] Without receiving the special revelation of Christ in Holy Scripture, we plummet into blindness and error every time.

Granted, some exclusivists try to soften their position on the overheated destiny of all those people who don't know Jesus by making exceptions for the mentally handicapped and children under the "age of accountability" (whenever that is). But these exceptions end up making exclusivist claims confusing and, perhaps finally, inconsistent. For example, consider the example of a young child who lives in a remote area where the gospel is unavailable. Buddhism is all she's ever known. She's supposedly "covered" by the "age of accountability" clause until she possesses the capabilities to understand and respond to the gospel. But do we want to say that, having reached this stage of accountability, her soul is in danger if she doesn't "accept Jesus," even though nothing in her external surroundings has changed that would make hearing the gospel even possible? Why is her lack of intellectual capability an acceptable excuse but not simple lack of availability? Notice that, in these exceptions, nothing positively is conceded to other religions and their ability to reveal God or communicate salvation.

29. Ankerberg and Weldon, *Ready with an Answer*.

30. Lindbeck, *Nature of Doctrine*, 16.

31. Rightly noted by Tennent, *Christianity at the Religious Roundtable*.

32. See, e.g., Clendenin, *Many Gods, Many Lords*.

33. Calvin, *Institutes of the Christian Religion* 1.4.1.

34. Calvin, *Institutes of the Christian Religion* 1.5.14–15.

The exceptions apply equally in areas where the gospel is and is not readily available.

Most semi-Pelagian evangelicals who want people to avoid hell by "choosing" Jesus don't realize that if you make exceptions for children and the mentally handicapped but not for lack of availability, then you've reversed into some form of weird geographic double predestination, because clearly God knew who was going to live in those periods of history and geographic areas where the gospel wasn't and isn't available. That position may be correct; that's not the issue here. My point is that making exceptions for someone's lack of intellectual capacity to understand the gospel but not their lack of opportunity to hear the gospel at all raises as many questions as it furnishes answers.

John Wesley understood the dilemma and said that many "heathen" didn't believe on account of a simple "want of light." Wesley said that Chicali, an old Native American chief, was once asked why the "red men" didn't know as much about God as the "white men." Chicali responded by saying, "You have the Word of God and we don't!"[35] Wesley said that on the day of reckoning this response will avail for millions of "modern Heathen" who've never heard the gospel.[36] Little given, little required.

The exclusivist perspective I've been describing is generally, but not always, wedded to a tradition model of apologetics in which one tries to validate or prove that the Bible is true (over against other religious claims) and therefore that Jesus is the "only way." Conversationally, this means I'm out to convince my conversation partner that Christianity is superior to his or her religion. So I'll try to demonstrate how the Bible's prophecies have been fulfilled or how Jesus' claims are unique amongst the world's great religious founders and demand an answer (e.g., C. S. Lewis's well-known "Lord, Lunatic, or Liar" trilemma).

To examine the assumptions hidden in these aims would take another book, but I'll say this much. Whenever someone says they can say they can "prove" the Bible is true, my initial response is, "Which parts?" The Bible is a composite of various writings scattered across several centuries. If you can prove some part but not others, have you proven that "the Bible" is true? I can prove that parts of the Qur'an or Buddhist sutras are true. Even if you can prove the central claim of the gospel, that Jesus rose from the dead, you still have to deal with the interpretive question, "What does this mean?" Peter's interpretation that God confirmed Jesus as both Lord and Christ (Acts 2:36) can't be proven in the same way that "Cleveland is 190 miles west

35. Wesley, "On Faith," §1.3 (*Works* 3:494).
36. Wesley, "On Faith," §1.3 (*Works* 3:494).

of Buffalo" can be proven. (I'm not exaggerating the difficulty with these remarks—gird up your loins and test your apologetic prowess on any state university campus.)

The weightier criticism is that attempts to "prove" the Bible invariably rest upon modern, rationalist assumptions about truth and proof that largely have been discredited (and that much of the non-Western world never bought into anyway). Much of modern apologetics was based on the notion that if we take the claims of the Bible and hold them up to a standard of rationality that everyone agreed upon, then people would have an "Aha!" moment and see that the Bible both made sense and was true. But, as I pointed out in the previous chapter, philosophers themselves can't agree on what this standard would look like. What makes sense in one culture sometimes seems ludicrous to another.

Many Christians still buy into this way of thinking without realizing it. I occasionally receive emails from people asking me to provide arguments or books that "prove" the Bible's claims over other rival religious claims. That's an odd request, if you think about it. On the one hand, you confess the divinely inspired character and claims of Scripture; on the other hand, you want to submit this same Scripture to another source for validation? If you could line up all the sacred writings of the world's religions and come up with the source (rationality? religious experience?) that would allow to adjudicate between these writings, wouldn't that source be your ultimate authority, instead of one of the sacred writings?

Inclusivism

Inclusivists occupy a moderating position. Christian inclusivists agree with exclusivists (and against pluralists) that Jesus is objectively the savior of the whole world, but they disagree with exclusivists by arguing that Christ can save those people who've never had the opportunity to hear the gospel. Roman Catholic theologian Karl Rahner, the most well-known exponent of Christian inclusivism in the last century, says that we can't seriously believe that the overwhelming majority of humanity will be damned through no fault of their own, while Scripture says explicitly that God wants everyone to be saved (cf. 1 Tim 2:4)—and yet only through Jesus is this salvation conferred.[37]

So how is it possible to say that someone who is not a confessing Christian has received the saving grace of Christ? Rahner's explanation involves unpacking what he means by an "absolutely moral commitment" within the

37. Rahner, *Theological Investigations*, 6:391; see also 10:31.

"present economy of salvation," but at the end of the day he basically means two things: love of one's neighbor and fidelity to one's conscience.[38] These two things demonstrate that one has been grasped by Christ's saving grace (the "present economy of salvation"); we can even call such people "anonymous Christians."[39] This is more or less the Catholic Church's position since Vatican II. The inclusivist perspective applies to all non-Christians, whether members of other faiths, agnostics, or atheists.

An inclusivist perspective isn't necessarily committed to speculating on how or to what degree other religions might convey grace to people. For example, a stripped-down version of inclusivism would maintain only that God's saving economy can embrace people apart from explicit reference to the gospel.[40] However, German heavyweight Wolfhart Pannenberg makes an important point (to which I'll return later in this chapter) that all inclusivists would agree on; namely, that if you do ask whether other religions can mediate salvation without being related to Jesus, the answer must be no.[41]

But the inclusivist position raises some serious problems; it's a double-edged sword, after all. Muslims and Hindus can just as easily refer to Christians as anonymous Muslims or anonymous Hindus. The great Hindu thinker Shankara has been referred to as a "concealed Buddhist" (*pracchanna-bauddha*).[42] However, would a serious practitioner of any faith accept the anonymous description—as though they didn't know who they really were?[43] Talk about an imperialistic attitude! That's a dialogical problem, but theological problems lurk here as well.

For example, it's all well and good for Rahner to talk about loving God and loving neighbor as evidence of being grasped by the grace of Christ apart from hearing the gospel, but can this grace truly be communicated through the dictates of conscience? Typically, Christians have said we can live this way on account of the sanctifying power of the Holy Spirit working through word and sacraments. I can imagine someone saying to Rahner, "You mean to say that people can love God and their neighbor as themselves simply by following their conscience? I thought our problem as sinners was precisely our inability to love!" In addition, "loving God" and "loving neighbor" quickly become abstractions apart from actual religious traditions that

38. Rahner, *Theological Investigations*, 6:239, 394.

39. Rahner, *Theological Investigations*, 6:391–92.

40. See, e.g., Sennett, "Bare Bones Inclusivism."

41. Pannenberg, "Religions from the Perspective of Christian Theology," 291.

42. Jayatilleke, *Buddhist Attitude Towards Other Religions*, 2.

43. Küng, *Theology for the Third Millennium*, 236.

attempt to answer the questions "Who is God?" and "Who is my neighbor?" No matter how much Rahner insists that the idea of "anonymous Christians" doesn't lessen the urgency of mission and evangelism, you can't escape the nagging suspicion that if people can receive the grace of Christ through conscience and lead a life of love without hearing the gospel and putting their trust in Christ, then maybe Christianity is nothing more than an easier way to do what everyone is already capable of doing.[44]

Lindbeck and his cultural-linguistic model also jump on the pile here. If Christian faith arises only in response to the word that comes to the self from without, and is shaped only by the Christian community and tradition, then, Lindbeck says, the notion of an "anonymous" Christianity present in the depths of other religions and a theory of salvation of non-Christians built upon it is just silly.[45] This would seem to toss Lindbeck back on the exclusivist pile, since there's no way your language-game can be reconciled with mine, but on account of his trust in God's mercy and fairness, he holds the hope that if someone hasn't heard the gospel in this life, they'll be confronted by it immediately after death. For believers and unbelievers alike, he says, only then is the final decision made for or against Christ.[46] But, seriously? At that point, who is going to reject the gospel? I can't imagine anyone saying postmortem, "I'm still not convinced." And if you did have genuine doubts in this life, wouldn't it make sense to hedge your bets until you got an indubitable offer in the afterlife?

In view of these problems, some Christian theologians attempt to show how other religious traditions explicitly contribute to or communicate salvation to their adherents, perhaps by finding parallels between how members of other faiths describe their relationship with God or the Absolute and the way Christians describe their relationship with Jesus. So you might look at a devotional form of Vaishnavism (a Hindu tradition dedicated to the worship of Lord Vishnu) and compare it to certain forms of Christian pietism, or what you might call "Jesus religion" (on this score, maybe Jesus is another avatar of Vishnu—or vice-versa!). Or you might look at Pure Land Buddhists' trusting reliance on the "other" power of the Amida Buddha and conclude that it's the Buddhist version of being justified by faith.

The problem with finding such "parallels" is that the entire context of such beliefs, the underlying metaphysics and worldviews, behind the examples can't be reconciled. Hindu and Buddhist conceptions of eternity, the human predicament, the status of the material world, and why you do what

44. Rahner, *Theological Investigations*, 6:398; 10:47–49.
45. Lindbeck, *Nature of Doctrine*, 62.
46. Lindbeck, *Nature of Doctrine*, 59.

you do in actual practice differ dramatically from Christian conceptions of the same. So the kinds of salvation other religions promise their adherents can't be compared in any coherent sense to the salvation promised by gospel. It's like trying to compare Christian apples to Buddhist oranges to Hindu mangoes. So inclusivism, despite good intentions, has its share of problems as well.

So Where Are We?

After looking at these attempts to come to terms with religious pluralism, let's take a step back and ask what's at stake in these discussions. All three positions have a sharp sense of the limitations of human knowing and the tragedies that result from bellicose religious claims. Pluralists distrust absolute claims based on special revelation, since so many religions make such claims on the special revelation given to them or their prophets. But instead of throwing their hands up in the air over the impossibility of judging between these claims and taking the agnostic position (like lots of people do), most pluralists try an "end run" around the problem by positing a common, mystical (noncognitive) core at the heart of all religious experience. Specific theological claims aren't a problem once you see that we can't seriously believe that our claims about God or the Ultimate accurately refer to much beyond our experience.

Exclusivists hold on to their special claims and agree that, yes, exclusivist claims have led to arrogance and even violence, but argue that there is no necessary connection between believing that you've found the truth and mistreating others. People make competing claims and argue for the truth of those claims in every area of life imaginable (from politics and economics to monster trucks and movies) but we don't believe that no one can be right simply because people have different opinions. Why should religion be any different? Besides, the whole point of special revelation is to address our confusion and overcome our limited capacity to know about divine things. Inclusivists share this perspective on special revelation, and at the end of the day I suspect most inclusivists and exclusivists alike have doubts as to whether pluralists are Christian at all, since they sound more vaguely theocentric than Christocentric. Related to this, neither inclusivists nor exclusivists think much of the "experiential-expressivist" dodge of pluralism, since if the divine or Absolute is finally inexpressible, then what's the point of talking about it anyway? Might as well go fishing.

Inclusivists, I think, have a sharper sense that while true exclusivist claims need not lead to mistreatment of others, they frequently have been used this way. But most inclusivists object to exclusivism not primarily on moral grounds (any good idea can be distorted and used to abuse others), but for theological reasons. Inclusivists share Rahner's concerns: it's monumentally unfair, unloving, and unscriptural to say God desires all people to be saved and then turn around and declare that only those people who have opportunity to hear the name of Jesus actually will be. "God is love"— but only to a tiny percentage of people? For the rest of you poor sinners who will never hear—through no fault of your own—the God of love is an abstraction; the actual God is a God of kick-ass *justice* who is giving you only what you deserve. Believe it or not, lots of Christians have no problem with this (that's for another discussion), but for those Christians who aren't so inclined, this seems to place the eternal destiny of those who have never heard the gospel on the shoulders of preachers and missionaries. Yikes.

Yet, oddly enough, the inclusivist rescue mission verges on the same kind of error that pluralists engage in. Somehow, what non-Christians really are expressing when they talk about Allah, Krishna, or nirvana is a pre- or supra-linguistic experience of Christ's grace. So what's ultimately important for members of other faiths is not what they confess explicitly, but what's behind such confessions—only in this case, instead of an ambiguous divine reality or mysterious Absolute (à la hick), behind it all there stands the sneaky face of Jesus. It's one more example of sitting around the picnic table and telling your cousins that *you* know more about their relationship with God than *they* do.

Is There a Way Forward?

In recent years, several theologians have attempted to address the shortcomings of the inclusivist paradigm. Two of the most intriguing theologians in this area, Episcopalian Mark Heim and Pentecostal Amos Yong, have attempted to broaden the context by developing nuanced theologies of religions instead of simply asking whether people of other faiths can be "saved" if they don't believe in Jesus. Is there a way we can talk about God in relation to the world's religions that doesn't amount to condemning them outright, or devaluing everything they have to offer except those bits that act as a kind of preparation for the gospel, or reducing all their messages to the same thing, even if they don't realize it (i.e., pluralism or inclusivism)? Following my quick and dirty summaries of what Heim and Yong are up to, I turn to John Wesley for some insights on this matter, and close by adding my own twist to the issues.

In a surprising move, Heim attempts to ground the diversity of the world's religions in the life of Trinity itself. Heim goes so far as to make the audacious claim that the Trinity is a kind of "map" that actually requires concrete truth in other religions, because it allows for a number of ways of relating to God.[47] Some religious traditions, such as Theravada Buddhism and Advaita Vedanta (Hinduism), speak of a more impersonal way of relating to the divine life, while other traditions' orientations (e.g., Judaism, Christianity, Islam) are more personal. Heim's proposal stands out among most inclusivists' projects insofar as it respects the integrity of each religious tradition's aims or ends.[48]

Heim has to nuance his proposal by bracketing the truth question, since not all religious claims can be true (some are flat-out contradictory). His asks only that we recognize the reality of different experiential states of religious fulfillment.[49] For example, when a Buddhist testifies to the experience of satori, or a Muslim claims to have submitted herself to Allah, we shouldn't have reason to doubt them. Heim's position doesn't require that all the metaphysical baggage a tradition associates with attaining that state are empirically true—but hey, it's a big universe out there—and there's no reason why a universe with a single religious ultimate couldn't be roomy enough to include several penultimate ends. So, on a Christian reading, other religious ends can be viewed as real—but nevertheless transitory— states on the way toward communion with God. Heim admits that, yes, this reading can be flipped on us. For example, Buddhists might interpret the Christian understanding of salvation as something like one of the pleasant layovers that Buddhists may enjoy between births as a reward for merit on their flight to final liberation.[50]

Heim's proposal is both respectful and creative, no doubt about it, but he's been criticized for pretty thin exegesis and for moving too quickly from finding parallels or correlations between ideas in Christianity and other faiths to announcing that the ends pursued in those other faiths are valid (if penultimate). It also strikes me that most religious believers believe that their experiences are legitimate because they somehow *are* in touch with the way the universe is. (To paraphrase Flannery O'Connor: if it's just an experience, then to hell with it.) In sum, Heim has a capacious and generous inclusivism going, but it's still a variety of inclusivism. And in terms of

47. Heim, "Trinitarian View of Religious Pluralism," 14–15. See also Heim, *Depth of the Riches*, 209–39.

48. Heim, "Pluralism of Religious Ends," 14. See also Heim, *Depth of the Riches*, 6–7.

49. Heim, *Depth of the Riches*, 25.

50. Heim, *Depth of the Riches*, 32.

dialogue, is there any real point to holding on to radical differences in terms of our respective ends?[51]

In recent decades, Amos Yong is foremost amongst a number of theologians who have tried to shift the way we look at other religious traditions from a christological to a pneumatological basis. The thinking here is that we get nowhere in interreligious dialogue if we start by asking the "Jesus question" in relation to members of other faiths. Instead, what if we start by asking if God has a role for the world's religions and what the Holy Spirit might be up to in the lives of these people in these various traditions.

We can appreciate the significance of Yong's approach best if we first consider the lack of pneumatology in the traditional exclusivist position, in connection with the idea of God's "general" or common revelation to all people. As an example, consider popular Baptist theologian Millard Erickson, on whose theology textbooks a generation of ministerial students cut their teeth, regarding the standard exclusivist-evangelical position on the limits of general revelation. Erickson writes that if someone who doesn't know the gospel were to "throw himself upon the mercy of God," not knowing upon what basis that mercy was provided, then that person would be accepted as were Old Testament believers. "The basis of acceptance would be the work of Jesus Christ, even though the person involved doesn't know that this is how provision has been made for his salvation."[52] In fact, Erickson claims that in Romans 2:1–16 (which speaks about general revelation through conscience) Paul seems to be laying open a "theoretical possibility" that one can be saved "without having the special revelation." But a massive qualification of this "possibility" follows.

> Yet it is merely a theoretical possibility. It is highly questionable how many, if any, actually experience salvation without having special revelation. Paul suggests in Romans 3 that no one does. And in chapter 1 he urges the necessity of preaching the gospel . . . so that men may believe. Thus it is apparent that in failing to respond to the light of general revelation which they have, men are *fully responsible*, for they have *truly known* God, but have willfully suppressed that truth.[53]

My eyes begin to cross when I give this passage a close reading. To begin, what does it even mean to say that Paul "suggests" no one experiences salvation without having special revelation? But, more to the point, is it conceivable that someone *could* "throw himself upon the mercy of God" apart

---

51. See Kärkkäinen's criticism in *Trinity and Religious Pluralism*, 150–51.

52. Erickson, *Christian Theology*, 172.

53. Erickson, *Christian Theology*, 173. Emphasis added.

from the work of the Holy Spirit? How else is conviction possible? Erickson doesn't acknowledge the role of the Spirit, however, which makes it sound like general revelation gives a certain (Spirit-free?) cognitive awareness of God, the suppression of which serves to condemn people. However, Erickson also says that people are "fully responsible," for they have "truly known" God, a statement that makes sense only if the Holy Spirit is at work (can one truly know God apart from the Spirit?). So a confusing situation results from this reading: if you acknowledge that the Holy Spirit works in general revelation, but that the knowledge obtained via such revelation is invariably suppressed, then the work of the Spirit in this instance is limited strictly to condemning people before God, unless the gospel is proclaimed—strange if the Holy Spirit is the Spirit of Jesus Christ.[54]

What, then, does a robust pneumatological approach look like? Yong's point of orientation is the Pentecost event—not surprising, since he's a Pentecostal theologian. What is surprising is his argument that, as language cannot be disconnected from culture (and that means religion), when the Holy Spirit redeems the various languages in Acts 2, the Spirit also redeems human religiousness where it can become, at least potentially, a vehicle for mediating the grace of God. Yong wagers that the Spirit of Pentecost, who enabled the diversity of tongues and the testimony to God's wondrous works, can also enable the integrity of other faiths *and* their ability to motor the good news of God's kingdom.[55] Both of these emphases are important, but this is a tricky act to pull off. Yong wants to respect the integrity of other faiths, and so avoid the inclusivist temptation to think we know what our conversation partners are doing better than they do, but he also wants to say that other faith traditions and practices can somehow contribute to the coming kingdom of God. Pneumatology and eschatology are inseparable. In this way, Yong's approach is a bit different than the usual Christocentric inclusivist ploy, but finally it does loop back around to Christ in view of the coming fullness of the kingdom.[56] Indeed, you could call Yong's approach an eschatological inclusivism. In truth, I don't believe that any Christian theologian who is serious about the relationship between the Trinity, atonement and eschatology can—or should want to—escape the tag of inclusivism.

Yong wagers that his pneumatological approach specifically provides a way out of the dialogical deadlock that Lindbeck's approach lands us in (namely, that since different religious frameworks are all-encompassing and

54. See Welker, *God the Spirit*, 219–27.

55. Yong, "P(new)matological Paradigm," 184. Emphasis mine.

56. Yong has always understood the danger that employing a pneumatological approach might end up functioning as pneumatological *criteria*, and therefore a detour away from Christ. See Yong, "Turn to Pneumatology," 437–54.

incommensurable, I'd have to convert to your religion to actually understand what you're saying). By contrast, rather than throwing his hands up in face of different religious systems, Yong believes that the Spirit who gave the capacity to speak in foreign languages on the day of Pentecost can enable a person to cross over into other faiths, experience to some degree those foreign realities "from within" (admittedly, in a carefully circumscribed way) and return to his or her faith.[57] So, at the end of the day, are we seeing a Pentecostal theologian's capacious pneumatology trumping a Lutheran theologian's narrow focus on the word? It sure looks like it.[58]

Yong doesn't mean that all forms of human religiousness can be sanctified. We have to carefully discern what the Spirit might be up to in the changing tides of the world's religions (even as we engage in such discernment in the Christian traditions).[59] Any "demonic elements" in the religions need to be confronted and purified so that if there is any truth, goodness, or beauty in them, these elements may be redeemed.[60] This discernment process might sound like an attempt to compare doctrines (à la cognitive-propositionalism), but Yong focuses primarily on praxis: ritual, devotion, morality, etc. So we look primarily at what God the Spirit might be doing in the lives of people, rather than at the theological statements they construct or what they say they believe.

Given my central metaphor in this book, I'm drawn to this emphasis on praxis, and in particular Yong's emphasis on hospitality—encountering and welcoming real people—as he unwraps the meaning of the Pentecost event. Pentecost reveals God's hospitality to all people, but, more than that, Yong argues that Christian hospitality can be realized only when it's reciprocated by those in other faiths. The Spirit who was been poured out on all flesh enabled Jews, Samaritans, and gentiles around the Mediterranean to open up their homes and hearts to the apostolic messengers. Particularly relevant to my concern is Yong's observation that the rules of hospitality in the primitive church revolved especially around the purity laws of table fellowship.[61] Eating together was a central theme in the missionary and evangelistic endeavors of the first century, as the church was convinced that

57. Yong, "P(new)matological Approach," 180.

58. Moyaert points out that the consequences of Lindbeck's position are fairly predictable, given his dim view of fallen creation, his narrow focus on the word and a limited role he ascribes to the Holy Spirit—in other words, on account of Lindbeck's conventional Lutheran commitments. See Moyaert, "Postliberalism, Religious Diversity."

59. For an example, see Yong, "Holy Spirit and the World Religions."

60. Yong, "Spirit of Hospitality," 57.

61. Yong, "Spirit of Hospitality," 64.

the new people of God birthed by the Holy Spirit were not separated by gender, ethnicity, class, race, etc., so that all could gather around a common table of fellowship. Now what would it mean for us if we could recover this neglected theme of hospitable table fellowship in our religiously pluralistic world?

For example, hospitality plays a central role in Buddhism (as it does in Christianity). In Christianity, hospitality is grounded in God's welcome in Christ to us all; in Holy Eucharist, we gather around the table where he feeds us of himself. (The early church used the image of a pelican plucking at her own breast in order to nourish her young with her own blood.) So any time Christians offer hospitality to the stranger, we do so out of the awareness that we've been welcomed by God and that our mission involves extending this welcome to people everywhere. In Buddhism, hospitality emerges from realizing that we're ultimately interdependent; hence, welcome is extended to all people, regardless of the artificial divisions we've erected (e.g., caste, religion, etc.). In the *Vinaya Pitaka*, for example, we read that, even after the general Siha (a Jain follower renowned for his generosity) became a Buddhist, the Buddha encouraged him to continue to show hospitality to the Jain monks.[62] Buddhist master Sangharakshita says that the Buddhist virtue of *dana* (generosity)is the first real sign of the spiritual life, since it indicates waning craving and attachment, and that *dana* is so central to Buddhism that you can't really consider yourself a Buddhist without exhibiting it.[63] If I understand Yong correctly, his point is that we don't sit down with our Buddhist friends and assume *we* know that, somehow, Jesus is welcoming others through them or they're welcoming Jesus without realizing it (and remember, a common saying amongst Indian Buddhists is "the guest is god").[64] Rather, through the practice of hospitality precisely as Buddhists understand it, and ensconced as it is within other Buddhist beliefs and practices, the Holy Spirit is enabling our Buddhist friends to contribute to the coming kingdom of God.[65] Is this pneumatological-eschatological inclusivism any less imperialistic than the Christocentric variety? Perhaps it is, in the sense that, when the kingdom arrives in its fullness, all religions—including, most severely, Christianity, will stand before the judgment seat of Christ.

So Yong's proposal is not theologically conventional, in the sense of trying to theoretically "solve" the problems of interreligious dialogue or to answer the question of the destiny of those who haven't heard the gospel.

---

62. *The Book of Discipline* (*Vinaya Pitaka*), 31.2–12 (6:318–23).

63. Sangharakshita, "Buddha's Noble Eightfold Path," 5.

64. See Rotman, "Buddhism and Hospitality," 115–22.

65. See Yong, "As the Spirit Gives Utterance," 299–314.

His theology of religions is a *performative* one, in which we trust the Spirit to open up a public space for reciprocal hospitality, a space in which we can testify to Christ while reining in any inclusivist tendencies to think we know what others are *really* saying or wanting, and in this way respecting the integrity of others to testify to their experience in their own language.[66] What would conversations with our cousins be like if we trusted the Spirit to move around, amongst, and within those seated at the table?

What I'm about to say may sound flippant or whimsical, but if we're serious about making hospitality and table fellowship truly performative, our theology must become gastronomy. There's no point in remaining on the level of theoretical constructs and abstractions in this business about "eating together." Table fellowship has to be embodied! It has to involve actual cuisine, where we bring food, share recipes and cooking tips, savor the offerings, and plan for our next get-together. Lin Yutang says that a good meal lowers the temperature of arguments and dials down the abrasiveness of our conflicts. Even if you put two friends together when they're hungry, they're bound to argue. Yutang quips that the Chinese have always understood that arguments are really settled at the dinner table instead of courts of law.[67]

And please leave the microwaveable noodles and prepackaged curry at home! On these occasions we share our best out of the abundance of our pantries and family recipes. The best cooking is always cooking with love for both our ingredients and the people we're serving. In doing so, we both sacramentally shadow the Great Gastronomy that is Holy Eucharist and prefigure that day when people will come from the four corners of the earth and take their places at the feast in God's kingdom (Luke 13:29). Hospitality, gastronomy, and eschatology go hand in hand.

A Pneumatological Approach to the Religions in View of the Cross

A pneumatological approach to the religions does have the advantage of bringing a more capacious view of God to the table, and being more sensitive to the nuances of cultures and human experience. But in the midst of our pneumatological musings, it is important to grapple seriously with Pannenberg's question, which I mentioned earlier in the chapter: Can any religion mediate salvation without being related in some way to Jesus? I say this because, in their attempt to avoid sounding imperialistically Christ-centered in matters of interreligious encounter, some well-intentioned

66. Yong, "Spirit of Hospitality," 66.
67. Yutang, *Importance of Living*, 44.

theologians distinguish between missions of Jesus and the Holy Spirit to the point where it almost seems like we're talking about two separate individuals working in their own sphere of influence.[68] If the particularity of Christ scandalizes members of other faiths too sharply, even in inclusivist terms, then our talk of the Spirit is supposed to have kinder and gentler edges. But this way of thinking about the triune persons is simply bad theology, for a variety of reasons.

Think about what's at stake theologically in Pannenberg's "no" to the question he raises: If salvation between God and creation doesn't come solely by way of the cross and resurrection of Jesus, or if what Christians mean by salvation is one way amongst other, equally valid ways to achieve salvation (variously described), then you have in fact ceded the game to the pluralists and any number of religious mediators. If you don't want to go down this road, then talk all you like about a pneumatological approach to the religions, but at the end of the day, you're going to have to connect whatever the Spirit is doing to the person and work of Jesus. Theologians who want to avoid the hazards of exclusivism's or inclusivism's Christocentrism with the non-starter question of "Who is saved?"[69]—perhaps in favor of a pneumatological approach—still have to come to terms with *the means by which* people are saved. As Kilian McConnell puts it, Jesus is the *what*, but the Spirit is the *how*,[70] and this relationship cannot be reversed.

No doubt this will sound imperialistic to some folks, but if we are all connected to the death and resurrection of Jesus because he is, in the words of the ancient church, not only one with God but one with us, then there's no getting around the centrality of atonement. Christology, atonement, and anthropology (not merely in the sense of what it means to be human, but how the human race is corporately related to the incarnation) either lie intertwined at the heart of what we mean by salvation, or else we'll end up spinning metaphysical abstractions about how the religions are related to each other or affirmations about some vague sense of divine grace in the religions. Again, because Jesus is the *what* and Spirit is the *how*, the latter does not communicate grace apart from the former. Before we lose sight of this, and for the sake of a little theological integrity, it's time that we recover the unity of the persons in the one triune God as per Basil's dictum: every act of God is initiated by the Father, executed by the Son, and perfected in the Spirit.

---

68. I am not accusing Yong of this.

69. Muck, "Theology of Religions," 14.

70. McConnell, "Trinitarian Theology of the Holy Spirit," 215.

Insights from John Wesley

Because John Wesley didn't enjoy the degree of religious pluralism that we do, and because many people assume that the Wesleyan-Methodist tradition has bought into the exclusivist paradigm, I suspect that most people don't know what Wesley had to say about other religions,[71] so let's address that. First of all, Wesley leaves no doubt about God's desire to redeem the entire human race (a position he sharpened in face of his Calvinist opponents). The God of love is willing to save all people.[72] But, unlike many evangelicals who would accept this point and then eviscerate it by making it dependent upon people's explicit confession of Jesus, Wesley relies on the traditional theological category of "invincible ignorance" to retain God's love and fairness. Truly invincible ignorance never did nor ever will exclude anyone from heaven.[73] God's sovereign and saving love for the entire human race can't be thwarted by circumstances of geography or limitations in human knowing; the God of the Christians is also "the God of the heathens."[74]

Therefore no one, says Wesley, has the right to sentence the entire "heathen" world to damnation.[75] We're not in a position to pronounce judgment on the eternal destiny of those who've never heard; rather, we leave them to the merciful God who accepts those in every nation who lives reverently before God and righteously.[76] If you were to press the question and ask *how* the "heathen" be saved without explicitly confessing Christ, probably the most well-known answer that's been picked up and passed down from Wesley is this: by living up to the light they do have.[77] Now, to some people this no doubt smacks of "works righteousness," meaning that a person has to prove the legitimacy of his or her faith by, e.g., keeping the law of conscience. But the situation in Wesley is more complex than that.

To begin, while it's true that Wesley ranks several sorts of deficient faith, from that of Materialists up through Deists, then heathens (he lumps Muslims in here), and finally Jews and Roman Catholics,[78] this formal classification breaks down a bit when it comes to actual individuals. Wesley

71. See Maddox, "Wesley and the Question of Truth," 7–29; Meadows, "Candidates for Heaven," 99–129.

72. Wesley, "On The Wedding Garment," §19 (*Works* 4:148).

73. Wesley, "Letter to John Smith (June 25, 1746)," §7 (*Works* 26:198); "On the Trinity," §18 (*Works* 2:386).

74. Wesley, "On Living Without God," §14 (*Works* 4:174).

75. Wesley, "On Living Without God," §14 (*Works* 4:174).

76. Wesley, "On Charity," §1.3 (*Works* 3:295–96).

77. Wesley, "On Faith," §1.4 (*Works* 3:494).

78. Wesley, "On Faith," §1.4 (*Works* 3:492–96).

acknowledges that among the "heathen" there are some whom God has taught "the essentials of true religion,"[79] meaning those "holy tempers" of the sort described in 1 Corinthians 13 (the chapter containing "the whole of true religion").[80] Whatever his detractors might say, at least for Wesley this "true religion" can never be attained through legalistic observance in any religion (including Christianity), a position consistent with his conviction that the merciful God considers our lives and tempers more than our ideas, and respects the goodness of our hearts rather than the clearness of our heads.[81] On this score, Wesley wishes that the lives of many "heathens" didn't shame so many of those who call themselves Christians.[82] We might say the same thing today.

But more importantly, Wesley believed that the "light" and "true religion" he spoke about was possible only on account of the work of Christ and the activity of the Holy Spirit. In a letter to someone who had joined the Quakers, Wesley's inclusivism comes out when he agrees that the benefit of Christ's death extends even to those who have no explicit knowledge of it. He affirms that these people may partake of the benefit of (Christ's) death, even if they don't know the story of the gospel, if they allow his grace to take place in their hearts in such a way that they are changed from being wicked to holy people.[83] And since Wesley firmly believed that we can do nothing, even by what we call our natural abilities, without the assistance of the Holy Spirit,[84] how much less would it be possible to talk about "true religion" without the Spirit's activity?

This means that when we see the Spirit at work, we must be careful not to criticize or forbid such work simply because those through whom the Spirit is working don't happen to share all our beliefs. In his sermon "A Caution Against Bigotry," Wesley says that, even if he saw one of the usual suspects on his theological hit list (which included Papists, Arians, Socinians, Jews, Deists, and Turks) casting out devils, he couldn't forbid such a person without convicting himself of bigotry.[85] But refusing to forbid such a person is only the beginning of our responsibility. Positively, we should speak well of whomever God is using, to the point where we defend their character and mission, and even try to enlarge their sphere of action. But

79. Wesley, "On Faith," §1.4 (*Works* 3:494).

80. Wesley, "On Charity," §1.3 (*Works* 3:293).

81. Wesley, "On Living Without God," §15 (*Works* 4:175).

82. Wesley, "On Faith," §2.3 (*Works* 3:500).

83. Wesley, "Letter to a Person (Feb. 10, 1747–8)" (*Works* X:178).

84. Wesley, "Letter to John Smith (June 25, 1746)," §7 (*Works* 26:199–200).

85. Wesley, "Caution Against Bigotry," §4.4 (*Works* 2:77).

then, Wesley adds this: We should continue to pray for such people, that God might save both them and the people to whom they are ministering.[86]

To be honest, when Wesley says things like even if he did see a "Jew, Deist, or Turk" casting out devils, he wouldn't forbid them, he's probably stretching the example to make his point about bigotry. Most likely he never expected to see such a thing. But when I look at Wesley's overall emphases on discerning the Spirit's activity, emphasizing "true religion" and paying attention to the actual lives of the "heathen"—coupled with his christological grounding—it seems to me that the theological trajectory he sets in motion finds resonance and a more sophisticated context in Yong's capacious pneumatology of religions.[87]

Around the Table with Our Cousins

So what can we take from all of this? First of all, we have no stake in pronouncing judgment on those who've never had the opportunity to even hear the gospel. Their salvation can't rest on the shoulders of missionaries, no matter how broad and fearless—it has to remain the prerogative of the triune God. Further, the determining factor in thinking about the eternal destiny of people is the activity and conviction of the Holy Spirit (who mediates the benefits of the atonement), not geographic or historical availability of the gospel or whether someone agrees to a set of propositions about metaphysical states of affairs. Eternal damnation can't be on account of simply holding wrong propositions, or failing to affirm those beliefs you *can't* know about, any more than holding right propositions ensures you have a share in the fullness of the kingdom. So saying that people are lost eternally if they resist the Holy Spirit is not the same thing as saying that they are lost if they fail to accept Jesus. Figuring out how and through what means (religious or otherwise) the Holy Spirit might use to get through to such people is an interesting speculative game for us to play, but beyond our ken and certainly our control to specify an answer that would be true in all times and places. So if you ask, "Is the Holy Spirit moving in Buddhism?"—Yong says the answer may be "yes" in this situation, or maybe "no" in that situation.[88] This state of affairs might bother us, but it shouldn't bother us any more than our Calvinist friends' insistence on God's secret counsel whereby some are ordained to eternal life and others to perdition.

86. Wesley, "Caution Against Bigotry," §4.4 (*Works* 2:77).

87. In fact, Yong has an appreciation for Wesleyan theology's contribution to interreligious encounter. See Yong, "Heart Strangely Warmed."

88. Yong, "Holy Spirit and the World Religions," 205.

Further, when sitting at the table talking about the gospel to cousins, I'm not particularly interested in arguing, along the lines of traditional apologetics, for the superiority of Christianity or why they really want Jesus even if they don't realize it, and I don't presume that the questions I'm asking are the questions my cousins are asking. *Some* religions and their adherents may be asking *some* of the same questions, and some may even be giving similar answers. Most religions, however, seem to me to be sufficiently *dis*similar both in their questions and answers and the way actual religious communities embody their answers that it seems far better to talk, not about why the gospel is superior or the answer to your deepest longing, but about what's *unique* about it. Of course, each religion can claim that what it offers is unique, but in my view the passion, death, and resurrection of Jesus as an event in God's triune life combine to kick over the standard metaphysical tables in the temple of the world's religions.

But more importantly, showing what the gospel *means* by introducing people to actual communities is far more effective than trying to argue or theologize someone into the kingdom. Lindbeck, for example, rightly said that you'd falsify the confession "Christ is Lord" if you confessed it while splitting the skull of an unbeliever.[89] If I can flip that observation on its head, people will best grasp what "Christ is Lord" *does* mean in a positive sense if they see it first in a community where Christians have renounced their claims to lordship and embody servanthood. That's much harder than arguing about theology! Apart from that embodiment, "Christ is Lord" remains at the abstract level and susceptible of being coopted into various ecclesiastical (or nationalist) schemes in which those in power can leech off the cachet of Jesus' lordship. May God deliver us from such betrayal.

89. Lindbeck, *Nature of Doctrine*, 64.

4

Talking with Outsiders

Agnostics and Atheists

For several years we lived in Melbourne, one of the world's most livable cities and home to great coffee. Turks, Greeks, and Italians have immigrated in droves to Australia, and these folks know what they're doing when it comes to handling the magic bean. Back before cholesterol was a worry in my life, I'd start most days with a croissant and espresso at a café in our neighborhood, served up by the ever-smiling Renata (not her real name). When our daughter Carolyn was still an "ankle-biter" (as they say in Australia), I'd sometimes take her with me, and Renata would fix her a *babyccino* (steamed milk with foam piled high).

The employees at this café were top-shelf: helpful, courteous, and hardworking. I'd often see one of the young women, Carlotta (again, not her real name), loading up a two-wheel dolly from a delivery truck and hauling around crates of fresh fruit and veggies early in the morning. There weren't many Americans in our neighborhood, and I was an odd duck in that café. Carlotta and I would joke around occasionally (usually about American politics). One day she came over to where I was sitting and saw the usual pile of books and papers.

"Jon, what's all this, then?"

"I'm writing an article on music and spirituality."

"Music and . . . *spirituality*?"

"Yeah, it's about how, through listening to music, we can get a sense of God brushing up against us."

If you don't know already, secularism runs deep in Australia. But after investing myself in Aussie culture for several years, I was confident in my ability to speak about spirituality to people who said they had no interest in God or organized religion. And I thought music was a great way to get the conversation started.

"I don't believe music has anything to do with being spiritual," Carlotta said, cutting me off at the conversational kneecaps. Aussies aren't shy about sharing their opinions.

"You don't?" I asked, surprised.

"No, no, no. Whatever you're experiencing when you're listening to music is just chemicals going off in your brain."

"Carlotta, you don't ever get a sense of something greater than yourself, and greater than the world around us, when you listen to music? That there's a dimension to life greater than what we're usually aware of?"

She laughed and looked at me as though my mother must have dropped me on my head when I was little. "Look, mate, be serious. There's nothing spiritual about music. Why do you have to drag God into this? I'm, what do you call it, a *materialist*!"

She remained entirely resistant to any connection I brought forth between music and God. It was like this woman had anti-apologetic superpowers; all the great and persuasive insights I'd culled from great thinkers like Jeremy Begbie and George Steiner bounced harmlessly off her. I continued to frequent the café, and Carlotta and I remained friends, but from then on she always regarded me as a bit of a nutter, poking around in airy-fairy nonsense.

A Growing Challenge

This group of conversation partners presents the greatest challenge: how do you talk about God with agnostics and atheists? We share some theological common ground with our cousins, but the conversational tectonics shift when we talk with people who have abandoned any religious beliefs, whether out of frustration, anger, or serious intellectual objections. Some are agnostic, some are full-on atheists, and some aren't sure what they are, only knowing that they're not religious. This group is growing considerably in the United States. In 2012, Pew Research published its survey on the rise of the nones, with a fifth of the public and a third of adults under age thirty saying they have no religious affiliation at all.[1] George Steiner, one of the most sensitive and erudite literary figures of our day, once referred to

1. Pew Research Center, "'Nones' on the Rise," para. 1. See also Lipka, "Closer Look."

agnosticism as the "established church of modernity,"[2] and at present this church is growing by leaps and bounds.

Pew Research has offered a few tentative theories about the root causes of the rise of the unaffiliated:[3] young people turning away from organized religion on account of its perceived connection with conservative politics, delays in marriage (meaning that once people get married they tend to become religiously affiliated), broad social disengagement, and secularization. As borne out in this research, why people don't believe has no easy answer. At the end of the day, you can find as many combinations of reasons as there are individuals. Regardless of reasons, however, it's clear that, given the trend, this group constitutes an expanding challenge for talking about the gospel in North America, and the challenges are even greater for our friends in Europe and Australia.

In this chapter, I want to explore what to keep in mind about agnosticism and atheism as religious or philosophical perspectives, what the real issues are in the debate between religion and science, and how to best approach conversations with agnostic and atheist friends (and enemies) when the subject of God comes up. To get at these issues, I need to undertake several tasks. First, I need to explain why the Bible and much of what passes for contemporary apologetics don't cut ice with many unbelievers, and what this means for our expectations in our conversations with them. Next, since Christians hope that their agnostic and atheist friends will come to faith someday, I want to ruminate on the oft-misunderstood issue of doubt and how conversion actually happens for most people. I'll then move into a discussion of the varieties of unbelievers (the wounded, perplexed, angry, and intellectual), since the approach we bring to the table should be scaled to our particular conversation partners. Following a look at Wesley's musings on the limitations of human knowledge and why Christianity (for all its great claims) seems to be so ineffective in this world, I'll close the chapter with some reflections on living peaceably with all people, especially with our unbelieving critics.

The Bible and Apologetics Aren't as Persuasive as You Think

I'll say it and then brace myself for the onslaught of emails: quoting Bible verses to atheists and agnostics isn't as effective as some apologetically-minded people think. (If you don't believe this, *get in the ring*.) While you

2. Steiner, *Errata*, 184.
3. Pew Research Center, "'Nones' on the Rise."

can find agnosticism and atheism in the ancient world, the Bible's concerns were shaped for the most part in a world of religiously pagan true believers. Outside of a few patches of natural religion found in the Psalms or jabs at unbelievers in Proverbs, the Scripture writers seldom respond to people who don't believe in any gods at all (or maintain silence about them). Quoting Bible verses to the nonreligious, and especially to those burned by the religious, is generally pointless and often counterproductive.

It might sound strange in our context (where agnosticism and atheism are common), but we'd be helped by recovering those elements of atheism within the Christian faith itself. One of the charges leveled against the primitive church by its pagan neighbors was that Christians are *atheists*![4] Christians refused to worship the gods of the Roman Empire, believing them to be demons (or, as Paul put it, "nothing"), and we still should refuse to bow our knee to any god wrapped in the flag or dragged in to justify abuses of power. Further, we should be among the first to declare ourselves "atheist" and protest that we don't believe in a Grand Puppeteer who condones the suffering of the innocent or in a convenient God of the gaps. If agnostic and atheists want nothing to do with those gods, neither should we.

The critical moment of our atheism is found above all in Jesus' cry of dereliction from the cross. The British apologist G. K. Chesterton said that atheists will find only one God who ever experienced their isolation, and one religion in which for a moment God "seemed to be an atheist."[5] Of all the religions out there, Judaism and Christianity take with utter seriousness the experience of God-abandonment, Christianity so much so that it alters what we mean by the word "God." Many Christians have so bought into the conventional idea of an *uncrucified* God that they don't understand this, but if you get what happened on the cross, you'll find that we share a kinship with atheists closer than any other religions.

If the Bible isn't terribly helpful in addressing atheism and agnosticism, neither are most conventional apologetics, concerned with "proving" things like God's existence, Jesus' resurrection, or the reality of the afterlife. For many people, that's an irrelevant enterprise. People disappointed in the church, angry at God, or stymied in the face of religious diversity for the most part don't need apologetic "proofs," and attempting this with them amounts to yet more "adventures in missing the point."[6] As we saw in the previous chapter, if one of religion's chief functions lies in structuring a community's life, then the church's more urgent apologetic task lies in

4. See "Martyrdom of Polycarp," 9–11.

5. Chesterton, *Orthodoxy*, 205–6.

6. The title of a book by Brian McLaren and Tony Campolo.

demonstrating how its beliefs inform its life. Dennis Hollinger puts it this way: the church needs to be the plausibility structure of the Christian life world.[7]

I don't want to overstate my case. Although the audience for conventional apologetics in the West is probably smaller than what we imagine (highly publicized debates between theists and atheists amount to little more than media spectacles), a place for apologetics remains. But this enterprise has limits, and the assumptions we bring to the table with agnostics and atheists differ from those we bring when talking with cousins. When matters of proof and doubt enter the conversation with cousins, such questions generally swirl around particular issues. For many of our cousins, you don't need to prove many of the things we believe in (e.g., you don't need to convince a Muslim that Jesus is returning). By contrast, we're treading on different ground when talking with our agnostic and atheist friends. They either won't grant you that God or a transcendent reality exists or, if they do, will deny that we can know much about it. And the more aggressive types (like the "New Atheists") take this one step further: your religious fantasies, prejudices, and violence threaten the progress and indeed the survival of the human race.

So what can we hope for in these conversations? How can we live peaceably with people who believe that religion is responsible for most of the trouble in the world? Although in any conversation about the gospel I hope to persuade my conversation partner of God's love for us, my immediate aims in these particular conversations are far more modest. At a minimum, I want to say this to our agnostic and atheist friends: "So many of your criticisms are spot on. Too often, the church has been on the wrong side of history and aligned itself lock-step with those ideas and causes we should have repudiated. At times, we've tried to compel people to believe. We've covered up abuses and sometimes justified them in the name of God. The church in the West in particular has a shocking history when it comes to women and people of color. We've often closed our eyes and substituted mythology and wishful thinking for science, and tried to censor the best literary minds of the age. Your intellectual and moral sensibilities are rightly outraged over these things, as ours should be, and we need to hear that from you."

Of course I immediately want to add, "but all Christians aren't like that." I want to say that most of us believe that hating and killing in the name of God runs counter to the core of the gospel. Most of us don't want to bulldoze religion into anyone's life. Most of us have personally experienced the

7. Hollinger, "Church as Apologetic," 191.

struggle of faith and realize that no one can be forced to believe anything. Most of us don't close our eyes to scientific research and many of us cringe at the thought of "creationism" taught in public schools as a legitimate scientific alternative. I want to say that most of us are alarmed at the idea of a theocratic government and oppose attempts to marginalize women or deny homosexuals their civil rights. Yes, Christian beliefs have been distorted and used to abuse and kill people, because *any* beliefs can be twisted, and heaps of fundamentalists consider agnostics and atheists to be our enemies. When Christians act this way, however, we betray the highest ideals of the faith and the One murdered in the name of God by the fundamentalists of his day. For our atheist critics to judge us based on what religious fanatics do in the name of God is as unfair as us judging them based on what communist regimes have done to millions in the name of atheist ideologies. Every philosophy or religion should be judged on the basis of its highest ideals and finest practitioners. (Muslims today grapple with this issue perhaps even more intensely than Christians.)

I want to say all that and more to agnostics and atheists, but most likely it would fall on deaf ears, given the number of examples our critics can point to. The words "most of us" repeatedly in the above paragraph is the problem. At what point does the sinful behavior of religion's practitioners outweigh the highest ideals of that religion? I'm not sure anyone knows the answer to that. A load of morally shocking material exists in the Bible itself, including descriptions of God in the record of Israel's history that are hard to swallow. Most of us (ha!), if we're honest, don't know what to do with these things. On that particular point, if there's any way forward at all, the best minds in the church have insisted that the story of Jesus is the key to helping us interpret the Scripture and make sense of who God is. The book of Colossians gives us our interpretive bearings when it declares that Jesus is the image of the invisible God, and that in him all of God's fullness dwells (Col 1:15–20). The first chapter of Hebrews likewise says that Jesus is the precise representation of God's being (Heb 1:3). I take this to mean that, when we're not sure what to think about other passages and how to comport our lives as Christians, we try to sort things out by following the gospel story—the story of a man who railed against many of the same things in organized religion that our critics point out.

Of course, we follow this story believing that he was more than just a man. And so I'd need to add this to the above statement: We believe lots of things our critics don't, and lots of things that many people think are completely bonkers. In fact, many of those beliefs turn out to be points of dispute between religious people themselves. As I've tried to show in the previous chapters, if someone has a hard time swallowing grandiose claims made by a religious tradition, all the cajoling or threatening in the world isn't going to help. Trying to force anyone to believe something always ends in tears or bloodshed, because belief doesn't work that way. For all the talk in Christian circles about the importance of the choices we make, coming to have faith in anything isn't simply a matter of choosing to believe something when you're troubled by doubt. How people come to navigate through their doubts and believe the gospel is a mysterious, Spirit-led process. So, come Holy Spirit!

Come, Holy Spirit! On Doubt and Persuasion

Beyond the conversational minimums I've been describing, Christians do want to see their agnostic and atheist friends at the table become Christians. Despite all the chatter about relationships and lifestyle evangelism, at some point we need to actually talk about the gospel! And all Christians would acknowledge that, so far as saving faith is concerned, rational persuasion alone will never do the trick. The Holy Spirit convicts people and gives the gift of faith, even if the Spirit works through proximate (e.g., conversational) means.

Because the Spirit's work is necessary, we all recognize it would be silly to urge someone *un*persuaded that Jesus is Lord to confess faith in him anyway, just to be on the safe side. That would constitute an existential act of bad faith (and you can't fool God, at any rate). Having said that, when someone says they're rejecting God or the gospel, you can't always be sure what they're really rejecting. A distorted, cultural expression of the gospel? An obnoxious Christian? What they've heard from a television evangelist? A bait-and-switch evangelism technique? A political platform in religious dress? Or simply unconvincing apologetics?

Sometimes rejecting someone's presentation of "the gospel" is the only decent and honest thing to do. Many Christians wouldn't be willing to make this concession, however, in which case an odd state of affairs emerges: You can't inherit the kingdom dishonestly, and you can't avoid hell dishonestly, which seems only right, but (oddly enough) this sounds like you *can* be damned precisely by being honest before God. So for those who struggle with objections and doubts about the faith, perhaps for years, and go to their graves still unpersuaded, punishment awaits? God is patient, but apparently, only to a point, even with those wrestling with legitimate questions. Hell brooks no exceptions for honest doubters.

It's a truism that faith is not a matter of mere logical persuasion. Anyone who says something like, "I looked at all the religions rationally and

Christianity made the most sense to me" needs to get out more often. "The third day he rose again from the dead," "ascended to heaven," and "whence he shall come to judge the living and the dead" are matters hardly susceptible of proof. When and how the Holy Spirit enables a person to make the breakthroughs necessary to believe remain hidden from view. Given this mysterious work of the Spirit, do we come to the point where we say to a doubting person, "Although your questions, reservations, and objections about the faith are legitimate, to the point that we acknowledge that our answers are not fully satisfactory, we know that the Holy Spirit would not lead you to the end of your life without fully convincing you inwardly. So the root of your resistance can't be a matter of legitimate moral or intellectual objections; it *must* be sheer hardheartedness"; in other words, sin. But telling someone to repent when they are neither convinced nor convicted is pointless. Again, you can't fool God. And so conversation seems to be at an end as an awkward silence descends on the picnic table.

Perhaps surprisingly, the Roman Catholic Church offers helpful insight when trying to work through these issues of doubt and persuasion (I say "perhaps surprisingly" because the church has hardly an unblemished record when it comes to gently persuading people of the truth). Nevertheless, Vatican II's Declaration on Religious Freedom, *Dignitas Humanae* (1965), offers this: "The truth cannot impose itself except by virtue of its own truth, as it makes its entrance into the mind at once quietly and with power."[8] So, in spreading the gospel, the faithful must never try to coerce people because no one can be forced to embrace the Christian faith against their will. As God calls people to serve Him in spirit and truth, we are bound in conscience but stand under no compulsion. And we must always obey the judgment of our conscience.[9]

"The truth cannot impose itself except by virtue of its own truth." What an odd thing to say! How does the truth do that? How does it make its way into us "quietly and with power"? To hear Christian apologists talk, you'd swear people become Christians through a process similar to that of buying a car. You do research on competing models, compile a list of pros and cons, and try to decide which make and model make the most sense for you. The overwhelming majority of people don't come to faith like this (thank goodness).

For most people, the process far more resembles the way John Gray (one of the Newer Atheists I'll talk about later in this chapter) describes Graham Greene's conversion to Roman Catholicism. Although Father

8. Paul VI, "Dignitas Humanae," para. 1.
9. *Catechism of the Catholic Church*, para. 1800.

Trollope confronted Greene with philosophical arguments for the faith, Greene felt that, in the good Father's presence, he was faced with "the challenge of an inexplicable goodness," and it was this force, rather than apologetics, that proved persuasive for Greene.[10] So if not arguments, then what *was* it that Greene accepted? Gray suggests that Trollope's way of life persuaded Greene, which is in effect an atheist giving a nod to the effectiveness of lifestyle evangelism. Theologically, Christians would want to explain that inexplicable goodness Greene encountered by talking about the Holy Spirit working in Father Trollope's life.

This event Gray mentions raises a couple of questions. First of all, there's little in Greene's own account of his conversion that deals with the claim of the gospel (it's not that important to Gray, at any rate), but surely at some point a person must deal with what the gospel actually says. We may not be argued into the kingdom, but neither do we merely believe in the power of belief or in an amorphous something out there. The Christian theological tradition has always recognized the difference between the faculty of faith by which something is believed and the content of what is believed, and theologians have generally focused on that content and how we negotiate our encounter with it. The other, equally problematic question is how Greene was able to respond at all to the gospel as it was lived out in Father Trollope's life, especially if, as the Christian tradition has always insisted, we're all sinners.

That question remains one of the most vexed in the history of Christian thought, and the answers put forward all try to triangulate the relationship between divine sovereignty, grace, and human agency. Although it might not seem so at first glance, understanding the basic issues in this discussion affects our approach to conversations with agnostics and atheists, since these questions bear upon how we think about doubt and how someone comes to faith. At the edges of the spectrum, you find the strict Reformed position on one end and Pelagianism (named after Pelagius, an infamous fifth-century heretic) on the other. The former holds that God, who alone is sovereign, has elected who will believe and who will be damned. God's decree is immutable and God's grace is irresistible. To allow any talk of human freedom in choosing to accept the offer of gospel is to obviate genuine grace, our Reformed friends say, since any real choice on our part means that salvation ultimately hinges on our response to God's "offer" of salvation. Pelagianism, 180 degrees removed from this, holds that human beings possess all we need in our natural capabilities to obey God and follow his commands. Contemporary Pelagianism surfaces whenever you hear people

10. Gray, "Can Religion Tell Us More," para. 3.

say things like, "God wouldn't want us to be robots! He gave us free will so we can choose to follow him."

Between the Reformed and Pelagian stances you find variations on a more difficult position that the majority of Christians have wanted to affirm, namely: Yes, our acceptance of the gospel is God's work throughout, but human beings are responsible, at least to the degree that we refrain from attributing anyone's damnation to God's eternal decree. The classic Roman Catholic and Arminian positions, for example, affirm that God gives prevenient grace to all people, enabling "whosoever will" to repent and believe the gospel. The eighteenth-century Arminian theologian John Fletcher said what most Christians have wanted to articulate, even if conceptually it's difficult to pull off cleanly: our salvation is of God, but our damnation is of ourselves.[11]

I'll go out on a limb and say that, on the question of how people are able to respond to the gospel, the classic positions seem to be abstractions of how it unfolds in real life. The Reformed perspective diminishes the spiritual narrative of people's lives as a real drama and renders the actual persuasive power of the gospel moot, since in the eternal counsel of God you were assigned to salvation or perdition. Despite Reformed protests to the contrary, despair or Antinomianism (living however you want, since it's all about grace) seem like perfectly reasonable responses to that theological position. Any struggle of doubt and faith to which an agnostic or atheist might testify is a pre-orchestrated experience, not a struggle with real consequences. On the other hand, as a Wesleyan I have to admit that the way people in my tradition often talk about the Arminian position seems to imply that people come to faith by successfully negotiating a series of grace-enabled choices, which seems to me both naïve and rationalistic.

Against both of these positions, I think that coming to faith is a lot more like being captivated by a compelling story or even drawn in unexpectedly by a beautiful piece of music. I'm flipping through a book in a bookstore and within a minute or two find myself following a story along. Or the radio in the truck is on in the background and I absent-mindedly begin tapping the steering wheel as I'm driving down the highway. I wasn't predestined to like the story or music, and I didn't simply decide to like it or not like it. My tapping turns into bobbing my head and rocking in my seat, and after a few minutes I say to myself, this music is great!

Now after I discover that I like what I'm reading or hearing, I may commit myself to reading the entire book or listening to that particular song again (or the whole album), and in retrospect I may try to piece together

11. Fletcher, *Zelotes and Honestus Reconciled*, 23.

how I came to love the work ("Yes, somewhere along the line I suppose I could have snapped the book shut" or "I guess I must have made some sort of unconscious decision to leave the radio on"), but in the moment I wasn't deciding for or against anything, and any attempt to tell me that I was pre-destined to like that book or music is an attempt to trump theory over real-ity and detract from the actual persuasive power of the piece. Every analogy has its limits, but the point I'm trying to make is that we don't really decide to believe something prior to and apart from that something entering "qui-etly and with power" and doing its work on us. We're imperceptibly taken hold of by something, via an interior tug-of-war in our heart and mind, in a process we don't fully understand but which involves rational coherence, emotional and affective needs, and sociological influences and pressures, until we reach the point where we cannot *not* believe and finally embrace that something (or something deep in our interiority tips the other way and we find ourselves rejecting what we're mulling). So maybe, instead of trying to argue people out of their unbelief or berating them for having doubts, our task should be to help them fall in love (or, for some, to fall in love again) with the music of the gospel.

A Taxonomy of Unbelievers

As we approach this taxonomy, it's important to keep a few things in mind. First, sometimes people are confused as to whether they don't believe in God at all or are disappointed with (or angry at) God or an idea of God they've inherited. To that degree, any believer who has cried out with Job isn't that far from our agnostic and atheist (or anti-theist) friends. Which is to say, the line between belief, agnosticism, and atheism is sometimes far fuzzier than it appears at first glance. In our darkest moments, when we wonder if anyone is out there, it's not a matter of *us* versus *them*. It's all of us seated at the table together, struggling through.

Second, pigeonholing people is unfair, and most agnostics and atheists fall into more than one of the groups mentioned above. (For example, some people who've been burned by the church want intellectual ammunition to back up their animosity against organized religion.) Any thoughtful Chris-tian could find themselves in any of the groups I describe in this chapter, and very well may at some point in his or her life. Again, it isn't a question of *us* versus *them* in an unqualified sense, because another fine line exists between believing something and hoping or wanting something to be true. Normal Christian experience includes ambiguity and doubt, and you can't make these experiences disappear by trying to force yourself to believe more intensely or sincerely. I often meet people who've been so shielded from doubt that when the slightest challenge creeps in and rattles them, the whole house of theological cards collapses. In my experience, if you've never been troubled by doubt, you haven't been wrestling with the right questions.

And third, beware of the seductions of *method*. In seminary, I took a course on evangelism, in which we were taught a method of persuading people to accept the gospel, which involved presenting the "bait" (i.e., starting a conversation by presenting Scripture passages and answering common questions) and learning how to "set the hook" (getting a commitment), but as a young seminarian I remember thinking two things: first, "fishers of men" aside, the extended metaphor demeaned people to the level of, well, *fish*, and, second, quoting Scripture passages to people might have persuasive purchase in a Christian culture, where residual piety remains even amongst the unchurched, but how is this supposed to work amongst people who have no respect for the Bible and who have rejected Christianity outright? (Where are these people who believe Bible verses you throw at them? I need their email addresses.)

At the end of the day, no foolproof method for convincing anyone of anything exists, least of all in something as mysterious and personal as faith. There are no secrets. These groups I'm about to describe are made up of individuals, each with personal histories and idiosyncrasies that emerge only after you get to know someone, and this makes the idea of stipulating a method rather silly. No one can be reduced entirely to the labels I'm about to use. Nevertheless, here are my labels.

The Wounded

For the most part, these people don't have substantial intellectual reasons for rejecting Christianity; they may still revere Jesus as an inspiring figure and even secretly believe that God exists. They *do* have horror stories involving the church, and (despite other reasons they may give for not believing), that's the reason they left the table. You've probably met scores of them: people who've been disappointed or abused in so many ways (emotionally, financially, spiritually, physically, you name it) by good church people, or who've been shocked by the corruption and hate-mongering they see in the church. If that's all you saw or experienced, of course you'd want nothing to do with the church or this God of love we Christians prattle on about. I frequently ask my classes to finish this criticism levelled at us: "You Christians are nothing but a bunch of . . . " and, without fail, the class responds in unison: "hypocrites!" We've heard it so often.

Let's be honest: most Christians could belong to this group. Who doesn't have stories of being let down by a church or wounded by "good Christians" who thought they were doing God's will? In a theology class, I include a class exercise in which I ask skeptical students, "Why do you think the church sucks?" Rarely do I hear responses about theology; they're almost always about the church's hypocrisy and how it has mistreated people. Several years ago, I even met a woman who was writing a formal academic thesis on what she called "spiritual abuse," a topic that came out of her own experience in the church.

Christians are notorious for rushing in and quoting Bible verses in order to correct people. Wounded people don't need to be corrected. The problem doesn't exist on an intellectual level. Rather than lecturing, we need to listen, take the Bible literally, and (as Wesley once put it) mix our tears with theirs.[12] If it's appropriate (although sometimes it's best to keep your mouth shut), share your own stories of being hurt and even how you've hurt others. If nothing else, you'll give your conversation partner at least one example of a Christian who confesses his or her brokenness and is honest about sin. Wesley advised that we always be ready to own up to our faults and failings. Far from hurting the cause of the gospel, our honesty and vulnerability will actually adorn the gospel and further it.[13] If I can put it another way, give Gandhi's maxim an ecclesiological referent: Be the change you want to see in the church.

As an academic, I'm tempted to slip into lecture mode with the wounded and explain that human beings have abused (and will abuse) every lofty philosophical and religious ideal, but as the ancient maxim says, abuse does not invalidate proper use. I want to jump in and explain that Christ himself was wounded by well-intentioned members of his own religion. But none of that will help. Like it or not, most people find it difficult if not impossible to separate beliefs from the behavior of people who hold those beliefs. Wounded people need healing, not answers, and unless I'm willing to sit in the ash heap with them, my answers might as well be salt rubbed in their wounds.

The Perplexed

These people believed for a time, and for many of them the gospel still holds a certain attraction, but they never received satisfactory answers to questions they think (or have been told by their churches) are central to the

12. Wesley, "On Pleasing All Men," §2.3 (*Works* 3:424).
13. Wesley, "Farther Thoughts," Q32 (*Works* 13:112).

Christian faith. They've grappled with the kinds of questions mentioned throughout this book. Do I have to believe in a literal six-day creation story in view of contemporary scientific understanding of origins? With so much evil in this world, how can I believe in loving God? Does God really pre-destine people to both salvation and damnation? What happens in baptism and the Lord's Supper? Why can't women hold leadership positions in the church? With so many religious claims out there, who's to say who's right? Are my Jewish and Sikh neighbors really going to hell because they don't believe the things I do?

The perplexed tend to fall into two groups: one group implicitly has agreed to play by a particular church's set of responses to questions like these and has said, in effect, "Yes, these answers are what Christians believe, so if we can't accept these answers, then we can't be Christians, even though there's a lot in the gospel we might admire." I call these people the *norma-tively perplexed*. People in the other group are more aware of the plethora of answers Christians have given to those questions and have more or less thrown their hands up in frustration over the bewildering array of answers. I call this group the *pluralistically perplexed*.

The normatively perplexed often don't know what to say or think when they find out I don't believe many of the things they've been told you must believe to be a Christian. Often they don't believe me! More than anything, these folks need exposure to the catholicity of the church and should meet Christians from a variety of theological backgrounds. In my classroom, I encounter a regular stream of students primed to become normatively per-plexed agnostics because they no longer believe the answers their church has told them they must affirm if they want to be Christians, and now that they're away from their church, they're ready to ditch what they've been told is the faith. So, sometimes the experience of meeting an array of people who claim to be Christians—but who answer their questions differently—can spin these students out. On several occasions I've observed students pub-licly digging in their heels on positions that they've told me privately they don't actually believe anymore! They simply don't know how to respond to a variety of answers to questions that they've been told must be answered *like this*. They're experiencing the philosophical equivalent of a hangover from rationalist evangelicalism.

The *pluralistically perplexed* have said, in effect, "With so many theo-logical opinions, who's to say who's right?" An honest agnosticism seems like the only reasonable position to take, given the history of infighting amongst Christians and between Christians and non-Christians. "You peo-ple kill each other over disagreements about invisible, metaphysical stuff? *Seriously?*" In their more charitable moments, this group might say *yes* to a kinder and gentler but amorphous spirituality, *maybe* to Jesus as an inspiring figure, but *no* to organized religion (the church). The aforementioned Pew Research revealed that, amongst the nones, many of those who had no formal religious affiliation still described themselves as "spiritual."

Many folks in this category often become angry toward "organized religion" for forcing people into a narrowly prescribed way of thinking and doing things. Now this rant against organized religion is pretty silly in itself, since "unorganized" religion quickly devolves into an incoherent vision quest or personal therapy. Whilst the pluralistically perplexed sometimes concede a vague apprehension of the Transcendent, they frequently protest that such knowledge remains out of reach for rationality and religious systems, and criticize the arrogance of institutions that claim to know "what God thinks" about this or that issue. Amongst those that grant some kind of concession to human knowledge, the assumption seems to be that, somehow, the various religions must all be aiming at the same end, albeit through different, screwed-up means (in other words, Lindbeck's "experiential-expressivism" gone to seed).

Frankly, many of the perplexed would be helped if they studied theology and the world's religions in more detail (my sense is that most of them don't understand matters as well as they think they do), and if they remembered that the sheer fact of complexity doesn't necessary mean that no one has any reliable answers to anything. It's difficult, of course, to push people to go deeper with theological questions, especially if they're tired of arguing about religion (and if they came out of a tradition that insisted it had all the right answers). In the case of the pluralistically perplexed, it's easy for people to slip into an intellectual laziness about ultimate questions, because surely if these questions were all that important, God would have made them easier to figure out. (On occasion I've tried to point out the egotistical fallacy of thinking that something is not important because it's not important *to you*, but that generally makes a person only dig their heels in deeper.) Some folks avoid grappling with questions about God until they experience a tragedy that forces upon them a rare moment of personal clarity. In that way, I suppose character does determine your theological destiny. But quite apart from those considerations, refusing to deal with theological question still means you've made a choice, because we all stand somewhere. So where are you standing and why? What *do* you affirm?

The Angry

The perplexed aren't satisfied with the answers they've been spoon-fed and still haven't found what they're looking for. The angry have made their frustration *personal*—against God! These people have had their faith crushed through experiencing one of the substantial objections to belief mentioned earlier: the problem of evil. It may strike some people wrestling with personal tragedy. How could a loving and all-powerful God have allowed (or worse, decreed) my loved one to die from cancer? It may strike other people when they contemplate global tragedies. How could this same God allow or decree [fill in the blank with your tragedy] to happen in this world? When I talk with these people, it seems to me that, rather than atheist or agnostic, they're really anti-theist. They're angry at a God they still grudgingly believe in (or think they should still believe in). Properly speaking, atheists shouldn't actually be angry at a God who doesn't exist. A true atheist's attitude, as Julian Baggini puts it, is that "Sometimes life is shit and that's all there is to it."[14]

Whenever someone declares herself an agnostic or atheist on account of personal tragedy ("Where was God when *this* happened to me or my loved one?"), there's a part of me that wants to respond, "You've become an atheist because something terrible happened to you personally? You haven't been paying attention! Read the news! What do you think goes on in this world every day!" (This wouldn't help the situation.) Some Christians who've left the table for this reason often come from churches where they were taught that obedience to God results in tangible blessings (health, prosperity, protection from harm, and so on). Then reality slaps them silly, and they don't know how or why to keep believing.

I always advise ministerial students in this way: when you're ministering to people struggling with tragedy, don't offer a theological explanation for what's happened to them or their loved one. "God needed another angel, so that's why He took your little boy" or "Everything happens for a reason." If you're thinking of saying something like that, then do us all a favor and shut up. If people suffering come up with a theological rationale that helps them make it through the night, fine. If you, on the other hand, try to convince someone of a theological explanation you've dreamed up, you're probably going to make things worse. And if you try this with someone already angry with God, you certainly *will* make things worse.

In my view, a big question mark should be placed above the enterprise of theodicy itself. We'll never solve the problem of theodicy by moving the

14. Baggini, "Yes, Life Without God," para. 5.

philosophical pieces of the puzzle around until they fit, and we're doing a deceptive and heart-breaking disservice to people in our churches by claiming that we understand why bad things happen to them. Marius Felderhof makes the point that engaging in the conventional enterprise of theodicy turns us into *voyeurs*, while instead we should be actively involved in *resisting* evil.[15] As much as the problem of evil is perplexing and faith-shattering, Jesus never lectured on theodicy. Consider the secrets of the kingdom Jesus shares with his disciples. He never says anything like, "Now lean in, boys; I'm going to let you in on a secret. The reason why God allows evil and suffering in the world is . . ." Instead, the gospel itself is how God addresses the problem of evil. Incarnation, cross, resurrection, Holy Spirit, church, eschatology: that's how evil is concretely and not merely theoretically confronted and conquered.[16]

I sometimes talk like this with former Christians who say they no longer believe in God because of the problem of evil; most of them look at me with blank stares. I suspect that, for all our talk in the church about Jesus' cross and resurrection, we've rarely helped people connect it to the problem of evil. We preach and teach about the forgiveness of sins, about becoming part of a community that resists the powers of this world and anticipates the coming kingdom, yet when it comes to the problem of evil we generally slip into abstract (and for the most part, pagan) conceptions of divine omnipotence. Maybe we'd do a better job in trying to respond to the angry if we admitted that we don't have an answer and refused to offer up religious platitudes or clichés, but just knuckled down and got on with the business of responding in substantial ways to suffering and evil.

The Intellectual

In my view, Western rationalism coupled with atheistic scient*ism* remains the most serious challenge to religions that maintain belief in the supernatural. In a legendary exchange, when Napoleon asked mathematician and astronomer Pierre-Simon Laplace why he made no mention of God in his theories, the latter allegedly remarked, "Sire, I have no need of that hypothesis." Laplace's remark might well serve as the motto for atheistic rationalists who find all they need for understanding life, the universe, and everything (à la Douglas Adams) in contemporary scientific method. Religion might be okay as therapy (for example, we've all read about the effects of prayer and convalescence), but as an explanation for how things work in the universe,

15. Felderhof, "Evil," 400.

16. On this point, see Pannenberg, *Systematic Theology*, 3:632–42.

you'd have to be crazy to believe religious accounts. We have groups like *Doctors Without Borders* and not *Witchdoctors Without Borders* for a good reason: Western science works. If you ask most people today if they'd rather trust reason and science or faith and religion to cure diseases, reduce carbon emissions, protect us from killer asteroids, and finally produce a decent low-fat salad dressing, the choice is obvious.

Serious atheists have been dominated over the past decade or so by the so-called New Atheists: brass-knuckled unbelievers who not only disagree with us but also let loose with invective. "Religion poisons everything," the late Christopher Hitchens pronounced.[17] Richard Dawkins admits that his description of religions as mind viruses is both contemptuous and hostile.[18] And Sam Harris charges that religion is "one of the most perverse misuses of intelligence we have ever devised."[19] Like the poor, we shall always have atheists with us, but after reading these critics for several years, my sense is that these New Atheists managed to capture the public imagination in large measure by appealing to human beings' mean streak.

In terms of the way they argue, the New Atheists seem remarkably obtuse when it comes to understanding people, and in particular how most people react to someone who is always raging at them about a cause (any cause). We probably all know someone who is on a constant crusade for (or against) something, isn't afraid to insult you to your face, who cannot ever, *ever* be wrong, or even consider that your opposing viewpoint might have some merit. After a few clashes you stop trying to talk with people like this, not because they've convinced you, but because you realize it's pointless and not worth your energy. They think they've shut you up because they've won the argument, while in reality you won't argue with them anymore because they're jerks and it's impossible to have a conversation with them. The New Atheists appear happily oblivious to the fact that this is the way most people operate.

When it comes to serious atheists' actual arguments, you cannot help but be struck by two things: the sheer predictability of their criticisms (and the theist responses) and the way that scientific and philosophical claims get folded indiscriminately together. (Atheism and theism are both philosophical perspectives that may or may not be supported by what one considers scientific "evidence.") Year after year, the parade continues: On the one side, Dawkins's *The God Delusion*, Hitchens's *God is Not Great*, and Harris's *The End of Faith*. On the other side, books like Gerald Schroeder's *The Hidden*

---

17. Hitchens, *God is Not Great*.

18. Dawkins, *Devil's Chaplain*, 117.

19. Harris, "Problem with Atheism," para. 13.

Face of God, Francis Collins's *The Language of God*, and Robert Spitzer's *New Proofs for the Existence of God*.

You hardly have to read these books to know how the "conversation" is going to go. Alister McGrath, in his book *Why God Won't Go Away*, lists three core themes that continually appear in the New Atheists' tirade against religion and its believers: religion begets violence, believers close their eyes to reason and choose to rely on blind faith, and science (not religion) tells us the truth about things.[20] Christians, of course, are going to say that our atheist critics have picked out the very worst examples or representatives of the faith in order to construct straw man arguments, but *any* belief can be distorted and abused. *Abusus non tollit usum* (abuse does not invalidate proper use). If only our New Atheist critics would read treatments by the best serious Christian apologists, they'd be able to see the rationale behind our belief. Indeed, you sometimes hear comments from Christians like "There's so much evidence; I don't have the faith to be an atheist."

Snarky New Atheists respond with their own chest-thumping, decrying serious Christian philosophers (like Alvin Plantinga) as obscurantists, and charging Christian scientists (like Francis Collins) with playing fast and loose with what they count as evidence. Just as a matter of how the world works, it's unlikely that any of the figures on either side would ever be convinced by the opposition (or at least admit that they are). Too much is at stake in terms of one's career and reputation. Christians sometimes mention Antony Flew, a long-time proponent of atheism, as a notable exception who came to believe in God, but the God Flew came to believe in hardly squares with the God of traditional Christianity.

Enter the Newer Atheists

What's interesting about this debate is the recent emergence of what British journalist Theo Hobson has called the *new* new atheists or, in simpler terms, the Newer Atheists.[21] Working mainly in the United Kingdom, these Newer Atheists have criticized the New Atheists for some of the same reasons that religious believers have: the New Atheists attack a crude, straw-man version of theism and possess an unrealistic faith in reason and the power of science. In brief, the New Atheists have turned out to be the atheist fundamentalist counterparts to religious fundamentalists. John Gray, a Newer Atheist philosopher at the London School of Economics, says that when Dawkins inveighs against religion in the name of evolutionary science, he's

20. McGrath, *Why God Won't Go Away*, 61–131.
21. Hobson, "Richard Dawkins Has Lost."

little more than an ideologue for the philosophical perspective of scientism. The funny thing is that Dawkins appears not to realize that, compared to Charles Darwin's cautious and humble approach to his own findings, he himself has become a kind of comic anti-Darwin caricature: arrogant, caustic, and without a trace of self-criticism (Dawkins is "a monument to unthinking certitude").[22]

These Newer Atheists admit that science can't be co-opted into either side in the religion versus science debate. Baggini (cofounder of *The Philosophers' Magazine*) says that atheists need to accept "that they are not of one flesh with science," and that their "love and admiration [of science] may not be requited as passionately as they suppose."[23] In his takedown of Sam Harris's *The Moral Landscape*, Baggini claims that if science has shown us anything, it's that we human beings are far less autonomous and rational than we imagine (secular humanists, take note). And while science can do things like reveal the physiological and neurological mechanisms that underlie the things we value in life, it can never tell us what we should value. In sum, "science is not such a large problem for religion as atheists suppose, but not such a small problem as the religious suppose, and not as much of an ally to humanists as they suppose. All of which means that science just isn't as central to the disputes between believers and atheists as almost everyone seems to suppose."[24]

This might sound terrible to some, but science can neither confirm nor deny the traditional concerns of apologetics (e.g., God's existence). To begin, science as a disciplined field of inquiry doesn't speak in a unified voice any more than philosophy does—only scientists and philosophers do after grappling with what counts as evidence to them. And what's convincing to one scientist may be entirely unconvincing to another. Furthermore, if God truly is Wholly Other than realities we study with microscopes or telescopes, then of course what's going to count as evidence is going to be different and susceptible to conflicting interpretations. So there's no slam dunk on either side; science possesses only limited utility for both theism and atheism. You sometimes hear Christians prattle on about how "science doesn't have all the answers," and while that's true in the obvious sense that no one has all the answers to everything, it's more difficult but more accurate to say that sometimes science and religion ask the same questions, and sometimes they ask different questions. Being able to differentiate these questions is the tricky bit.

22. Gray, "Closed Mind of Richard Dawkins," para. 22.
23. Baggini, "Science is Independent of Humanism," para. 9.
24. Baggini, "Science is Independent of Humanism," para. 10.

These questions are hardly new to thoughtful Christian scientists. Dennis Alexander (Faraday Institute for Science and Religion, Cambridge), summarizes four basic models found in science and religion conversations: the conflict model (science and religion exist in opposition), the independence model (science and religion ask different questions), the fusion model (using science to construct religious systems or vice versa), and the complementarity model (science and religion address the same reality but from different perspectives).[25] Alexander adopts what seems to me to be a sane and nuanced perspective, namely, that no single model is capable of encompassing all the complexities of the relationship (although he leans toward the last model), given the vast subject areas and questions that could be examined.[26] It's possible that, on different issues, science and religion could be irrevocably at odds with each other, they could be asking different questions, they could be capable of being "fused," or they could be addressing the same reality but from different perspectives. Given the complexity of the issues, both atheists and theists should recognize that pitting science against religion is a caricature.

John Gray says that the New Atheists' inflated claims for science is based on what he calls a "childlike faith in reason." We've come to know a great deal about human beings, but "one of the things we know for sure is that we're not rational animals. Believing in the power of human reason requires a greater leap of faith than believing in God."[27] Science, Gray says, may well confirm that irrationality is hardwired in us. We might like to think that we base our beliefs on carefully analyzed experience, but the opposite seems to be the case: "human beings block out of their minds anything that disturbs their view of the world."[28] Religion provides, if nothing else, at least an antidote to the naïve faith in the boundless capacities of our minds. What should give the New Atheists heebie-jeebies, Gray says, is the idea that religion, a universal phenomenon amongst human beings, might actually serve an *evolutionary* function. "What if the upshot of scientific inquiry is that a need for illusion is built into the human mind?" Gray asks. And "if religions are natural for humans and give value to their lives, why spend your life trying to persuade others to give them up?"[29]

Make no mistake; these Newer Atheists (especially Gray, Baggini, and Alain de Botton) truly *are* atheists. They don't believe the question of

25. Alexander, "Models for Relating Science and Religion," 1–4.
26. Alexander, "Models for Relating Science and Religion," 4.
27. Gray, "Child-Like Faith in Reason," para. 2.
28. Gray, "Child-Like Faith in Reason," para. 9.
29. Gray, "What Scares the New Atheists," para. 30.

whether religious claims are true is even worth pursuing, and remain critical of anything that smells of the supernatural. Gray goes so far as to claim that, in most religions themselves, "belief has never been particularly important," as opposed to *practice*.[30] One of Baggini's "Articles of 21st-century Faith" (his attempt to offer an olive branch to believers) proposes that contemporary self-critical religions shouldn't require belief in the supernatural.[31] Yet several of the Newer Atheists recognize that we can still learn from both the content and form of religion. Gray, for example, says that some of the ancient myths we inherit from religion are more truthful than the stories the modern world tells us, insofar as the former "tell us something about ourselves that can't be captured in scientific theories," and that "you don't have to believe a story is literally true in order for it to give meaning to your life"[32] When's the last time you heard an atheist affirm the practical effects of religion and encourage you, as Gray does, to "just go into the church, synagogue, mosque or temple and take it from there"?[33]

Similarly, Alain de Botton recognizes the salient practical effects of religion. In his book *Religion for Atheists*, de Botton recognizes that religions have served two important needs that secular society hasn't addressed very well: the need to live together in harmony and the need to cope with pain and tragedy.[34] So de Botton proposes a secular version of what religion has been able to pull off with considerable success, constructing a list of Ten Commandments for atheists,[35] and imagines a secular analogue to the Mass, called the Agape Restaurant, which could replicate the ideals of welcome and community without the religious superstition.[36] (I'm not sure if de Botton is aware of the love feast practiced by the Moravians and early Methodists.)

I don't think most believers would rest comfortably with the Newer Atheists' dismissal of religious truth claims, even if they recognize the practical effects of religion. Many believers would argue that they wouldn't practice their faith unless they believed it was true—that Jesus really did rise from the tomb, or that Allah really did speak through the angel to Muhammad. But the Newer Atheists recognize the immense power for good in the world's religions and the importance of talking with believers as we

30. Gray, "Can Religion Tell Us More," para. 11.
31. Baggini, "Articles of 21st-century Faith."
32. Gray, "Can Religion Tell Us More," para. 17.
33. Gray, "Can Religion Tell Us More," para. 33.
34. de Botton, *Religion for Atheists*, 5–6.
35. de Botton, "Alain de Botton's 10 Commandments."
36. de Botton, *Religion for Atheists*, 40.

navigate extraordinary challenges together, and we dare not ignore that open invitation.

Baggini argues convincingly that believers and nonbelievers need a basis of coexistence more than the simple need to get along. He says that a much firmer basis can be found by starting with "a recognition that we are all flawed human beings with prejudices formed from our social backgrounds and limitations created by our education, intellectual weaknesses and other cognitive blind spots," and therefore in the search for common ground in the religion debate, we should seek to foster the unfashionable virtues of sincerity in our attempts to seek the truth, charity toward those with whom we disagree, and modesty in acknowledging the limits of our understanding.[37] Clearly, Baggini has had his fill of the shrill New Atheists; he even admits that he's "often had more fruitful dialogues with some Catholics and evangelicals than with some fellow atheists," and that "the most important divide in the religion debate is not between believers or non-believers, but between those who show the virtues of reasonableness and those who do not."[38] In his "Heathen Manifesto," he proclaims that "religion is often our friend" and that "we believe in not being tone-deaf to religion and to understand it in the most charitable way possible."[39] Let that sink in for a moment. Have you ever heard a Christian say that he or she was prepared to listen to an atheist in the most charitable way possible? It seems like you could invite an atheist like Baggini to sit at the picnic table and have an actual conversation with him.

What I'd Like to Talk About at the Table

After taking a look at the New and New*er* Atheists, what are the central issues that we need to talk about with our atheist and agnostic friends at the table? Before I offer a few suggestions, I have a confession. If it's not already apparent, I quite like the Newer Atheists. On a range of issues I've found Gray, de Botton, and Baggini to be sensible and clear thinkers. I can recommend to any reader, religious or not, de Botton's *The Consolations of Philosophy*,[40] Gray's *Straw Dogs: Thoughts on Humans and Other Animals*,[41] and Baggini's *What's It All About? Philosophy and the Meaning*

---

37. Baggini, "Give Me a Reasonable Believer," para. 4.
38. Baggini, "Give Me a Reasonable Believer," para. 11.
39. Baggini, "Atheists, Please Read," para. 19.
40. de Botton, *Consolations of Philosophy*.
41. Gray, *Straw Dogs*.

of Life.[42] Gray has been featured on *BBC Radio 4*, and his contributions to the *Uncertain Minds* series (hosted at St Paul's Cathedral) in 2011 were the finest offered by any guest speaker. Baggini's *Philosophers' Magazine* and de Botton's *School of Life* video series (available on YouTube) have done more to put philosophy in the hands of non-philosophers than any other attempts in recent memory. All of our critics aren't as thoughtful and measured as these thinkers, and there's no way to predict how a genuine conversation is going to go, but I think the following three issues need our attention as we continue conversations with critics of similar good will.

A Messy Relationship Exists between Reason, Faith, and Doubt

Many atheists and agnostics talk as though *reason* and *what is reasonable* is as plain as day, and if the human race could just get its act together and follow reason, all would be well. Yet over the past century, any easy appeal to universal reason and what we think of as rational has been exposed and critiqued by a variety of thinkers on the philosophical spectrum. Alisdair MacIntyre, for example, has shown that what we think of rational enquiry is always embodied in particular traditions.[43] Max Horkheimer, given the horrors of the twentieth-century, offered a devastating exposé of how rationality works against itself and spirals into irrationality.[44] And Jean-Francois Lyotard, in one of the most well-known "post-modern" treatises, argues that what we in the West accept as knowledge is always legitimated by overarching "metanarratives" promising progress and liberation, metanarratives that people increasingly find hard to believe.[45] But if all you read were some of the contemporary atheists (of the New variety in particular) and their huffing and puffing against the irrationality of religious people, you might never realize that such criticisms of the nature of reason even existed. When anyone proceeds to tell me what is reasonable in terms that amount to little more than "as anyone can clearly see," I'm pretty sure some philosophical sleight of hand is going on. This is not an argument for irrationality, of course, only that atheists should be more wary of allowing the word "reason" to come rolling off their tongues too easily.

John Gray, at least, amongst the Newer Atheists recognizes that the doctrine of original sin contains "the vital truth—there are impulses of

42. Baggini, *What's It All About?*
43. McIntyre, *Whose Justice? Which Rationality?*
44. Horkheimer, *Eclipse of Reason.*
45. Lyotard, *Postmodern Condition.*

irrational destructiveness in every one of us"[46] that reason simply can't root out. As Pascal once said, the mystery farthest from our ken, that of original sin, is that very thing we require to possess knowledge of ourselves. Similarly, Alain de Botton says the doctrine of original sin rightly reveals that "the faults we despise in ourselves are inevitable features of the [human] species," so therefore we can admit to such faults and "attempt to rectify them in the light of day."[47] The Christian tradition, of course, has always insisted that we can't simply mount up and rectify such faults "in the light of day" (whatever that means); that's exactly why we need the Holy Spirit working through the means of grace given to the church. So when de Botton, for example, writes in glowing terms about the future nonreligious Agape Restaurant, he misses the point that we come to the Lord's Table not merely because we recognize our sin and disconnection from each other, but because we also realize we can't save ourselves from our failure to love. Nevertheless, Gray and de Botton have pointed out a chink in reason's armor (and in human nature) that, coupled with the criticisms mentioned earlier, more atheists need to take seriously.

We also should bring to the table our conviction that reason isn't opposed to faith and faith isn't opposed to doubt. The fact that we can have reasons for believing certain things to be true and still entertain some doubts about our judgment reveals that in our thinking process we've engaged in messy things like following hunches, drawing on past experiences, constructing mental patterns, or connecting the dots, and that we acknowledge some of these connections are tenuous and a matter of faith. John Henry Newman once remarked that "how a man reasons is as much a mystery as how he remembers."[48] Rather than proceeding methodically (the Western philosophical tradition in particular is enamored of method), Newman says the way we reason is more like a mountain climber, "who, by quick eye, prompt hand, and firm foot, ascends how he knows not himself, by personal endowments and practice, rather than by rule, leaving no track behind him, and unable to teach another."[49] We try to surmount a difficult question similar to the way a mountaineer ascends a literal crag. And such, Newman reckons, is the way all people generally reason: "not by rule, but by an inward faculty."[50] In other words, we make a string of fiduciary commitments and leaps in order to be able to present a coherent case for believing

46. Gray, "Child-Like Faith in Reason," para. 10.

47. de Botton, *Religion for Atheists*, 82.

48. Newman, *Fifteen Sermons Preached*, 259.

49. Newman, *Fifteen Sermons Preached*, 257.

50. Newman, *Fifteen Sermons Preached*, 257.

what we do, but of course those commitments could be (and frequently are) wildly misplaced. To talk as though we make, or can make, most of our decisions based on rationality alone until we arrive at certainty seems to me to be naïve and untrue to human experience.

The Irish Dominican priest and philosopher Herbert McCabe observes that people typically take up one of two opposite positions when it comes to believing a religious proposition. They might say that having faith in a proposition has nothing to do whatever with having reasons for it (the blind faith that atheists frequently charge us with) or that believing a proposition is exactly the same as having reasons for it. Against these extremes, McCabe argues for a middle way between holding that faith has nothing to do with reason and argument and that it's nothing but a matter of reasons and arguments.[51] (This position seems to me to be consistent with most of Christian tradition.) Religious beliefs are "mostly matters of fact plus interpretation."[52] So, rather than providing rock-hard evidence, arguments for belief might at least show that believers aren't crazy, eccentric, or unreasonable in holding their views.[53] For believers, our faith is more than just a matter of probability, but whatever certainty we testify to isn't incompatible with the experience of doubt that attends all fiduciary commitments, given our limits as human beings. "Our belief can, and indeed must, go with a certain kind of searching and questioning, a certain kind of doubt."[54]

Religious Language Presents Tricky Challenges

The New and even some of the Newer Atheists tend to attack the crudest renderings of theological language, as though believers possess childlike intellects and think that God literally sits on a throne or that the flames of hell refer to actual fire. But sophisticated thinkers in any theistic tradition could tell you that all language about God is ineluctably symbolic. Gray "gets it" when he criticizes Dawkins's literal-minded rant against Christian belief and the Genesis narratives. Dawkins and his ilk "overlook the vast traditions of figurative and allegorical interpretations with which believers have read Scripture."[55] Believers acknowledge the complexity of religious language as part and parcel of dealing with a reality that overflows the banks of our cognition and description, but our critics typically think this is taking

51. McCabe, *Faith Within Reason*, 4–5.
52. McCabe, *Faith Within Reason*, 2.
53. McCabe, *Faith Within Reason*, 9.
54. McCabe, *Faith Within Reason*, 40.
55. Gray, "Closed Mind of Richard Dawkins," para. 11.

refuge in obfuscation and woolly-headed thinking. In light of this, McCabe rightly says that the task for Christians is to explain how holding a doctrine is true is different from and related to other ways of holding a proposition to be true, and many Christians through the centuries have done precisely that. In my view, then, it's unfair for our atheist critics to criticize childlike renderings of the faith and then turn around and complain when believers offer more sophisticated renditions.

As an example of religious language that often throws our critics, consider the way we talk about "knowing" God. Obviously, this kind of knowing isn't the same kind of activity we have in mind when we say we know other people or things. Whatever their devotional value, old Pietist hymns that claim Jesus walks and talks with us leave a wrong impression if anyone thinks this knowing is a straightforward affair (over-the-top charismatic claims don't help the matter much). When Christians talk about knowing God, we're essentially talking about a process of discernment. John Barton suggests that knowing God is something akin to knowing a text intimately, in the sense that, as we follow a text along, we have to be willing to be surprised and keep our minds open as the otherness of the story is disclosed.[56] This kind of knowing requires self-involvement, and contains emotional as well as intellectual components, but this is true of human understanding and interpersonal knowledge in general. This might not satisfy a critic's claim that such "knowing" is not very scientific, but Barton quotes Austin Farrer in response: "To look for God by the methods we use for examining nature would not be scientific, it would be silly. A microscope is a scientific instrument, but it is not scientific to look for a note of music through a microscope."[57] T. F. Torrance reminds us that the nature of what is to be known, as well as the nature of the knower, determines *how* something can be known.[58] To put it another way, if you set out the conditions under which you want to know something, you'll be disappointed when it comes to God. Any religious tradition will tell you that you cannot know what we're talking about if *you* set the terms of the arrangement.

Belief in Supernatural Intervention and Miracles Presents a Problem for Many Believers as Well

Atheists both New and Newer generally set their crosshairs on religious belief in miracles at some point in the conversation. Only intellectual rubes

56. Barton, "New Atheism," 41.

57. Barton, "New Atheism," 42.

58. Torrance, *Theological Science*, 10.

devoid of understanding how the universe works could possibly believe in miracles. In response, some believers have expended no small amount of energy in explaining that objections to the supernatural or miraculous based on a closed, deterministic view of the universe (often attributed to Isaac Newton) and the "inviolable" laws of nature (David Hume) are faulty objections,[59] and that the contemporary scientific understanding of the quantum world with its random and probabilistic character breathes new life into the legitimacy of miracles.[60] Various theories of "non-interventionist" divine action purport to show how God could act in the realm of quantum probabilities in such a way that doesn't require us to claim that God "breaks" into the natural order and throws its regularities to the wind. So maybe what we think of as a miracle isn't all that miraculous at all (in the conventional sense of the term), even if it's surprising and spectacular.[61]

Even if these objections against a deterministic view of the universe hold fast and quantum mechanics does open up new apologetic possibilities, Christians should proceed with caution in this area.[62] It's one thing to claim that what we call a miracle is theoretically possible, but it's another matter to prove that such an event actually happened, and the chance of getting egg on your face is pretty high when you undertake such a venture. Clearly, no Christian can accept Baggini's proposition that contemporary self-critical religions shouldn't require belief in the supernatural,[63] but we need to be judicious in deciding where to engage the debate. The resurrection of Jesus, of course, remains the lynchpin of Christian belief, and gallons of ink have been spilled trying to defend the truth of the gospel report that the tomb was empty. While that's a worthy endeavor, we also should be prepared to discuss other closely-related questions that arise when we talk about the resurrection. For example, if (as the New Testament claims) God's

59. See, for example, Plantinga, "What is 'Intervention,'" and Louis, "Miracles and Science."

60. Cramer, "Miracles and David Hume."

61. For an account of non-interventionist divine action theories, see Wildman, "Divine Action Project." For a critique of these theories, see Plantinga, "What is 'Intervention.'"

62. The randomness of the quantum world can be variously interpreted (is it true randomness or simply apparent randomness caused by the limits of our understanding?). Steve Horst warns us that "not all interpretations of QM [quantum mechanics] are compatible with miracles, and at present one's choice of interpretation tends to reflect philosophical taste more than a choice between empirical alternatives" (Horst, "Miracles and Two Accounts," 333). On some of the problems associated with attempting to demonstrate the legitimacy of miracles on the basis of contemporary science, see Jaki, Miracles and Physics.

63. Baggini, "Articles of 21st-century Faith."

future has broken in on us now in Jesus' resurrection, is resurrection *the kind of event* that can be investigated and confirmed through conventional historical methods?[64] (After all, no one saw Jesus walk out of the tomb.) A closely-related question, given the way Paul talks about resurrection in 1 Corinthians 15, is *what kind of thing* is Jesus' resurrected body, seeing that the apostle rules out the idea of merely a resuscitated corpse (no zombie-Jesus), a disembodied spirit (no ghost-Jesus), and a "resurrected" memory of the Lord in the life of the disciples (no metaphorically-risen Jesus)? What exactly are we claiming?

Problems related to miracle reports in general exist on the level of popular perception as well. Miracle stories embarrass many Christians in the West, due in part to things like charlatan faith healers and bogus miracle reports. (To be honest, and perhaps to our discredit, how many of us pray for miracles?) The fact that many of our brothers and sisters in the global south take for granted that *of course* Christians believe in and expect "signs and wonders" complicates the discussion even more. Like it or not, the charismatic renewal movement of 600 million plus constitutes the most important force in Christianity today. That's a big target, and our critics see it. So without writing off much of the global Christian movement as naïve or superstitious, we need to exercise a deft touch in acknowledging that religious people often possess, as John Henry Newman once characterized the piety of the woman who reached out to touch Jesus' garment, "a faith tinged with superstition,"[65] while insisting that condition in itself constitutes no argument against the possibility of what we call a miracle.

Some Christians would say that if Jesus' resurrection is true, then *any* miracle is possible (which would open the floodgates), but I suspect this attitude, uncoupled from a critical eye in the best sense of the term, would only increase non-believers' perception of believers as credulous. Since many believers are already primed to accept the miraculous, they accept miracle reports as confirmation of the gospel and as a comforting testimony to God's continuing activity in the world. But try using these reports when your conversation partners are hostile to religion. Many of these folks remain unimpressed with what we call miracles (we live, after all, in an age of nano-technology, virtual reality, and interplanetary exploration) or simply find other, reductionist ways to explain such reports. In our context of religious pluralism, we also have to take up the challenge of responding to Hume's objection that the claims of miracles in competing religious traditions cancel

64. See Braaten, "Resurrection Debate Revisited," 147–58.
65. Newman, *Fifteen Sermons Preached*, 245.

each other out,[66] and still have to establish a context in which the meaning of an event can be correctly interpreted, which may be as difficult as proving beyond all doubt that something miraculous happened.

Wesley on the Edges of Unbelief

Wesley doesn't provide a great deal of help when it comes to our task of responding to modern atheism and agnosticism in matters pertaining to why someone should believe. He reckons that the actual number of atheists during his day was considerably smaller than what some atheists might have led one to believe—which is probably true for Wesley's time, before the ravages of modern secularism came full bloom. For that small number of actual atheists, Wesley exhibited little appreciation or sympathy. He likened a real atheist to a toad living inside a hollow tree trunk, insensitive to the light of the Holy Spirit and morally malformed.[67] Those who rejected the Christian revelation on account of "overvaluing" reason were sadly mistaken if they thought their reason could produce faith, hope, or love.[68]

Despite these nonstarters, in other places dealing with the topic of reason and the limitations of human knowledge Wesley exhibits some intellectual and moral virtues worth emulating when we talk with our unbelieving friends, virtues that resonate with what the Newer Atheists in particular prize. In a manner that separates Wesley from some other figures in the Pietist tradition, he has nothing but praise for the faculty of reason insofar as it assists us "through the whole circle of art and sciences," and is necessary for just governance and resolving many cases of conscience.[69] Wesley couples this, however, with a profound sense of humility regarding the extent of our knowledge in any area, including theology. This might surprise you, since many theologians give the impression that they know the deep secrets of the universe and God's preferences on everything from global affairs to the best sports teams.

You might get a whiff of this hubris in Wesley's sermon "On Faith," for example, in which he indulges in flights of metaphysical fancy when speculating on the life of disembodied spirits (e.g., how they can travel and recognize each other, whether they might run errands for God or Satan, etc.).[70] However, you do get the sense that Wesley knows he's romping around on

66. Hume, *Inquiry into Human Understanding*, 129–30.
67. Wesley, "On Living without God," §2–8 (*Works* 4:169–72).
68. Wesley, "Case of Reason Impartially Considered," §2.1–10 (*Works* 2:593–98).
69. Wesley, "Case of Reason Impartially Considered," §1.4,7–8, (*Works* 2:591–92).
70. Wesley, "On Faith," §8–13 (*Works* 4:193–98).

a metaphysical playground when in a couple of sober moments he admits that, in truth, we know very little of the invisible world.[71] This sober assessment of the limits of what we can know also can be heard in his sermon on "The Imperfection of Human Knowledge." We know what is necessary for human survival, and while our knowledge of the world is increasing, vast dimensions of the natural world and their secrets remain hidden from us.[72]

If we know comparatively little of the natural world, Wesley says, how much less do we know of the inner workings of the divine life and the ways of Providence in the world? You can't help but chuckle when Wesley quotes a celebrated theologian who defines divine eternity as "the at once entire and perfect possession of never-ending life" and then asks how much wiser we are for this definition. What does that definition even mean?! "We know just as much as we did before."[73] On this point at least, Wesley edges toward that modesty prized by Baggini, certainly to a greater extent than shown by other theologians. For so many questions we have about the divine ways (why God does this or that in history, why the apparent unfairness in God's dealings with the human race, etc), we simply have no answer. Wesley even admits that this state of affairs isn't an objection to Christianity only; he believes that it challenges natural religion as well. Why do some people "get it" and others don't?[74]

The way Wesley scrambles through this theological thicket, however, wouldn't satisfy our unbelieving friends and critics. He says that if our inability to reconcile the ways of Providence with apparent injustice were conclusive, "it would not drive us into Deism, but flat Atheism. It would conclude not only against the Christian revelation, but against the being of a God."[75] We can avoid the force of this objection to belief, Wesley says, only by "resolving all into the unsearchable wisdom of God, together with a deep conviction of our ignorance and in ability to fathom his counsels."[76] What? How is that a resolution at all? Wouldn't agnosticism, at the very least, be a more reasonable position?

But Wesley refuses that option. He instead proceeds to draw a few lessons about the life of faith, namely, that we must learn to trust the invisible God farther than we can see him, resign ourselves to his will, and adopt a

71. Wesley, "On Faith," §14 (*Works* 4:198).

72. Wesley, "Imperfection of Human Knowledge," §1.5–12 (*Works* 2:569, 572–77).

73. Wesley, "Imperfection of Human Knowledge," §1.3 (*Works* 2:570).

74. Wesley, "Imperfection of Human Knowledge," §3.2 (*Works* 2:583).

75. Wesley, "Imperfection of Human Knowledge," §3.2 (*Works* 2:583).

76. Wesley, "Imperfection of Human Knowledge," §3.2 (*Works* 2:583).

stance of humility toward what we claim to know about God.[77] At this point, religious experience comes into play. We'd be stumbling at every step in our lives were it not for "an anointing from the Holy One" that abides with us and helps us in our weakness.[78] Unbelievers find this strategy predictable and exasperating. When the questions get too difficult, believers take the jump into mystery or spirituality or "having a relationship with Jesus"; in other words, theological obfuscation.

At some juncture in a conversation with atheists, the jump to spiritual experience is both inevitable and necessary. The problem is that some Christians either take it too soon in the course of the conversation (in the attempt to cut off questions they'd rather not face), or refuse to take it when they should (in the attempt to prove the rationality of Christian belief). But if we know the resurrected Jesus through the power of the Holy Spirit, then clearly the faith can't be reduced to rational terms one could understand apart from the Holy Spirit. As Kilian McConnell puts it, you either know God through the Holy Spirit, or not at all.[79] At its heart, Christianity announces an encounter with the living God, which is supposed to change everything. This encounter evades wholly rational analysis, remains irreducible to proofs or a series of propositions, and *has to be* more than a philosophy of life you could compare to humanism, materialism, or any other isms. An outsider will doubt that disciples ancient and modern have met the risen Jesus, and may serve up all sorts of reasons why it isn't possible, but when all is said and done, Jesus' disciples know they've met him!

Now, even if you can't satisfy an unbeliever's standard of proof for such an encounter, you'd think that the effects of such an experience should be clear. Having one's sin forgiven, being inhabited by the Spirit of God, being transformed more and more each day to the image of Christ—surely if millions of people experienced this, it would make a tremendous impact on the world. So maybe even our critics would be forced to say, "Wow. I'm not persuaded by these Christians' arguments for God's existence or Jesus' resurrection, but given the changed lives I see, maybe there's something to it after all." Even if the gospel was a load of codswallop, merely believing that it was true should have significant impact, right?

Wesley himself pondered why Christianity has been so ineffective in the world. Why don't we see the results of the medicine given to us by the Great Physician? "Thou hast given us medicine to heal our sickness; yet our

---

77. Wesley, "Imperfection of Human Knowledge," §4.1–3 (*Works* 2:584–85).

78. Wesley, "Imperfection of Human Knowledge," §4.1 (*Works* 2:585).

79. McConnell, "Trinitarian Theology," 222.

sickness is not healed."[80] Wesley tries to do the math. He reckons that five-sixths of the world's population in his day was entirely ignorant of Christianity, so that accounts for a good chunk of its ineffectiveness. He also thinks that most Christians in places like Russia and the near East don't know true Christianity, and even doubts whether most so-called Christians throughout western Europe actually know the faith in a living and vibrant manner.[81] So he's whittling down the regions in the world in which you could reasonably expect to see the effectiveness of the gospel. But surely in Ireland and England, where "scriptural Christianity" is well known, you should see its effects unmistakably.[82] Well, hardly. But *surely* among the renewalist sect that goes by the name of *Methodist*! I mean, if any group of Christians should have its holiness act together, it'd be the Methodists. Right?

Nope. Wesley persists with his line of inquiry "Why is not the spiritual health of the Methodists recovered?"[83] The question displays, on Wesley's part, painful personal honesty and remarkable charity (another of Baggini's virtues) toward any critic of Christianity who might throw the charge of ineffectiveness in our faces, taking to heart those criticisms that could be directed in particular against the very movement he initiated. Talk about a bracing question! Wesley doesn't give a theologically complex response; in fact, his answer is almost a let-down because it's so practical and mundane, but the practical character of his response resonates precisely with this-worldly concerns held by many contemporary nones who are suspicious of organized religion.

Wesley says the early Methodists were great at following part of his advice in his sermon on "The Mammon of Unrighteousness," specifically his admonitions to "gain all you can" and "save all you can." But scarcely any could be found who heeded his third admonition to "give all you can." "And yet nothing can be more plain, than that all who observe the first two rules without the third, will be twofold more the children of hell than ever they were before."[84] (The Methodist Children of Hell? It sounds like a Wesleyan theology death-metal band.) Wesley accuses these two-thirds Methodists of not caring for even indigent Christians, let alone poor folks in the wider circles of society. Why has Christianity done so little good? Because those of us who should know better have refused to take seriously the Lord's command

---

80. Wesley, "Causes of the Inefficacy of Christianity," §2 (*Works* 4:87).
81. Wesley, "Causes of the Inefficacy of Christianity," §3–6 (*Works* 4:87–89).
82. Wesley, "Causes of the Inefficacy of Christianity," §7 (*Works* 4:90).
83. Wesley, "Causes of the Inefficacy of Christianity," §8 (*Works* 4:90).
84. Wesley, "Causes of the Inefficacy of Christianity," §8 (*Works* 4:91).

to deny ourselves, take up our cross daily, and follow him.[85] We don't take up this self-denial for its ascetic value, but specifically so we can share out of our abundance what others need to live. Wesley hears the objections: "But is it possible to supply all the poor in our society with the necessaries of life?"[86] To be blunt, given the wealth Christians have amassed for themselves: *yes* (an answer that would give many Christians fits today).

The early Methodists had gotten themselves into a dilemma. They'd grown rich on account of their diligence and frugality (which Christianity engenders), but along with wealth comes "pride, love of the world, and every temper that is destructive of Christianity." Hence it seems, oddly enough, that "true scriptural Christianity, has a tendency, in process of time, to undermine and destroy itself."[87] Is there no way to prevent this? Wesley's prescription splashes the ice water of practical Christian living on the face of a self-deceptive holiness. "If you have any desire to escape the damnation of hell, *give all you can*; otherwise I can have no more hope of your salvation than that of Judas Iscariot."[88] (What about that don't you understand?) Perhaps we don't think of Baggini's virtue of sincerity expressed in frank terms such as these, but Wesley's straight talk here exemplifies his advice to avoid flattering your hearers and always speak from the heart[89]—not always easy to do when you're talking with people who should know better, whether in the eighteenth or the twenty-first century.

Around the Table with Atheists and Agnostics

In sum, what should we keep in mind when talking to our atheist and agnostic friends and critics? First, if these folks say they don't want to talk about religion, then we shouldn't force the issue—and let's not find sneaky ways to bring up the topic. (Talking about politics, by the way, is perhaps the worst way to bring up the issue of religion with people.) We're not as clever as we think, and agnostics and atheists wary of Christians trying to "witness" to them can smell a ruse at a great distance. Many people in this camp have been burned by the church, and if we try to push religion on them, we'll turn potential friends into enemies. We'll never have to bring up the subject of faith if we live out lives of gracious conviction and hospitality;

85. Wesley, "Causes of the Inefficacy of Christianity," §13 (*Works* 4:93).
86. Wesley, "Causes of the Inefficacy of Christianity," §10 (*Works* 4:92).
87. Wesley, "Causes of the Inefficacy of Christianity," §17 (*Works* 4:95).
88. Wesley, "Causes of the Inefficacy of Christianity," §18 (*Works* 4:96). Emphasis mine.
89. Wesley, "On Pleasing All Men," §2.7 (*Works* 3:425).

they'll ask *us* questions. I suspect that if we caught the wave of the kingdom Jesus set in motion, most atheists and agnostics wouldn't care what else we believed about God, as long as we didn't try to hound them. We're never going to convince anyone that we're salt and light *by arguing* that we're salt and light.

In connection with this emphasis on practical living, only the rabidly religious believe that agnostics and atheists lead meaningless lives or lack any moral resources for compassion and honesty, and it's counter-productive to try and convince our atheist and agnostic friends that they're miserable or bereft of basic morality. For every book coming out with accusing titles like John Bevere's *Good or God? Why Good without God Isn't Enough*, you can find thoughtful atheist treatments on morality and ethics like Greg Epstein's *Good Without God: What a Billion Non-Religious People Do Believe*. Having said that, while self-critical atheists like Baggini maintain the humanist party line that right and wrong don't require religious teaching, he also recognizes that it's no easy task for an atheist to ground morality, and acknowledges that the possibility of atheist morality must be distinguished from its inevitable actuality![90] While morality is just as murky for us religious types (grounding ethics in theology isn't a walk in the park), Baggini admits that at least believers have some metaphysical bedrock (albeit delusional) that gives us reason to believe that morality is real, whilst in an atheist universe, morality can be shucked off at any point, and, without a foundation for it, that's what happens sometimes (but, in fairness, this is probably not any different than when Christians decide to chuck their morality when it becomes inconvenient).[91]

Second, as painful as it might seem, we should maintain relentless honesty about our questions and doubts. Our conversation partners will respect us if we respect them enough to admit that a lot of popular apologetics is nonsense and that sometimes the Bible makes even our eyes cross. The last part of that sentence may raise some eyebrows, but while we believe the Bible is an inspired book, it's also ancient religious literature composed over many centuries, and (as is true in interpreting all ancient literature) no straight lines run from the past to the present. Christians don't view the Bible as Muslims view the Qur'an, and I often tell my students that if they can't tell me the difference, then they don't understand what Christians historically have meant by "inspiration." This doctrine remains one of the most misunderstood and abused doctrines in Christianity, but whatever else it means, it doesn't mean that the Bible is a book of magical incantations

90. Baggini, "Yes, Life Without God."
91. Baggini, "Yes, Life Without God."

whose verses easily answer every question we have or guarantee peace and prosperity.

We'd be better off, I think, viewing the Bible closer to the way some early Talmudic scholars viewed the Scriptures: respect coupled with intense study (and not mere lip service about the Bible's authority), but with a sense that each generation needs flexibility in its interpretation as it grapples with this ancient text, and a willingness to follow its trajectory beyond a wooden reading. For example, in the Jerusalem Talmud, Moses asks the Lord to teach him the law so there will be no doubts about it. The Lord's response is surprising. God says that were he to reveal the law in its finality, there'd be no possibility for a range of argument over it. Each generation must grapple with what the law means and come to a majority determination.[92] In the Babylonian Talmud, R. Joseph reports that R. Yohanan claimed that Jerusalem was destroyed only because judgments were pronounced there in accordance with the laws of the Torah. Come again? Isn't that what faithful interpretation is all about? R. Joseph comments that R. Yohanan's point is that, while the people based their decisions strictly upon the Biblical law, they did not go beyond its requirements.[93] I suspect that, if we don't find a way to go beyond the letter of the text to the life-giving Spirit animating the text, we'll have a hard time convincing anyone that the Christian life is one worth pursuing.

Third, we Christians in North America aren't helping ourselves by publicly whining about how we're sinned against by hordes of godless atheists and the liberal media. This complaining makes us sound weak and paranoid. Even given the rise of the nones, the US population continues to be massively churched, and to claim that we're a persecuted minority is to persist in a "poor-me" delusion. (I'm making no claims about Christian minorities in other nations.) Especially since the Supreme Court's green light to same-sex marriage, many Christians have acted like their religious freedom is being trampled because they have to respect the civil rights of people with whom they disagree. This isn't helping our case—none of our non-Christian friends believe we're being oppressed, and I can't imagine anyone wanting to get to know us if we persist in lashing out against enemies, either real and imaginary.

Of course Christians will experience opposition in this world, but as Luther once remarked, how we respond to opposition is the real test of our Christianity and the "Lydian touchstone" of genuine love.[94] By nature, Luther

92. *Talmud*, 11.
93. *Talmud*, 181.
94. Luther, "Lectures on Galatians—1519" (*LW* 27:353).

says, we love praise, can do good works, and speak well of others as long we've not been offended. But, apart from God's grace, when we're offended or opposed, then our true colors come out; our "love" falls away and we resort to hatred, shouting, and malice. This simple test, Luther says, will reveal how far along we are in our Christianity.[95] If you know a little about Luther, you'll know that by his own standards he would have hardly passed the test when it came to responding to his opponents—but that's not to say that the test is illegitimate. Wesley similarly stresses the necessity of undeviating love in his exhortation to "let *love* not visit you as a transient guest, but be the constant ruling temper of your soul. See that your heart be filled at all times and on all occasion with real, undissembled benevolence, not to those only that love *you*, but to every soul of man."[96] If an atheist can imagine an Agape Restaurant, how much more should we be ready to sit at the table with our atheist and agnostic critics and find out if our claim to love passes the test?

95. Luther, "Lectures on Galatians—1519" (*LW* 27:354).
96. Wesley, "On Pleasing All Men," §2.1 (*Works* 3:422). Emphasis original.

Conclusion

Can We Listen?

Can We Listen to Each Other?

Uncle Bub didn't have kids of his own, but he never lost the opportunity to lecture us nephews and nieces at family reunions. He'd sit across the picnic table from us kids, cross his farmer's sun-tanned arms, announce yet again how "If I had children, I'd teach them to fear the Lord!" and then launch into one of his standard sermons on why the world was "going to hell in a handbasket" and what we young folk needed to know if we were going to make it in this life. Not that Uncle Bub had any actual connection to the church, of course. That ended somewhere in his childhood. His was a cultural Christianity, in which you could talk about "the Lord" and America as a "Christian nation" without any mention of the church. And yet, if you had pointed this out to him, then *why of course* he was a Christian. What else would any hard-working, self-respecting citizen be?

Looking back, it's clear that no conversation was happening during these encounters. Uncle Bub was well-intentioned, but he acted out of a mix of self-appointed authority and fear. The world he knew was slipping away, and the only thing he knew to do was deliver a good talking-to for a captive audience, which he knew wouldn't talk back to him. He talked, we listened (or at least that's the way it was supposed to work). He didn't trust what was happening to the country, nor did he trust the younger generation to know how to respond to the changes. As far as we kids were concerned, we didn't trust that he understood us very well (or even wanted to understand us), and we had no intention of taking to heart anything he had to say. So instead of listening, his words rolled off us like water off a duck's back. On one occasion, when he repeated that he would have taught his own children to fear the Lord, I remember thinking, "You mean you'd have taught them to *fear you.*"

There are a couple of things I've learned from experiences like this. In the church, we often adopt the Uncle Bub strategy of dealing with people who disagree with us. If only I could sit down with them at the table and give them a good talking-to, I could sort out their problems, help them see the error of their ways, and bring them back into line. We may say that's not what we're doing, and protest that we really are listening (how many people would admit they're not a good listener?), but sitting quietly for a few minutes while we allow the other person to speak is no guarantee that we're listening. Often it's merely an interlude for catching our breath and preparing to launch another assault, while their words bounce off us with little or no effect. As any parent or teacher can tell you, you shouldn't mistake a young person sitting there silently in front of you with someone who is listening.

Talking *with* someone is far different, because genuinely listening is a humbling exercise in which we admit we don't have all the answers figured out ahead of time. It involves the difficult and patient work of developing empathy, in which we try to slip out of our skin and imagine what the world looks and feels like to someone else. Sometimes when a student comes to my office, plops himself in a chair and shares a lengthy disaster story about his romantic life or starts to rant about the unfairness of the academic world, I have to restrain myself and not speak too soon, even if after a few minutes I have a pretty good idea of where the story is going and how I'll probably respond.

The other thing I've taken from Uncle Bub encounters is that there's a close relationship between being willing to listen and having trust in your conversation partner. Now the questions come thick and fast: On what basis and to what extent should I trust you? Do I trust you enough to believe that you want to have an actual conversation, and that you'll take what I have to say as seriously as you want me to take what you have to say? Do I trust you enough to believe that you won't slaughter me on social media if our conversation goes off the rails? Trust remains the most difficult and gossamer-like bond to build between people, and the most easily lost. Simply put: no trust, no listening.

In each one of the areas I've written about, there's a listening deficit on account of a trust deficit. Let's be honest. After centuries of infighting, and despite the modern ecumenical movement, how much do Christians from different traditions trust each other (fundamentalists and charismatics? Calvinists and Arminians?)? To say nothing of the lack of trust between the religions, between Christians, Jews, and Muslims, or between Hindus and Muslims. Not that there aren't positive examples you could point out in official dialogues or conferences, but what are the actual attitudes held by the rank and file in any tradition toward religious Others?

Then consider the lack of trust between the religious and nonreligious. Atheists and agnostics harbor their own unique doubts about us religious types, asking questions such as these: "Can we trust that you'll be honest about your own doubts, instead of giving us plastic answers? You talk a lot about how we're all sinners. Can we trust the church to be transparent in its dealings and confess its own sin? Given your message about heaven and the sweet bye-and-bye, which you string like a carrot on a stick in front of believers, can we trust that you're interested in real world issues? Given the church's record on the history of faith versus science, can we trust that you're interested in serious intellectual and scientific issues and that you won't shut us down when we have legitimate questions? How can we sit at the table and listen to you if we don't trust you?"

Of course the preeminent example of what lack of trust looks like in the church is the current debate over homosexuality. If Phyllis Tickle is right, the fight over the interpretive issues involved in this debate will have consequences as momentous as the Protestant Reformation.[1] With rare exceptions, the Right and the Left don't trust each other enough to listen to what the other side has to say. The Right can't hear anything but the "homosexual agenda"—all biblical scholarship and theological reflection supporting homosexuality is in principle suspect. Such work can't be carried out in good faith, so it doesn't need to be considered seriously. The Left can't hear anything but condemnation or the cold counsel to either celibacy or counselling. Anyone on the Right who says they're trying to stay faithful to Scripture or tradition is either hermeneutically stuck in the Dark Ages or using their "faithfulness" as an excuse to hate or exclude.

Most people realize by now that neither side is going to come up with an interpretation or argument that hasn't already been put forward and refuted by the other side. The theological chessboard allows only so many moves you can make. We already know what the other side is going to say, we know what our riposte will be, and so we don't trust that conversation can take place. So what can we expect? A string of more pointless books that reinforce what *your* side or *my* side believes? More churches and religious bodies discharging their religious obligation to stand for the truth by issuing official "statements" that function as little more than rhetorical trench warfare?

The issue of homosexuality is *the* issue dividing the church in the West presently, and when you add a host of other culture war questions,

1. See Tickle, *Great Emergence*, 98–101.

the picture looks hopeless indeed. So the big question I've been mulling over lately is this: What's the endgame for the church? Where does it all lead? In the political arena, it is when our side wins. But what about in the church? Can we be satisfied with denominations voting on motions that solve nothing and produce nothing except more divisions, with religious leaders saying exactly what their followers want to hear and continuing to make things worse? Without trust, there's no way forward.

Show Us Your Scars

Perhaps the most important lesson that my students have taught me through the years as I've discussed theology with them is this: If you want us to trust you and listen, show us your scars. This vulnerability doesn't come easy for clergy or religious professionals; we're supposed to be paragons of expertise and spirituality, and many of us have had role models who exuded arrogance and an aura of infallibility. Too often, we've pretended that, since we believe in "absolute truth," we're the guardians and dispensers of that truth. Too often, we act as though we know what Jesus would say in any situation and take it upon ourselves to act as his spokesperson.

If you want us to trust you and listen, show us your scars. I believe my students aren't the only ones saying this. Of course, being vulnerable is a cliché in Christian circles today. Lots of people talk about it, far fewer try it. What would it cost us to reveal at the tables that we are a *scarred body*, with wounds old and new, sins and failures, shortcomings and addictions, all of this and more in the one, holy, catholic, apostolic church? Would people get up from the table and leave in disgust, or would they then trust us enough to want to talk?

One thing seems clear. We're never going to build that trust online, precisely the place where we spend more and more of our time. In her book *Reclaiming Conversation*, Sherry Turkle points out that our ability to develop a sense of empathy with others shrinks the more we forsake flesh-and-blood conversation for online social media.[2] I've observed that, while using social media might support or even improve good relationships, such use rarely makes bad relationships better, and far too often makes them worse. (How often have you witnessed ordinarily civil people turn brutal the longer a disagreement on Facebook goes on?) Attempting to use social media to carry nuances of complex issues is, frankly, laughable. Whatever else social media might be good for (cat videos?), it doesn't help us talk graciously about volatile issues like sexuality, immigration, gun control, or health care.

2. Turkle, *Reclaiming Conversation*, 168–73.

Most online conversations about these issues result in a trust hemorrhage. As a theologian, it's always seemed to me that we land ourselves into a performative contradiction by blathering on about the importance of incarnation and embodiment, but then resorting to shouting and grandstanding via disembodied social media when we try to work through the most difficult issues confronting us. Face-to-face conversation? No thanks. We'd rather tweet—nay, *bark*—at each other on Twitter. Without actual conversation, we might as well be making animal noises: snarling, growling, and barking.

As I've tried to make the point throughout this book, if ever we're going to make headway in these conversations, it's going to happen through real encounters with those other people at the table, listening to each other's stories, telling each other why we hold certain things dear (and, frankly, what we fear about the other side), and coming to see each other as more than a bundle of opinions on issues. All of this takes time and commitment, and there are no shortcuts. Apart from patiently and painfully coming to the point where we have a modicum of trust restored in our conversation partners, what we're presently arguing about will never be resolved except by voting—which will only make things worse.

The prospect of endless rounds of denunciations and recriminations reminds me of Alan Kirby's description of one of the characteristics of the digimodern age: *onwardness*.[3] Unlike the textual properties of a conventional book, where you read the last chapter and where perhaps a writer unwisely tries to pronounce the last word on a topic, in the digimodern age the whole idea that you can bring an important conversation to a conclusion seems a bit silly. (For example, think about the comment section following an online article, which may go on for weeks or even months and take multiple paths sideways.) Recognizing the *onward* character of the conversations we're presently having in the church, I'm not foolish enough to believe in the digimodern age that I can pronounce anything close to the last word on the issues we're debating. But perhaps we can listen to the gospel and trust the Holy Spirit to not end the conversation, but move it forward in fruitful ways.

Can We Listen to the Gospel?

I said in the introductory chapter that the Bible doesn't give us detailed instructions or helpful examples for negotiating disagreements. That was true enough to grab your attention, but also somewhat misleading, because the Scripture writers themselves write out of an awareness of the conflict that

3. Kirby, *Digimodernism*, 52.

Jesus and his message generates. So, I want to wrap up this book by examining two passages in the Gospels that speak to such conflict. Jesus' actions and words in both passages are suggestive and oblique rather than straightforward; they invite us to deliberate on the arc of the gospel story instead of giving us proof texts. Luke 9:51–56 recalls the disciples encountering opposition from the Samaritans, and Jesus' rebuke to his disciples (James and John) who want to call down fire from heaven, and Matthew 10:34–38 contains Jesus' warning to his disciples that he hasn't come to bring peace but a sword, and that even family members will be set in opposition to each other on account of him.

Jesus Rebukes the Bros

> When the days drew near for him to be taken up, he set his face to go to Jerusalem. And he sent messengers ahead of him. On their way they entered a village of the Samaritans to make ready for him; but they did not receive him, because his face was set toward Jerusalem. When his disciples James and John saw it, they said, "Lord, do you want us to command fire to come down from heaven and consume them?" But he turned and rebuked them. Then they went on to another village. (Luke 9:51–56)

First, a bit of background: At this point in Luke's story, Jesus is traveling from Galilee to Judea on his way to Jerusalem, but he has to pass through Samaria. Jews tried to avoid Samaria if they could, and would sometimes travel on the east side of the Jordan, but if you couldn't, you shifted your donkey into high gear and powered through Samaria as quickly as possible. You did this because of the thorny relations between Jews and Samaritans, which were far worse than what the average Christian might glean from the story in John's Gospel about the woman at the well, who mentioned to Jesus a long-standing antagonism: "Our ancestors worshiped on this mountain, but you say that the place where people must worship is in Jerusalem" (John 4:20). Where to worship? That doesn't sound like a deal-breaking dispute: sort of like hymns versus choruses or immersion versus sprinkling. (Thank God we don't split churches over minor issues, right?)

This dispute over the right place to worship was just the tip of the iceberg. To someone who studies different religious traditions, the Jew/Samaritan relationship is interesting because it's about orthodoxy and a heretical other rubbing up against each other. Of course Jews knew that pagan Roman religion had nothing to do with the story of Israel's God. But it was different with the Samaritans and their religion. They descended from the people who had lived in the northern kingdom of Israel, some of whom remained there after it fell to the invading Assyrians and the leading citizens were deported. Some of these remaining folks married into the pagan people the Assyrians brought in to recolonize the land. Second Kings says that this all led to the rise of religious syncretism.

By Jesus' time, the Samaritans were strict monotheists, but the Jews never let the Samaritans forget their dodgy ancestry. Theologically, Samaritans believed that only the first five books of the Bible were authoritative and insisted that Mount Gerizim, not Mount Zion in Jerusalem, was the correct place to worship; in fact the Samaritans built a temple there in the fourth century BC. But here's the thing about that temple: when the Seleucids were harassing Judea in the second century BC, the Samaritans wimped out and sent a letter to the Seleucid king disavowing any relationship to the Jews or their God. They even asked that their temple be renamed the temple of *Zeus Hellenios*, so *they* escaped persecution while many faithful Jews lost their lives. When the Jews won a brief time of independence for Judea, it was all about payback. They destroyed the Samaritan temple.

So there's bad blood between Jews and Samaritans, both claiming to be the true worshipers of God, that went back for centuries. According to Jewish tradition, three hundred priests and three hundred rabbis once gathered in Jerusalem for a big curse-fest to dump all the curses in the Mosaic law upon the Samaritans. You might remember when the Jewish leaders wanted to curse Jesus (John 8), they called him demon-possessed *and* a Samaritan in one breath. You had to make him the vilest false messiah ever. It wasn't enough to call him demon-possessed; they had to call him *a Samaritan* on top of that.

So you have two groups of people who share a common religious heritage, but one of them has a dodgy history that makes them a problematic other. You're feuding cousins who don't trust each other, and you try as much as possible to avoid each other; because we all know that arguments with relatives are the worst. It's not surprising, then, that the Samaritans don't want to receive Jesus. What you might find surprising is the reaction of James and John. With my off-kilter imagination, I picture a couple of cocky frat boys, baseball hats turned around, chests puffed out, inflated egos mortally offended. "Why won't you receive us, huh? You wanna start something?" Having reached the red line, they—bizarrely—ask Jesus if he wants them to call fire down from heaven and destroy them. "We can do that for you, Jesus. No problem. 'Cause, you know, they're really asking for it!"

Where'd they get this idea from? When Jesus commissions the disciples, they're to preach the gospel, heal the sick, and cast out evil spirits;

their commissioning includes no flamethrower provision. Most likely, James and John were thinking of the story in 2 Kings 1:1–16, when Elijah calls fire down from heaven to consume the arrogant military commanders who came to bundle him up and take him back to the king of Samaria. Apparently the disciples are hanging on to an event that happened over eight hundred years prior, and still hoping they can get in on some heavenly action. (Hope springs eternal, I guess.)

James and John act like what I'm calling "bros," a term that shouldn't need clarification in contemporary parlance, but if you haven't discovered the next big thing called the internet, I'm using the term here to refer to young men who are impetuous and way too overconfident, and who try to handle any challenges with bravado and chest-thumping. Jesus calls James and John "sons of thunder" in Mark's Gospel; I reckon that's sarcastic Jesus speaking. Their behavior in this passage isn't an isolated instance of broish behavior. In the immediately previous passage (Luke 9:49–50), John effectively says this to Jesus: "We saw this dude casting out demons in your name, and we told him to *step off* because he doesn't hang with us." Imagine *that* conversation. (Talk about awkward! "Hey buddy, *relax*. Because it's better for that person to be demon-possessed than, you know, be freed in the wrong way.") Jesus must have facepalmed before reminding John that whoever isn't against us is for us! In view of thousands of denominations, it's worth remembering that people aren't our enemies just because they don't have the secret password to our respective ecclesiastical tree forts. Sometimes we have so much troubling distinguishing our friends from our enemies.

If Jesus had given the go-ahead to summon fire from heaven, James and John would have probably taken a selfie with Samaria in flames behind them. (Can you imagine how they would have responded to the suggestion of sitting at the table with Samaritans?) But how did Jesus respond? Luke doesn't give us a verbal response from Jesus; he says that the only thing Jesus did was turn and rebuke the disciples, and then they moved on to another village. What might Jesus have said? In some older versions of the Bible, you read in verse 56, "For the Son of man is not come to destroy men's lives, but to save them " (KJV), but this isn't found in any of the best early manuscripts. Apparently a bare rebuke from Jesus was too much for someone to simply leave in the story, so at some point in the history of the church someone thought they had to insert a comforting Sunday School lesson to lessen the severity of the passage. But earlier in this same chapter, when Jesus hears that his disciples couldn't cast out a demon, we read, "Jesus answered, 'You faithless and perverse generation, how much longer must I be with you and bear with you?'" (Luke 9:41a). I wonder if the rebuke here was along similar lines: "How long have I been teaching you and you *still* don't get it? You of all people should know better by now!"

No, Jesus doesn't want them to command fire to come down from heaven. He rebukes them and moves on to another village. He's focused on his mission, as if to say: "James, John, listen: Instead of spending our energies on invective against people who won't receive us, we need to stay the course. We need to stay focused on proclaiming the God's kingdom and making it happen in real life with people. It's so easy to get sidetracked, bros, but you need to follow me to Jerusalem. You need to follow the way of the cross."

In order to make the offense of this passage sink in for us, what if we performed a little thought experiment and substituted a group of people we find offensive or heretical for the Samaritans in this passage, people who we would never consider inviting to sit at the table with us, and upon whom we would maybe like to see heavenly retribution poured? The passage itself, of course, doesn't stipulate what kind of people that must be, but I do know that if we're content to let this passage speak to us only about Samaritans in the ancient world, then we've disarmed the story and consigned it to a museum. Because I don't think anyone reading this today has a grudge against actual Samaritans. (And if you do? Wow. You need a life.)

I'm not suggesting that beliefs don't matter. Jesus didn't condone Samaritan theology or practice. Nowhere does he say "Samaritan theology, Jewish theology, it's all good!" But Samaritans do keep popping up when Jesus wants to make a point about God's kingdom. In the parable of the Good Samaritan in the next chapter (Luke 10), Jesus doesn't say, "How much better the Samaritan's actions would have been if he had better theology." Jesus' point is, "He's closer to the kingdom than you are!" In the story of healing the ten lepers in Luke 17, Jesus doesn't say, "You there. The leper. No, not you. The Samaritan leper. Let me drop some correct theology on you before I drop some healing on you." The point of the story is this: "How is it that *this* man, whom you despise and don't trust, knows what gratitude is, when members of the true faith don't?"

What group could we substitute for the Samaritans if we're going to retain the offense of these passages and allow them to speak to us today? We may not call down fire from heaven onto those who oppose us, but sometimes we'd sure like to. We certainly resort to calling down Facebook fire! Let loose with religious howling and snarling! Rather than daring to sit at the table with those who disagree with us, let's make them out to be as vile as we possibly can—even call them demon-possessed, and send them a tweetstorm of judgment and brimstone! Sometimes I think we imagine Jesus as a kind of evangelical Thor, a god who'll throw down thunder and lightning on our opponents, thereby transforming Christianity into a pagan Jesus religion. (The god of thunder *would* be the perfect patron deity for bros and the sons of thunder, no?) Are we known more for our raging against all *those* people, rather than following Jesus to the next village and on to Jerusalem, and staying focused on our mission? Can we listen to the rebuke of Jesus?

The Word of Jesus and the Cross of Jesus

> Do not think that I have come to bring peace to the earth; I have not come to bring peace, but a sword. For I have come to set a man against his father, and a daughter against her mother, and a daughter-in-law against her mother-in-law; and one's foes will be members of one's own household. Whoever loves father or mother more than me is not worthy of me; and whoever loves son or daughter more than me is not worthy of me; and whoever does not take up the cross and follow me is not worthy of me. (Matt 10:34–38)

Jesus knew that his message of "Repent! For God's kingdom is coming to you!" would stir up sharp disagreements. One of the great ironies in Matthew's Gospel is that, while in chapter 5 Jesus pronounces peacemakers "blessed," when he gives instructions to his disciples about their mission in chapter 10, he says in so many words, "Oh, by the way, don't think that *I've* come to bring peace. I haven't come to bring peace, but the sword." (Good job, Jesus. Thanks for your help.)

Jesus isn't being a jerk here. What he means is that controversy will arise around him as a predictable consequence of his message, so that even close family members will be at odds over who he is and how we should respond to what he says. Who is this man? A rabbi? A prophet? A blasphemer? Or is he the very hope of Israel, God's own Anointed? The gospel, in short, recounts the dispute over this man's identity and God's ultimate vindication of him.[4] But if Jesus *is* who he says he is, then the capacious and radical love to which he calls his disciples must break our conventional boundaries, so that all other loves (even of parents and children) need to be reordered. Following this Jesus means being caught up in a love that calls us beyond ourselves and beyond the familiar. It extends beyond family, beyond ethnicity, beyond political affiliation, beyond national boundaries, beyond our natural inclination to bark like dogs at strangers coming into

---

4. See Jenson, *Systematic Theology*, 189.

our backyard, and instead calls us to welcome at the table those who are unlike us, even those whom we think are eminently unlovable.

The context of this passage in Matthew refers to the controversy Jesus knew would be stirred up amongst people who heard the message for the first time. Who is this man? Could Jesus have foreseen the day, however, in which the "sword" he brought would pit son against father and daughter against mother in his own church? Maybe you think I'm stretching the reading, but ask yourself: Hasn't this in fact happened in the church? Aren't Jesus' own brothers and sisters, parents and children, currently flipping over the table and accusing each other? "You don't know who this man *really* is! If you did, you wouldn't believe X. You don't preach Christ like we do. Your church doesn't know what he wants, like my church knows. *My Bible* says such-and-such."

The sword metaphor in this passage should trouble us, since the only other place where Jesus mentions a sword in Matthew's gospel is in his warning for us that those who take up the sword will perish by the sword (26:52). We might not literally take up the sword in the church (at least not yet), but it's clear that we've waged the culture wars in the body of Christ to the point where it seems like two Christianities have emerged. If you're firmly ensconced in one side, there's a good chance that if you attend a worship service on the other side, you'll leave wondering if you belong to the same faith. Am I exaggerating? You might insist that we both believe in and worship the same Lord, but scarcely a week passes in which some high-profile church leader accuses the other side of not really being Christian. If you try to occupy a middle ground, you most likely will be accused of compromising the truth and betraying the side to which you're supposed to belong. Given the sword we've taken up, will God allow the credibility of the church in this country to perish?

The warning is frightening in its clarity: whoever doesn't take up the cross and follow Jesus isn't worthy of him. If you were among Jesus' first followers and believed he was who he said he was, taking up the cross and following him might very well end in your death. But you couldn't call yourself one of his disciples and *refuse* the cross. So much has been written about "taking up the cross." What can this even mean today? It's not merely soldiering on under adverse conditions in life. Supporting a horrible football team might be a painful way to spend your Sunday afternoon, but it's not taking up your cross. Serious matters like enduring an illness or putting up with a wretched job isn't taking up your cross. It clearly isn't a matter of shouting your theological opinions at people out of a misguided sense of religious obligation— nobody ever convinced anyone of anything by turning up the volume and wearing them out. Taking up the cross *may* include experiencing active persecution (as many of our sisters and brothers around the world have experienced), but if that's all it means, then most of us who come from safe places like Buffalo or Toronto or Omaha will never know what it means.

In essence, taking up the cross means shouldering the burden of patiently and painfully learning to love people who are unlike us, even those we consider to be our enemies, no matter the cost to us—because this is the pattern of how God saves us. The apostle Paul says that God demonstrates his love for us in that while we were still God's enemies, barking and snarling at him, Christ died for us (Rom 5:8). In this passage, we hear Jesus say that whoever doesn't take on this pattern of living, of loving in the face of bared teeth, isn't worthy of him, which means we shouldn't call ourselves by his name. Jesus even said that if you love only those who love you, *big deal.* Don't even people who *don't* call themselves by Jesus' name do the same (cf. Matt 5:46–48)?

To put it another way, there's no taking up the cross of Christ without taking up the love of Christ. Over and over again, I've heard "good Christian people" object to this: "You simply don't want to alienate anyone—but the gospel *is* offensive, and when you speak the truth you'll always end up offending someone." But this objection entirely misses the location of the offense. The offense of the gospel lies in the fact that the Christ of God has taken the way of the cross, suffered the consequences of our sinfulness all the way to death, and in doing so has kicked over our conventional view of deity and exposed the way we justify our own desire for power and glory based on that idol. The "offense" of the gospel *isn't* an abstract trump card we can throw on the table in the midst of tough conversations in order to excuse our hatred in the name of Jesus, under the pretense of proclaiming the truth. Of all people, we should know the dangers of attempting to justify ourselves; if anything, taking up the cross calls us to constantly repent of that sin. Can we listen to Jesus' call to take up the cross?

In terms of the metaphor I've been pushing throughout this book—the table at which we are sitting is *cruciform.*

Staying at the Table and Figuring It Out

There are no easy answers here. Throughout this book I have not been delineating a technique, but recommending an ethic grounded in the gospel's call for us to love even our enemies, and raising questions that will help us become more thoughtful conversation partners as we try to figure things out. Figuring out how to love in the face of opposition isn't a sufficient condition for answering difficult questions or making decisions; neither is it a luxury. But it is necessary, and it is the only Christian way to proceed if we're to avoid a major break in the Western church. If we don't want to take this route, we can keep calling ourselves Wesleyans or Baptists or nondenominationals, and reserve spaces at the table with those who look and tweet and bark exactly like us, but we shouldn't call ourselves Christians.

The practical upshot of this means that I have to stay at the table and figure out how to love people who hold a different view of sexuality than I do, without betraying the integrity of my exegetical and theological convictions. I have to figure out how to welcome desperate refugees who don't look like me or speak my language, and also love my neighbor who believes those refugees are bringing crime and taking jobs. I have to figure out how to respond to a feral visitor in my office who begins barking at me, without barking in return. It's *so* hard to know how to love people when you're opposed to what they say or do; figuring this out takes a lot of fumbling and making mistakes and saying "sorry" and trying once again. The larger task, of course, is that as the church *we* have to figure it out, amongst ourselves, lest we betray the way of the cross. And if we don't start figuring it out, our shelf-life in this culture may be coming to an end. After all, who *out there* is going to want to join us at the table if all we're doing is barking louder than anyone else? Let Wesley have, not the last word, but a word that will encourage us to stay at the table and talk with each other graciously as we figure it out. In the conclusion to his "Farther Appeal to Men of Reason and Religion," Wesley sums up his response to opponents:

> Why do you not acknowledge the work of God? If you say, "Because you hold opinions which I cannot believe are true," I answer: believe them true or false; I will not quarrel with you about any opinion. Only see that your heart be right toward God; that you know and love the Lord Jesus Christ; that you love your neighbour; and walk as your Master walked; and I desire no more. I am sick of opinions. I am weary to bear them. My soul loathes this frothy food. Give me solid and substantial religion. Give me a humble, gentle lover of God and man; a man full of mercy and good fruits, without partiality, and without hypocrisy; a man laying himself out in the work of faith, the patience of hope, the labour of love. Let my soul be with these Christians, wheresoever they are, and whatsoever opinion they are of.[5]

5. Wesley, "Farther Appeal, Part 3," §4.10 (*Works* 11:321).

Appendix
Unconcluding Conversational Postscript

List of Characters

Helen Campbell ("Nanna") Grand Dame of the Campbell family (Bruce†)

    Campbell Children

        Robert† (Linda†)

            Daughter Claire (Jan)

        William "Bill" (Teresa, aka "Treece")

            Daughter Jesse (James)

            Son Stephen (Ian, boyfriend)

        Theodore "Ted" (Kate, aka "Deuce")

            Daughter Tilly, aka "Happy" (Benny, aka "Clappy")

            Son Samuel (Abbie, girlfriend)

        Fiona (divorced)

            Daughter Emily†

        Angus (confirmed bachelor)

Neighbors

    Chayton and Hetty

    Sanjay and Saanvi

Anticipation

"We drive five hundred miles to a family reunion that's going to be painful for all involved, and it's coming down in buckets. Perfect." Jan had the wipers on high and was still having trouble seeing through the rain. "Jeez, look at that lightning. Maybe it'll strike us all dead before we get there."

"It'll be okay. They have a big porch with a roof. We'll be fine," Claire said, not looking up from her phone. "Jesse just texted me. She and James are running a little late out of the city. Traffic's a mess."

"Great. So we're trapped on a porch with your relatives and . . . " Jan's voice trailed off as he shook his head. These family reunions were notorious for arguments about politics and religion, and usually the two topics couldn't be distinguished from each other. On the one end of the spectrum, some family members got their news from *True Christians for America. com*. Or was it *Real Patriots for Jesus.com*? Jan couldn't remember. At the other end, some were hunkered down in that fetid morass of atheism, Leftist ideology, and identity politics—the state university. And when Right and Left clashed, did the fur ever fly! Although he and Claire attended church, Jan was skeptical about religion in general and tried to avoid hot issues at these get-togethers. His main strategy at these reunions was to keep his mouth shut, and his main objective was to leave mentally and emotionally unscathed. He was already suffering from a pre-reunion headache.

"Your Uncle Bill always smells like booze," Jack said from the back seat. Jan laughed.

Claire perked up and glanced at the back seat, strewn with fast-food wrappers and electronics. "How would you know that? You haven't seen him in three years. You remember that?"

"Because Dad said."

"See? You're creating memories in him."

"Well, he does smell like booze." Jan murmured, trying to avoid potholes. "My God, don't they ever fix these roads? Hours of *bumpa-bumpa-bumpa*."

"*Well*," Claire said, mimicking Jan's voice, "we're turning out one cynical sixth-grader."

Jan glanced in the rearview mirror and smiled. "My boy."

"Daaad . . . "

"Lou, honey, I told you. We'll be there in about fifteen minutes."

"You said that an hour ago." Louise sighed, looking out the window. She was nine and not enjoying herself in the back seat.

"Yeah, well, you know the old saying: time crawls when you're going to meet relatives you don't want to see."

"I don't think that's a saying, Dad." Louise smirked and put her forehead against the cool window.

"It is now," Jan said. A peal of thunder shook the car. "That was close."

Claire sighed. Since she lost both her parents a few years ago, her Aunt Treece and Uncle Bill were the closest she had to a mom and dad, and she wanted this reunion to work out. "Okay, everybody, let's try to stay positive." Then they all saw the road sign, "Springville 17 Miles." They were almost there, and began watching for the Duckworth Road exit. The Campbell family reunion was happening that evening, rain or shine. Probably rain.

Preparations

"Bill, let's try to be civil," Treece said as she brought plates and cutlery out to the picnic tables. "Sure wish this rain would stop." The rain's steady rhythm pelted the porch's metal roof.

"I'm always civil. The problem is that some people don't like to face reality," Bill said, glancing at his smoker, which he loved more than some of his relatives. "Probably time to get the coals ready. Smoked and *grilled* meat! A victory for carnivores everywhere! 'Course, some of our tree-hugging vegan nieces and nephews probably won't think so."

"Could it have anything to do with the carcinogen-fest you're serving up?" Treece asked. Bill *hmmphed* in response. "And do you think maybe we could avoid 'reality' for a few hours?" she probed, looking hard at him. She knew her husband's moods too well. "We don't get together very often anymore; let's not ruin it with politics, okay? And you really should change your shirt before everyone gets here. By the way, you need to position that grill so the smoke won't choke us to death."

"No problem. No one's gonna choke on anything tonight, except maybe chicken bones. I've got it covered." He moved the grill right to the edge of the porch, judging where the wind would take the smoke away from the tables, then glanced down at his "Led Zeppelin US Tour 1975" shirt, stained with ashes, barbecue sauce, and various substances found by the state of California to cause cancer. "What's wrong with my shirt? It's got character. And I'm not gonna ruin anything. But if certain Libtard family members bring up issues, I'm not backing down either."

"I think you're itching for a fight."

Bill laughed and didn't say anything.

Treece was back in the kitchen when she heard a knock at the front door. She glanced through the living room and saw their next-door neighbor

Chayton with his arms full, standing on the front porch. "Come in, Chayton," she called, "and shut the door."

The big Sioux walked into the house, carrying a cooler. "Pretty soggy
out there today, Treece. Got some nice fish for the grill. Thanks for the invite. Hetty will be along shortly. Said the biscuits weren't quite ready." For
much of his life, Bill had suspicions about Native Americans and their work
habits; that is, until Chayton and Hetty moved next door. Chayton was a
veterinarian and well-known throughout the county. He also happened to
be an avid outdoorsman, and over the years he and Bill spent many days
fishing and hunting together. Chayton was the most decent man Bill knew,
but Bill never told him that. They developed that kind of punch-you-in-the-
shoulder rapport where they could call each other "Chief" and "Paleface"
and have a good laugh about it, but they knew they could never talk like that
in public. *Politically correct bullshit*, Bill called it.

Treece wiped her hands on her apron and gave him a big hug. She
hugged everybody. "Glad you both could come. Bill's out on the back porch
doing his caveman thing with meat and fire. Maybe you could get him to cut
back a little on the whiskey before everyone gets here."

"I'll see what I can do," Chayton said, and walked through the kitchen
out on to the back porch.

"Hey there, Chief," Bill looked up from the charcoal he was spreading
out on the grill. Chayton sat the cooler down on one of the tables.

"Been out on the river this week, Bill?" Chayton asked. "Fish've been
biting like crazy. Got some big 'uns to put on the grill." He picked up a fat
trout from the cooler and grinned, holding it up with both hands.

"That's a nice one. Hell no, I haven't been out for a while. And with all
this rain, the river will be out of shape for the rest of the week. Leg's been
sort of acting up again, anyway. Hey, how about some spirits to lift your
spirit? I think a certain Mr. Daniels knows exactly what you need."

"Maybe a splash, Bill. You know, you really should have that knee
looked at. Pretty amazing what they can do now."

"Ha. Yeah, you'd love to cut on me, wouldn't you!"

"Cutting on you wouldn't be any different than any other old horses I
treat, 'cept they drink less and smell better. But seriously, there wouldn't be
much cutting. Minimally invasive. Plus, Uncle Sam would take care of the
bill." Bill was retired Army Corps of Engineers.

Bill *hmmphed*. "I'll think about it." Chayton knew he wouldn't. They
clinked the whiskey glasses together.

Chayton's wife Hetty arrived shortly thereafter, carrying in enough hot
biscuits to feed half the county and fussing about her husband not helping
her. Hetty was a whitebread girl raised in the Midwest, right down to the

strawberry-blonde hair, freckles, and blue eyes, and when she and Chayton moved into the neighborhood, there was some gossip in Treece's quilting group about that "mixed couple" on Duckworth Road. And so it was that gentle Treece, friend to every stray cat and wayward child in the neighborhood, became a legend on Duckworth Road for finally losing her cool one night. Treece, whose real name was Teresa but who people sometimes called Mother Treece on account of her gentleness and hospitality, told the offending Mrs. Williams straight out to "grow up or go to hell." Those words had never before or since left Treece's lips.

Bill's younger brother Ted and his wife Kate then walked through the door. They lived only a few miles away on Duckworth Road. The younger people in the family thought it was hilarious that two of the Campbell boys had been named William (Bill) and Theodore (Ted), which proved to be an endless source of bad, retro-pop-culture jokes. There was never any doubt that Kate ruled her roost and kept Ted in line. Possessed of a rapier-like mind and tongue, few people wanted to get into a verbal fencing match with a former assistant DA. Given her ferocious courtroom style, in the early years of their marriage, Ted (also retired USACE) jokingly referred to Kate as "Ma Deuce," the nickname given to the old Browning fifty-caliber M-2 machine gun used in the First World War. The name stuck, so that only people outside the family referred to her as Kate. To family members, Kate was always "Ma Deuce," or "Aunt Deuce," or simply "Deuce." A veteran marathon runner and prosecutor, Deuce brought her long-haul mentality and tenacity to any argument she tackled, in or out of the courtroom.

Ted talked even less than Bill, and his vocabulary for the most part consisted of expletives. He communicated the whole spectrum of human emotion with a simple *goddamn* or *sonuvabitch*: amazement, disgust, agreement, resignation, you name it. Bill often joked that Ted was an artist who painted the air in expletives. What made things strange was the fact that Ted could often be heard absent-mindedly humming and half-singing under his breath church hymns he had learned growing up. He said those songs reminded him of better days, and he felt peaceful when he sang them. So he could go from cussing out those *sonzabitches* in the *guvment* to mumble-humming "A Mighty Fortress is Our God" within a few moments and without the slightest apparent inconsistency.

"Goddamn," Ted whistled when he saw the trout on the grill. "Those are big fish." Chayton shot him a crooked smile. Ted came dressed tonight in his usual formal wear: camo hat and threadbare USACE T-shirt.

"Ted," Deuce raised her eyebrows. "Language, remember? All the kids are going to be here tonight."

"Goddamn," Ted stage-whispered and winked at Chayton, who had the good sense to feign frustration at Ted's language when Deuce glanced him.

Guess Who's Not Coming to Dinner?

"So, Bill," Ted asked, "How many we got coming here tonight? I know all the kids and their kids will be here. But what about Fi and Angus?" Fiona (or Fi) was number four, and the only daughter amongst the Campbell siblings, and Angus was the youngest.

"Fi's not coming. Not surprising, I guess." Bill was poking at the meat on the grill. "Said there's gonna be to be too many fanatics and hypocrites here."

Fiona had taught Sunday school at Springville Community Church until it came to light that the Reverend Richard Enright and the Christian education director couldn't keep their pants on when they were together. Half the church wanted him out, and half wanted to keep him on the condition that he complete a "restoration" process. Both groups lobbed Bible verses at each other in support of their position and claimed that God was on their side. The social media carnage went on and on. Fiona, who had friends on both sides, was disgusted at the hypocrisy and hatred she saw in the church she had attended for years, and now wanted nothing to do with church or Christians. Since her messy divorce and the loss of her daughter Emily to an overdose, Fiona had been wrestling with questions about God for a few years, and this church scandal finally broke the Sunday school teacher's back.

Bill, who also attended Springville Community, was more philosophical than his sister when the church split. He and Treece left with the members who started a new plant a few miles down the road. Officially they were the New Community Church of Springville, but the locals all imaginatively referred to the new church as "The New Church." When he had heard the news about Pastor Enright, Bill only shrugged and said, "People are people, I guess." He never talked much about the split, but from then on always took delight in referring to the Reverend Richard Enright as "that former Pastor Dick we had."

"Goddamn, Bill. You're hardly a fanatic. A hypocrite, maybe," Ted winked at him. And then, as he rearranged some coals on one of Bill's grills, he hummed a few bars from "Praise to the Lord, the Almighty, the King of Creation."

"I think both of you are barely Christian, let alone fanatics," Deuce offered, setting down a pitcher of iced tea. "Real models of Christian virtue, you two. First Church of Cussing and Whiskey Drinking." Bill and Ted chuckled. Ted didn't attend church much anymore, but occasionally tagged along with Deuce to traditional mass at St Mary's. He jokingly referred to Deuce as his Latin lover. Most people would have been surprised to learn that he still thought of himself as a Christian, and that he even prayed occasionally.

"Anyhow," Bill continued, "Angus called last night and said he decided at the last minute not to come. Said he would come if it was just Stephen, but not if Stephen brought his 'friend.'" Stephen, Bill and Treece's son, had only recently come out as gay, and planned to bring his boyfriend to the Campbell reunion. It had been a talking point in the family for a couple of weeks.

"We kind of got into it on the phone last night. Again. Shit, Ted. He called Stephen an abomination in the sight of God and started quoting Bible verses at me, and then went off at me and Treece again, asking what kind of parents were we and all that. Nothing I haven't heard before." Among themselves, Bill, Ted, and Fiona referred to their youngest sibling Angus as "Angus the Ayatollah." If the New Church was conservative, the church Angus attended was so far to the right that it was nearly falling off the edge, which was fitting, given that a few flat-earthers attended there.

"Sonavabitch. Typical Ayatollah stuff. Sorry to hear that." Ted said, reaching for the whiskey. "Stephen's a good boy."

Bill noticed Treece listening across the table, hands on her hips. "Bill, you didn't tell me that last night. You said he couldn't get the time off."

Bill lowered his gaze. *Oh boy*, he thought. "I didn't want to upset you, honey, right before the reunion. But you know Angus. He's just being the Ayatollah."

"He's just being mean and ugly," Deuce corrected him. "I mean, there's Angus, as dishonest and greedy a businessman who's ever lived, quoting Bible verses about Stephen, one of the kindest people you'd ever meet. You tell me who'd be more likely to give a homeless Jewish preacher a welcome."

"Well, there's nothing for it, I guess. *Anyhow*," Treece said, doing her best to stay upbeat and keep the conversation on track, "all the kids and their kids will be here, plus I invited our new neighbors down the street, Sanjay and Saanvi and their kids, since they just moved to the neighborhood and hardly know anyone. So all those plus the six of us adds up to twenty-eight, I think."

"*Sandjay* and *Sandvee*?" Ted asked, intentionally mispronouncing the names. He looked at Bill. "Neighborhood's sure changing here, huh? Much different . . . complexion than it used to be. *Hindoos*, I reckon. Goddamn."

"You be *nice*," Treece said. "They're good people, Ted. Sanjay works in IT at the hospital. Their kids are having a hard time making friends in school, though."

"Imagine that. An Indian working in IT," Bill said, mock-puzzling. Deuce chucked the end of the dinner roll she had been munching on at her brother-in-law's head. "You be nice, too," she warned him. Bill ducked and laughed.

Arrivals

Over the next hour or so, a steady stream of Campbell children and grand-kids straggled in, Claire and Jan and their brood followed by assorted cousins and grandchildren. Finally, Nanna Helen, the Grand Dame of the Campbell family, made her regal and anxiety-producing entrance. Ramrod-straight, white-haired, imperious, Nanna Helen was a force of nature and old-school Scottish Presbyterianism. She was only a baby when her parents had emigrated from Scotland, and on special occasions Helen wore the Campbell plaid and a small brooch that was her mother's. Now in her late eighties, Helen recently had her driver's license taken away, and had agreed after much discussion to live with one of her granddaughters and her family.

Decades ago, when the last of the old guard at the petrified Presbyte-rian church in the area finally went to sort out Jesus, Nanna Helen held her nose and began attending the First Methodist Church of Springville, but she never really trusted those Arminians, because what was the point of listen-ing to a sermon every week and writing a tithe check if you weren't sure you were among the elect? When First Methodist started calling themselves Springville "Community" Church, she was convinced they had lost the nerve to even admit they were Methodists. And when the church scandal split the congregation, she was, of course, one of those who began to attend New Community. So for years Nanna Helen felt herself in denominational exile, sole guardian of orthodoxy, providentially ordained to worship with people who didn't know the glories of the Westminster Confession. But that was better than attending her granddaughter's charismatic church, where things were not even close to being done decently and in order. Still, her grandchildren treated her well, and she was grateful that they ushered her faithfully to Springville Community every Sunday morning. This wasn't dif-ficult for the family to work into their schedule, since the chaotic Spirit-fest they attended tragically broke from the historic tradition of the church and offered a Saturday evening service. Nanna Helen often prayed for them and their weak grasp of the faith.

"Lovely to see you all, especially my *great*-grandkids," she said, sitting down in the living room, as the little ones crowded around for hugs and sweets that magically appeared from the folds of her dress. She scanned the porch. "I don't see Fiona or Angus here."

A moment of awkward silence, and then Claire spoke up. "Well, Nanna, they . . . couldn't make it tonight."

"Couldn't make it. Hmmm. I suspect there's a lot you're not telling me. I'll let it go for now. Now who's *this*?" she motioned towards Sanjay and Saanvi. Mother Treece made the necessary introductions, after which everyone began to find a place at the tables.

"Alright everybody, we're going to sing before we eat," Mother Treece announced. Jan often puzzled at the mix of religion in this family and glanced at everyone on the porch as they made a circle and got ready to sing. Some of them attended "non-denominational" churches, which all seemed pretty vague to Jan. Then there were some harmless Methodists and Catholics, some slightly more dangerous *happy clappy* Pentecostals, Nanna in her hardline Presbyterianism-in-exile, and a black-sheep cousin in his dogmatic atheism. Jan didn't know a lot about Native American religious beliefs or Hinduism, so he didn't know what to think of Chayton and Hetty or the Indian couple he just met. If you mentally included the absent Angus (the Ayatollah) and Fiona, the former in his cantankerous Fundamentalism and the latter in her pissed-off and broken antagonism, you came up with a mixed bag.

Everyone linked hands to make a misshapen circle on the porch and Claire got them started on the doxology. Nanna Helen always insisted on the Old Hundredth, and everyone gave it their best. Almost everyone, anyway. Some of the kids giggled all the way through, and Claire's atheist cousin and his girlfriend looked at the ground without saying anything. And, surprise, surprise, Jan couldn't be sure, but it looked like Sanjay and Saanvi were trying to sing along. For a moment there was this strange, peaceful moment on the Campbell's back porch as they lurched through the hymn, accompanied by the steady rhythm of rain on the metal roof. *Such a cliché*, Jan thought, *but what the hell*. He smiled anyway and enjoyed the moment.

The Spice of Life

The Campbells knew how to eat well, so there was entirely too much food, but that's what everyone expected at these gatherings. Bill and Ted privately talked about the family in terms of two groups: the meat-eaters and "those people," and harbored suspicions about the patriotism, personal hygiene, and basic humanity of "those people." The carnivores in the family tucked into the steaming piles of flesh, while "those people" chose the veggie burgers, lentil loaf, and other vegetables pretending to be meat. Every salad combination in the history of the West appeared to be on the tables, including that monstrous green Midwestern "jello salad" that lies on your plate like alien placenta and melts when you put it next to hot food.

Ted, not normally adventurous when it came to food, was working his way down the line of dishes laid out, humming a line or two from "O Sacred Head Now Wounded." Jan overheard him, nearly laughed out loud, and thought, *This guy's so weird*. Ted carefully avoided those dishes that looked like a mix of beans, stems, and flowers. *Fucking hippies*, he thought, and mainly chose foods that had parents. He had nearly filled his plate when he smelled and poked at a dish at the end of the line. It was a curry that Sanjay and Saanvi brought. Ted put a glop of it on his plate next to a grilled chop and found a seat at one of the tables next to the *Hindoos*.

"You folks brought this?" he asked.

"It's a mild curry. Something we thought most people's palate could tolerate," Saanvi smiled.

"Go ahead, Ted," Sanjay said. "Try it. Tell us what you think."

Ted took a bite and after a moment felt the combination of ginger, turmeric, and chili powder do its work on his throat. "Goddamn," he said. "That's hot. But, you know, that's really good." He grinned at Saanvi.

"So," he said to Sanjay, "you don't sound . . . Indian." Ted always felt uncomfortable when he had to make small talk."

"Not by nationality. I was born in San Diego. My dad was stationed there."

"Stationed?"

"Yup. Thirty-Second Street Naval."

"Your Dad was a Navy man? US Navy? Goddamn." Ted laughed softly to himself.

"Saanvi's from India," Sanjay continued. "We met when I was back in Varanasi visiting family. She's a new orthopedic surgeon at St. Mark's." Saanvi smiled at him.

"Orthopedic surgeon? Goddamn. You should talk to Bill about his knee."

Saanvi raised her eyebrows and tilted her head a little. "Bill doesn't seem like the kind of guy who wants to talk about his knee."

"Oh, he's rough, but okay once you get to know him. Bit like me." Ted winked at her. Saanvi wasn't sure she could get past the rough bit any time soon.

South America Calling

At another table, Bill and Treece were catching up with their daughter Jesse and her husband. Bill enjoyed winding them up. He always thought it was hilarious that Jesse had married a man named James, and never tired of cracking "wild, wild west" and Robert Ford jokes. After Bill joshed them, asking if they were still running from "lawdogs," Jesse and Treece exchanged a few glances when Bill started to turn serious and made a few cracks in front of James about "big government." James, who lived a life of quiet desperation working at a soul-killing post in the EPA, wasn't taking the bait, grunting half-hearted "uh-huhs" when Bill delivered one of his standard lectures on how all those damned regulations were killing this country.

Bill eventually turned his attention to Jesse. "How are things in that liberal love-fest you call a church these days? Hiring any tree-hugging pagans yet?" He thought he was being clever and good-natured.

"Dad, there's nothing wrong with taking care of the planet. And things are going quite well at the church, thank you very much. I'm working with community outreach a couple days every week, and we're sending a relief team next month to Chile to help with the rebuilding effort after the quake." Jesse could read her Dad's mood and had resolved to do her best to stay off politics. Bill had different ideas.

"Hey, I'm all for taking care of the planet. But I don't think you social justice eco-warriors have thought things through very well."

"Bill," Treece said in a soft voice, looking at him. James took a deep breath and closed his eyes for a moment. *Oh shit. Here we go*, he thought.

"Oh, I'm sure *you've* thought it through, Dad. That's why you've got that enormous new truck parked out back."

"Ha-ha! You saw that, did you? Four hundred horses under the hood! What a deal I got, Jesse! Three thousand in trade for the old Ford! And I bet I'll use less fuel in that new truck over the next year than what it costs to send one person on your relief team back and forth to Chile. So I'm contributing even less than you people to all that nonexistent climate change you keep yapping about."

"And I'll bet you *don't* use less fuel. But the point, Dad, is that they're going down there to help people." As soon as she said it, Jesse realized that she had taken the bait.

"Like I don't help people around here with my truck? Ask Chayton about what I did last spring when his people got flooded. And you mean to tell me there aren't any people in Chile with basic construction skills? You have to fly people all the way down there to lay concrete blocks and put up drywall? We've got lots of people right here in this country who need help, you know."

"Bill," Treece said again softly, raising her eyebrows.

"I'm just saying that you don't need to go halfway around the world to help people, that's all."

"Look Dad, can we agree that people here *and* in Chile need help? And by the way, the team down there rebuilding the school campus could use someone with engineering experience. Remember Tim Witzouski? The skinny redhead on St. Stephen's softball team? He's going to supervise the work."

"What?" Bill put his fork down and screwed up his face like he was in pain. "Wit's a moron. Wouldn't know his ass from a hole in the ground. Especially in South America. Hey, Ted, you hear that? Tim Wit's goin' to South America to head up the rebuild on a school campus."

Ted looked up from the next table over and said between mouthfuls: "Wit? Goddamn. He'll burn the place down."

"You know," Jesse mused, "it's not too late to join their team. I'm sure they'd welcome two engineers. You could put all your experience to good use down there. *Helping people*, remember? Better than sitting on your asses every day up here, complaining about the government. Or Tim could do the work, I suppose."

"You're really going to use that strategy on me? Next thing I know, you'll be telling me to think of the children down there," Bill half-laughed, as he watched his own grandkids running circles around the porch, exulting in mayhem as his dog, barking, chased them. Bill hadn't been abroad for years, and no one knew it, but he secretly hankered to travel again.

"South America, huh? Guess I could think about it. But only because I can't stand the thought of that idiot doing the work. Hey, Ted," he called over to another table, "you wanna go to South America with me?" Ted laughed to himself and swore softly.

"Dad, you can be played so easily when you think someone is going to screw up a project." Jesse laughed and Bill snorted. He had to hand it to Jesse, though. Chalk one up for the social justice warrior in the family.

Not in Front of the Company

Sanjay and Saanvi were both going up for seconds when they ran into Ted's daughter Tilly and her husband Benny. Known in the family as Happy and Clappy, Tilly and Benny attended Falling Fire Pentecostal Fellowship, and didn't hide their charismatic religion under a bushel at the reunion. After making small talk with Sanjay and Saanvi about the trials of settling into a new neighborhood, Saanvi mentioned how her children were having a rough time adjusting in the local school.

"You know, our church runs a private school." Benny said. "It's smaller and feels more like a family. Maybe your kids would have an easier time of it there than in the public school."

Saanvi smiled but felt uneasy. "That's very nice of you, but . . . you know . . . we're not Christian, so I don't know how comfortable our kids would feel."

"Oh, there wouldn't be any pressure." Tilly said, "We're only trying to provide an environment that's healthier than what you find in secular schools. What the kids are exposed to in public schools is horrible." Saanvi believed Tilly was sincere, but most likely wrong about the lack of pressure to become Christian.

"But isn't there a lot of Bible reading and lessons about your religion?" Saanvi asked.

"Well, it *is* a Christian school, so the curriculum is based on the Bible." Now it was Benny's turn to feel uncomfortable. It suddenly dawned on him that he didn't know anything about Hinduism, and here he was about to explain a Bible-based curriculum to a Hindu.

"I don't really know what you mean, like how their subjects are based on the Bible," Sanjay said. "Don't the students study things like math and science and history?"

Benny tried to give a couple of examples to clear things up. "Yeah, but from a Christian perspective. So they study science based on what the Bible says and they study American history from what our founding fathers had in mind."

"Science based on what the Bible says? Don't they study science based on what . . . scientists say?" Sanjay asked. He glanced at Saanvi, who was hoping her husband would be tactful. Making new friends can be so tricky.

"What *Christian* scientists say," Benny said.

Saanvi was still puzzled. "I'm still not sure what you mean. Is that different from what non-Christian scientists say?"

"Sometimes it is. Like when we talk about the creation of the world. Christian scientists don't believe in evolution or that the world is billions of years old." Benny realized he was verging on controversial topics, but didn't know how to stop, and began recalling Bible verses to bolster his courage. Years of Bible quizzing as a child had given him a formidable arsenal, and now he had the opportunity to be a witness to a young couple imprisoned in an idolatrous religion.

Claire, overhearing snippets of the conversation as she went back to the table for coffee, wasn't happy over the picture of Christianity that Benny was painting for Saanvi. A biologist by training, Claire had clashed with her cousin's husband several times over this issue.

"Look, I couldn't help but overhearing, Ben." Claire said. "Lots of Christian scientists would disagree with what you just said. Including me."

Benny shot her a look that fairly pleaded, *Please don't screw up my chance to witness*. Claire, ignoring the desperate look in his eyes, instead said quietly, "Saanvi, you *can* be a Christian and not hold to those ideas."

"A liberal Christian," Benny said, in a flat voice. *I need to speak the truth in love*, he thought.

Jan had come up beside Claire and caught the last bit of the exchange between the two cousins. *Oh boy*, he thought. *We need to stay off this topic*. "Hey guys, you know, maybe we shouldn't have this discussion in front of our new friends," he said, motioning towards Sanjay and Saanvi. "Do we really want to keep talking about religion at a family reunion?"

But Sanjay, always the inquisitive one, said: "You don't need to feel uncomfortable in front of us. I think it's okay to disagree about religious things. We call our religion the *eternal teaching*, so who can figure out all the details of what's eternal? God is greater than our thinking."

"I can agree with that." Benny said, nodding. "But you do believe some definite things, right?"

Sanjay nodded. "Sure, sure. Every religion has things you have to believe to be a part of it, I suppose."

Benny continued, "That's all I'm trying to say. Our school is based on some definite Christian beliefs. But the thing is, some people who call themselves Christians want to cut corners on those things." He looked at Claire. Jan was thinking, *For God's sake, can we stay away from religion*?

Against her hopes for this reunion, Claire was getting drawn into a discussion that she preferred to not have, especially in front of new friends. But she couldn't let Benny's comment pass. "Ben, I think that's really unfair. I mean, what are you saying? That we're not real Christians? We say the Creed and pray the Lord's Prayer and take Holy Eucharist. We sure do all the things that Christians do."

Benny laughed a little. "And you think that's what makes someone a Christian? Lots of people do all those things and still don't have a relationship with Christ." Ben got as close as he could to calling Claire's tradition a sham, without actually crossing the line and getting personal.

Sanjay appeared to be enjoying this. A former member of the debate team at his university, he had never lost his love for spirited discussion.

Things were different for Benny. He was inwardly worried that his witness to Sanjay was being hampered by his wife's liberal cousin.

"I don't think 'having a relationship with Christ' gives you the right to judge other Christians who disagree with you," Claire said. Jan knew Claire wasn't going to back down. He loved his wife, but he was thinking *My God, can't anyone in this family ever just drop anything?*

"And I think that being a Christian means more than being tolerant," Benny shot back. *Speaking the truth in love*, he thought again.

Sanjay pressed the issue. "But, Benny, being tolerant *is* a good thing when it comes to religion, right? Look at the fighting over religious differences. Muslims, Christians, and Hindus have killed each other for centuries. And for what?"

"I'm not suggesting anything even close to violence," Benny said to him. "But, with all due respect to your beliefs, being a Christian does mean that I believe Jesus is Lord. That Jesus is God." As he said that aloud, he was inwardly reciting, *Whosoever shall confess me before men. . .*

Claire and Sanjay spoke at the same time in response. Claire stared squarely at Benny and said simply, "We believe that too, Ben," while Sanjay asked, "So that means God isn't found in any other religion?" Jan and Saanvi traded knowing glances and shook their heads. Saanvi was hoping Sanjay wasn't blowing their chances at making friends in a new neighborhood. Jan was hoping for a quick exit, but reckoned he was stuck there.

The conversation attracted the attention of Tilly (Benny's wife), who moved closer but didn't say anything. Chayton, who wasn't a Christian, also perked up from the next table when he heard the last exchange. He was all-too aware of what white Christian settlers had done in the story of his people, and through the years had grown suspicious about conservative Christians talking about other religions.

"Wait," Claire continued, closing her eyes and shaking her head. "We confess the same basic things about Jesus that you do. Ben, we do. But you seem to be suggesting that, to be *real* Christians, we'd have to agree with you on those other things you mentioned? That doesn't seem fair. I mean, who appointed your church to be the guardian of what it means to be Christian?"

"I didn't say that," Benny said. "I'm just saying our church keeps closer to the Bible, if that's important you. We interpret it literally. It's about honoring God's word, Claire."

"And *I'm* just saying that your way of interpreting the Bible doesn't necessarily mean that you're 'closer' to it than anyone else," Claire countered. "Last year I was reading Nadia Evans, and she said the Bible . . . " Claire stopped mid-sentence when Benny shook his head from side to side, signalling his disapproval.

"What? What's wrong with her?" *Oh my god*, she thought, *it's always something with this guy.*

"She embodies most things I disagree with. For her, it's all loosy-goosy interpretation. You know what I mean. Questions rather than answers, peace and justice and the environment rather than the gospel, tolerance instead of truth. Claire, we need to be people of the truth and support people who preach the truth."

Sanjay had been waiting to get back into the conversation, only now he felt genuinely confused. "Benny, I thought asking questions and being tolerant of each other were good things. And shouldn't we all want peace and justice? I don't know a lot about Christianity, but didn't Jesus teach about peacemaking and loving your enemies?"

Benny was getting irritated, but tried not to show it. "Sanjay, yes, of course we should love each other. But it's more complicated than that."

Sanjay plowed ahead with his questions. "I'm also not sure what you were implying when you said that Jesus was God, as though that means no other religion has God? Think about Hindus, Buddhists, Muslims, Jews. None of them knows God? Maybe Jesus is in some way God, but God can still be *more* than Jesus, can't he? Isn't He everywhere and in everything?" Chayton, from his place at the table across the porch, liked where this was going. He picked up his coffee and moved to sit closer to the conversation.

Benny scratched his beard and looked around. He was fumbling now and he knew it. "I don't know that I would put it exactly like that, Sanjay. I mean, the Bible says that Jesus is the only way. And I choose to believe that."

"But every religion claims that it knows God. That it has the answer," Claire interjected. "All kinds of sacred books make those claims. Simply choosing to believe a claim doesn't make it true."

Benny lowered his voice. "The Bible is God's word, Claire. We have to decide what we're going to stand on."

"You don't see the problem with that answer?" Claire asked. "I have good questions. Sanjay has good questions. And your response is little more than *the Bible says*, as though that settles the issue, when you know lots of churches don't interpret the Bible like you do."

"We don't interpret it, Claire. We really don't. We just read it and believe it." *You are so blind*, Ben thought.

"Lots of churches say the same thing. And still there are thousands of denominations. Why?" *I can't believe he doesn't get this*, Claire thought.

"So what are you saying, Claire. That nobody's right? That all interpretations are equally true? You believe what you believe and I believe what I believe and it's all good? That's relativism. Surrendering to the world's values, pure and simple."

"That's not what I'm saying at all. I'm saying that maybe we should concentrate on the big issues we *can* agree on, and agree to disagree about minor issues. Because if it's all or nothing, Ben, then we're going to forever divide amongst ourselves. And these family reunions? We're always going to be walking on eggshells, tiptoeing around religion." Jan, at least, thought there was nothing wrong with a good tip-toeing, and would have gladly tip-toed into the next county at this point. The very thing he didn't want to happen at reunion was happening.

"Okay, Claire, I'll play along. So how do *you* know what those beliefs are that we should agree on? I mean, what's important to *your* church might not be important to my church and vice-versa." Benny was sure he had backed her into a corner.

"I'm not a theology expert, Ben. I suppose, ideally, we could study what different churches believe and find out what they have in common."

"Snooze fest," Ben snickered, shaking his head. "Plus, we'd have to slog through a lot of dangerous teaching and heresy."

Claire ignored the comment and continued. "Okay, then maybe the best place to start is *here*, with all of us keeping the conversation going and trying to learn from each other and giving each other the benefit of the doubt. I can't imagine we're going to be able to work through this without coming to trust each other. Maybe we could even visit each other's churches when we get the chance."

Sanjay's imagination was bubbling. "It's like if I asked you to compare Indian food to American food, and all you did was read Indian recipes. How could you compare? You have to experience it." Then Saanvi finally dared to speak up. "Were you there when Ted tried the curry we brought? If he didn't try it, how he could say he liked it or not?"

Benny looked skeptical, but Claire saw Saanvi's point, and added: "Right. It can't be just about describing what we believe. It's too easy to kid ourselves. On a deeper level it's about the way we live our lives day in and day out. You know, Ben, I'll bet we have more in common than what you imagine."

"I don't know," Benny said. "I mean, I'd be happy if you and Jan visited our church, or any Spirit-filled, Bible-believing church, for that matter. But I don't see us sitting through a dead service in a church that doesn't believe the Bible, and—frankly—I don't see what I have to learn from you."

"I get it. No one can force you. But then you *have* made a decision about how you want things to be between us. I'm not sure how you can square that with Sanjay's comment about Jesus and peacemaking and every-thing, but I guess you'll have to answer to God like we finally all will."

"I have to stand on the truth, Claire," Benny said softly. "I can't compromise on truth because someone's feeling might be hurt."

"Well, this isn't about feelings," Claire said. "At least not the way I see it. It's about not thinking you have someone else all figured out before you take the trouble to get to know them. It's about listening instead of shutting people down because you have a lock on the truth."

Benny was getting frustrated with this conversation. *What is wrong with this woman?* he thought. "Look, Claire, even if I did agree with what you're saying, how far do you want to extend this little experiment of yours? I mean, should we say, 'Oh, let's get a little taste of other religions. Let's learn about God from Muslims and try worshiping at a Hindu temple'?"

"I'm not saying there aren't boundaries, Ben. I mean, if Sanjay and Saanvi came for a visit at our church, we wouldn't expect them—and I don't think they would expect—to take Holy Communion. I'd want them to get to know us—inside the church, outside the church. To become friends. I think that's the only way."

"I'm still not convinced, Claire. I'll have to think about it," Benny said. He didn't plan to think about it.

"That's all I'm asking," Claire said.

Convictions

Ted's son Sam eventually sat down across from him. Sam had brought his girlfriend Abbie with him to the reunion. Both graduate students at the state university, Sam was studying physics while Abbie was immersed in an arcane and angry branch of cultural studies, replete with subjects that had descriptors like "post-Marxist" and "postcolonial," wholly impenetrable to those outside that academic tribe. Somewhere along the line, Sam had become a fervent evangelical atheist, and never lost an opportunity to berate the family members who were religious. It was difficult to know how much of Sam's atheism stemmed from his studies and circle of friends at university and how much of it was a reaction against his religious upbringing. Fashionable, self-confident, and unhindered by the slightest trace of self-awareness, Sam and Abbie were the only ones to have shown up at the party without bringing any food, and looked sheepish when they realized their faux-pas.

When they had first arrived at the reunion, Deuce scrutinized them as they stood there in the doorway furiously texting and ignoring everyone in the room, and thought about saying something, but decided it wasn't worth it. *Kids*, she thought. She loved her son, and knew he was regarded as a genius at university— or at least he thought he was—but she wondered when his emotional maturity would catch up to his intellect. Sam's girlfriend was still an unknown quantity, but Deuce thought Abbie must genuinely love Sam to put up with his rants.

Sam and his Dad were always a volatile combination when they got together, and Abbie had heard enough tales to already feel uncomfortable. Abbie, one of "those people" Bill and Ted joked about, had picked her way carefully through the various dishes on the tables, loading her plate so as to announce to the world her disagreement with the Slaughter, as she called it. She sat down next to Sam and her potential father-in-law. Ted glanced at Abbie's T-shirt, which had RESIST emblazoned across the front.

"Resist," he grunted with his mouth full. "What's that? Some new band I never heard of?"

Abbie hemmed and hawed, unsure of how to respond. *This damned shirt*, she thought. She hadn't considered her choice of attire, and because she still hadn't figured out her place in the family, didn't know how much she could get away with when she opened her mouth. "It's like . . . It's kind of an activist thing." She picked at a quinoa something-or-other on her plate and hoped Ted wouldn't continue down this path. Sam had a feeling he knew what was coming.

"Okay," Ted said, between mouthfuls of pulled pork. "But resist what?"

"You know. Like authority. Like we should question authority."

"All authority?" Ted asked, not looking up from his plate. "Just because it's . . . authority?"

"He's *army*, remember," Sam said, making a face and glancing sideways at Abbie.

"I think we should, like, be sure the government's telling the truth, that's all." She threw the comment out nonchalantly and adjusted her glasses on her nose, trying to cover her nervousness.

"You don't trust the government," Ted said. Abbie couldn't tell if he was making a statement or asking a question.

"I mean, you know, the whole military-industrial thing," Abbie said.

Ted stopped chewing and looked her. "Goddamn." Abbie didn't know how to interpret that, either. She was feeling mental paralysis starting to set in.

"Words, Ted. Use words," Deuce said. Sam and Abbie didn't realize Deuce had been standing behind them at the table, listening. Sam thought his father was a right-wing dinosaur with a limited vocabulary and fairly easy to outmaneuver in a conversation, but he didn't want Abbie to tangle with his mom.

Ted took a breath and tried to collect his thoughts. "Well, Abbie, I worked for that military-industrial complex, and . . . "

Sam cut him off. "And what, Dad? It put food on the table and put me through college? And if we don't like it, we should move to Canada?"

"Sam, stop," Abbie nudged him, before Deuce had a chance to object.

Ted put his knife and fork down and looked straight at Sam. "Nope. Jesus, Sam. What's gotten into you? You're such a know-it-all anymore. I was gonna say that I was part of that complex thing for years, and—goddamn— I have my own questions, sure. Everyone knows the *guvment's* full of ass-wipes. But, Abbie, do you believe everything they tell you at the university?"

She didn't meet Ted's gaze. "Well, no. Not, like, everything." *Jesus*, she thought, *this is turning into an inquisition.*

"Alright, then. So we both don't trust the *guvment* or the university. So I guess we're both okay." Abbie would have been fine to let the matter drop right there.

"That's too easy," Sam smirked. "It's not simply about all of us mis-trusting the government or the university. We've gotta be specific, Dad. *You* don't trust *the Left* because you're sure there's some kind of grand conspiracy they're planning. They want to . . . do what? Take your guns away? Use tax dollars to help people murder babies? Weaken the military and take Amer-ica down a notch? *We* don't trust *the Right* because too many of them are puppets to Big Business, push through policies that favor the top 1 percent, and turn a blind eye to racism and environmental problems whenever it becomes inconvenient for them."

Deuce sat down at the table next to Ted, and trained that fearless gaze of hers on her son. "So now that you've drawn a line in the sand, Sam—not that anyone here actually needed to see it—what do you expect us to do? Have everyone on the Right sit *here* and everyone on the Left sit over *there*? Not talk to each other? Have everyone complain about everyone on their car rides home? Bitch about each other on social media? What do you ex-pect us to do here? Why do you have to do this every damned time we get together?"

"We should be able to talk openly about our differences," Sam said, sitting up straight but looking down at his plate.

"We should. Yeah, we should. But we're family, Sam. We're going to be family no matter who's in office, whether there's another economic melt-down or natural disaster, or if World War III starts. We pull together."

"Mrs. Campbell," Abbie interjected, "I'm sorry I started this. I didn't know, like, how to explain myself and it was kind of, like, diarrhea of the mouth." She tried to laugh a little.

Deuce, eyes softening, looked at her. "It's okay, Abbie. This is par for the course when Sam and his dad get together, I'm afraid."

This conversation was starting to attract a crowd. Sanjay was leaning forward in his chair, looking at the floor but listening carefully. Most of the cousins felt apprehensive. Bill had slouched back in his lawn chair and played with the label on his bottle.

"You *can* love your country and still have your questions. I do," Ted offered.

"Maybe I shouldn't say this," Sanjay offered, hesitated, and then: "But my parents came to this country because of the opportunities it had and what it stood for." Saanvi also wasn't sure her husband shouldn't have said that. She and Sanjay were new to the Campbells, and she didn't want to be seen taking sides in an internecine family war.

"Loving your country doesn't really have anything to do with anything," Sam protested, and ignored Sanjay's comment. "The whole topic is a distraction. The real question in this country today is who's looking at reality and who's persisting in a fantasy. Reality won't bend to any stupid idea we happen to have. It's a matter of what is actually the case, not what we hope or want it to be."

Deuce took a deep breath. "All of that may be true, Sam, but you act like you somehow have direct access to reality, while anyone who disagrees with you doesn't. I wish you could see how much like your Uncle Angus you are. He does this with his interpretation of the Bible, and you do it with your faith in science. Sam, I don't know. You may or may not see reality more clearly than the rest of us, but we're never going to get closer by drawing battle lines. These things are going to take time. We might find agreement in some places, and we might come up empty in others. I don't know. But we're never going to get closer like this."

"Mom, all you're saying is that we should be *nice*. I expect more from you. I've *seen* you in a courtroom." Deuce had a reputation. "You know, we go round and round on the same things. Over and over and we never get anywhere, year after year." You could hear the frustration in his voice.

Deuce spread her hands out in front of her, palms up. "Where would you like us to *get*? That we'd finally all think alike on everything? Really? That's what you want? You think that could actually happen?"

"But that's what Dad and Uncle Bill and a few other people here want, only on the Right side of things," Sam said, poking his finger a few times on the tabletop for emphasis.

"Goddamn," Ted said, shaking his head in disagreement.

"That's bullshit, Sam," Bill said, crossing his arms and staring hard at his nephew. "Your dad and I have been around a while. We know we're not gonna change you, because people don't change very often, or very much when they do. I think you're full of shit about a lot of things, and I know you think the same thing about me. But I also know that, in this country, you've got the right to be wrong!" he laughed.

"I know you're a smart guy, Sam," Bill continued, "but, you've gotta understand this. The Lord has blessed this family with so much. We're all thankful for what we've been through and for each time we can all be together. Your Dad and me, you know, we're rough old sons a' bitches. But we know we've been blessed, even if we don't talk about it much. So when we get together we gotta try to find a way to get along. Unless you don't want to. No one can force you, that's for damned sure."

"God. God again, Uncle Bill?" Sam sighed, shaking his head. "That's not simply a throwaway line you use to sound pious? Seriously? You think God underwrites everything in this family? That he's blessed us? With all the shit that's happened to us?" At this, a few people at the tables exchanged glances, as if to say, *Brace yourselves, a theology storm is coming.*

"Nothing more than what's happened to any other family," Treece offered. Deuce continued Treece's line of thought. "Everybody goes through tough times, Sam. That doesn't mean God doesn't exist, or doesn't care."

Sam dismissed these comments, brushing them aside in the air with his hand. "Aunt Treece, I wouldn't expect you to say anything different." Sam realized that came out more rudely than what he had intended, yet he plowed on, scarcely taking a breath. "But *Mom*, you should know better. You always taught us to weigh evidence for and against a claim. So, like I've asked you all a thousand times, where's the evidence for this God?"

Sanjay waded in once more. "In our religion we say that God is like salt dissolved in water. If you taste the water and someone says 'bring me the salt,' you can't, because it's completely dissolved. God is so close to each of us, it's not easy to come up with proof that takes what we experience out of the picture."

Most of the Christians around the table weren't sure if this was a good response or not. Jan thought maybe it wasn't. But Ben and Tilly, charismatics who emphasized having a "personal relationship with Jesus" and the "baptism in the Holy Spirit," were big on experiential religion, and wondered, surprisingly, if in Sanjay they had an ally of sorts in this conversation.

"Sanjay, I don't know you, and I'm trying not to be rude, but you can prove anything by personal experience. Everything from alien abductions to Jesus appearing in a tortilla."

"God is a mystery," Sanjay protested. "Just because we can't fully explain something doesn't mean it's not real." Sanjay, who had advanced degrees in computer science, didn't know a whole lot about physics, but he also didn't believe that scientists had the universe and the deepest questions of existence completely figured out.

"Ah, mystery," Sam chuckled, "religion's convenient default position when it can't answer questions. Sanjay, with all due respect, *mystery* is obfuscation. You know, I think this is really something," he said in a mock-hurt voice. "Everybody—Christians and Hindus both—seems lined up against poor old Sam. When *you* people"—he motioned to Sanjay and Benny—"otherwise wouldn't agree on anything. Once again I guess it's fallen to me to be the sole voice of reason in this family." Sam relished his self-appointed role as the perpetual outsider.

It was Tilly's turn to offer a few thoughts of her own, knowing that Sam would likely dismiss her simply because she was his big sister. "You're a scientist, Sam, and you're always going on about wanting evidence, but what kind of evidence would you accept? That all of our problems would disappear and God would write, 'Hey everybody, I exist!' in the sky? That everything would be great all the time? It's not that straightforward when it comes to God. *That* God's a heavenly Santa Claus."

"Oh, come on, Tilly!" Sam chuckled, not bothering to hide his scorn. "How many times as kids did we listen to Uncle Angus drone on about how he never saw the righteous forsaken? No, I don't think that if God existed, everything would be okay. But some things would be different, surely. At least the people who claimed that he talked to them every day would be different, for Christ's sake!" Sam's tongue was looser than normal tonight. Abbie and a few other people wondered if he had tipped back a few too many.

Sam turned to his cousin Stephen, sitting nearby with his boyfriend Ian, who had been quiet during most of the evening. "You know why that good, Bible-believing uncle of ours didn't come today, Stephen? Can you guess?"

"Uncle Angus refused to come because of me?" Stephen asked. Angus the Ayatollah, who was never afraid to pass judgment, and whose own children had left the church, the family, and the state entirely, once told Bill and Ted that he couldn't decide which of their sons was worse. Bill's son Stephen was gay, while Ted's son Sam was straight but had become an atheist and now had a live-in girlfriend who was a socialist, didn't shave her legs, and probably practiced yoga. Angus figured regular hell was too good for people like that.

"I'm so sorry," Ian said. "I'm the one who shouldn't have come."

"No, no," several of the nieces and nephews said, nearly in unison, shaking their heads. "Uncle Angus has issues," Claire said. Jan snorted, "He just a bigot."

"No, he's not 'just a bigot,'" Nanna said. "He happens to believe very strongly some things that the Bible says. It's an abomination for a man to lie with another man."

"Nanna, those verses . . . ," Stephen sighed, shaking his head. Ian, uncomfortable, looked away.

"I know, I know, Stephen," Nanna Helen continued. "I know people have different ways to get around verses like that. But you can't write off your Uncle Angus because he has the courage to live up to his convictions. He also doesn't like your Uncle Ted's bad language, and I happen to agree with him on that." She fixed Ted in her gaze. "You shan't take the name of the Lord your God in vain. That's what the Bible says, Theodore." Ted adjusted his hat and tried to not look at his mother.

"See?" Sam said. "That's what I'm saying. Uncle Angus lives up to his 'convictions.' *Convictions*? Convictions like refusing to see his own family? With no evidence whatsoever backing it up, religion makes people nuts. It gives you a license to condemn anyone who sees things differently than you do, all in the name of pleasing some spirit in the sky or obeying an ancient book." Abbie put her hand on Sam's forearm, hoping he would stop for the sake of family harmony. She had more commonsense than he did.

"Think about it." Sam said, shifting to full jackass mode. "All the years we spent in church. Aunt Fiona doesn't want to have anything to do with us anymore. Uncle Angus, a complete fundamentalist asshole. Religious convictions!" He laughed.

For Jan, this was too much. He thought of himself as a Christian, but even if he didn't have all the theology worked out, he knew what he *wasn't*. He took a deep breath and tried to find the right words. "Sam, if you're going to judge us all based on what Angus is like, then I guess none of us have a chance with you. But we're all here trying to make it work despite our disagreements. And I'll bet that you don't want us to judge all atheists based on how you've been talking to the family tonight. You know, it really is possible that God exists, but that the people who claim to follow him are good at screwing up."

"Yeah, yeah. Christians aren't perfect, just forgiven. I've heard it all before. Nice theology for religious hypocrites to hide behind." Jan scowled at Sam's comment. He knew people back at his own little church whom he would never accuse of hypocrisy, plus he knew that hypocrisy was hardly the exclusive province of religious people. He thought about saying something more, but kept his mouth shut. *It's not worth it, and it wouldn't change a thing,* he thought.

Claire, not wishing to get dragged into this conversation as well, had remained silent, hoping that Sam would eventually drop the subject or that an earthquake would happen or that the Four Horsemen of the Apocalypse would crash the party. None of that was happening. So she jumped in. "Sam, I'm not going to say that I never act like a hypocrite. We all know each other here. But I think that most of us believe that, however badly we might try to describe it, and however badly we might try to live it out, God is love, and that should make some difference—it does make *some* difference—in the way we lead our lives. Sam, it would be easy for us to say to hell with these get-togethers, and to hell with people like you, who just want to divide us. But we don't want to do that. Loving people is hard, Sam, even those people who see things the same way as you do. But loving those people who see things much differently than you do, that's damned difficult."

"Claire, I wish I could believe that you Christians were serious about that. But from where I stand, you have little evidence to believe that a God even exists, and that, even if he did, there's very little connection between what you say you believe about him and the way Christians behave."

Claire took a deep breath. "Sam, it seems like this never ends with you. We run through this script every time we get together. We think there *is* evidence, only not the kind you'll accept, and we're trying to live out what we believe as best we can. And you shoot us down on both counts. I don't know. Is there anything left for us to talk about? Should we even try to get together anymore if you're constantly on the attack? Are we really all that confused or stupid? What do you want to do, Sam?" At this point, all eyes were on Sam.

"I dunno, either," Sam mumbled. He, too, seemed tired from the conversation. "Maybe for me there isn't a point in coming to these reunions anymore." He looked at Abbie, and they both wandered off to an empty table. Abbie was on the verge of tears.

It took some time for normality to return, people talking quietly in corners, nibbling on apple pie and blueberry crumble. The rain had almost stopped. The tense conversation hadn't affected the kids, who continued to terrorize their elders with squirt guns, water balloons, and the occasional frog. After a few minutes, Jesse noticed that Sam and Abbie had made their way to the door. She managed to disentangle herself from a passel of kids wanting her attention, walked up and caught her cousin's sleeve.

Jesse did her best with the conversational tatters left over. "Are you guys leaving? Look, I wanted to say before you take off . . . Sam, whatever problems you have with us, we still love you and don't want you to cut yourself off from us. We don't . . . none of us here . . . have all the answers to the questions you have, but we can still try to keep loving each other and listening. And Abbie, you're always welcome to come. Maybe next time things will be a little more peaceful." Abbie smiled and looked at Sam, who didn't say anything. They slipped out the door before anyone else came up to say goodbye.

Shall We Meet on That Beautiful Shore?

The conversations around the tables continued long into the night. After a few hours, people sensed that their time together was drawing to a close and began clearing the tables. But the final curtain couldn't come down before the traditional Campbell closing. Treece whipped out her harmonica and played a bit of the *Star Wars* theme music to warm up, which made all the kids laugh. Bill broke out his banjo and Ted began tuning his ukulele. They were ready to play. And Nanna Helen, in that quavering voice that had raised the rafters in the church for years, long before the Methodists lost their nerve and started calling themselves a "community church," started in on "In the Sweet Bye and Bye." Ted would continue humming the tune long after the party ended.

Bibliography

Alexander, Denis R. "Models for Relating Science and Religion." *Faraday Paper* 3 (2007) 1–4. https://faraday-institute.org/resources/Faraday%20Papers/Faraday%20Paper %203%20Alexander_EN.pdf.

Ankerberg, John, and John Weldon. *Ready with an Answer: For the Tough Questions about God.* Eugene, OR: Harvest, 1997.

Baggini, Julian. "The Articles of 21st-century Faith." *The Guardian,* November 21, 2011. http://www.theguardian.com/commentisfree/belief/2011/nov/21/articles-of-21st-century-faith.

———. "Atheists, Please Read My Heathen Manifesto." *The Guardian,* March 25, 2012. https://www.theguardian.com/commentisfree/2012/mar/25/atheists-please-read-heathen-manifesto.

———. "Give Me a Reasonable Believer Over an Uncompromising Atheist Any Day." *The Guardian,* March 15, 2012. http://www.theguardian.com/commentisfree/belief/2012/mar/15/believer-atheist-coalition-reasonable.

———. "Science is Independent of Humanism, Atheism and Religion." *The Guardian,* October 21, 2011. http://www.theguardian.com/commentisfree/belief/2011/oct/21/science-atheism-humanism-religion.

———. *What's It All About? Philosophy and the Meaning of Life.* New York: Oxford University Press, 2004.

———. "Yes, Life Without God Can Be Bleak: Atheism Is About Facing Up To That." *The Guardian,* March 9, 2012. http://www.theguardian.com/commentisfree/2012/mar/09/life-without-god-bleak-atheism.

Barton, John. "The New Atheism: Reflections of a Biblical Scholar." *Modern Believing* 53 (2012) 34–47.

Beardsley, Monroe. "Metaphor." In *The Encyclopedia of Philosophy,* 284–89. New York: MacMillan, 1972.

Bell, Rob. *What We Talk About When We Talk About God.* New York: HarperOne, 2014.

Bevere, John. *Good Or God? Why Good Without God Isn't Enough.* Palmer Lake, CO: Messenger International, 2015.

Blomberg, Craig. "Jesus, Sinners, and Table Fellowship." *Bulletin for Biblical Research* 19 (2009) 35–62.

The Book of Discipline (Vinaya Pitaka): Volume IV (Mahavagga). Translated by I. B. Horner. Lancaster: Pali Text Society, 2007.

Braaten, Carl E. "The Resurrection Debate Revisited." *Pro Ecclesia* 8.2 (1999) 147–58.

Buddharakkhita, Acharya, trans. "Kakacupama Sutta: The Parable of the Saw." https:// www.accesstoinsight.org/tipitaka/mn/mn.021x.budd.html.

Calvin, John. *Institutes of the Christian Religion, Vol. 1.* Edited by John T. McNeill. Translated by Ford Lewis Battles. Philadelphia: Westminster, 1960.

Canons and Decrees of the Council of Trent. Translated by H. J. Schroeder. St. Louis: Herder, 1941.

Cantacuzino, Marina. *The Forgiveness Project: Stories for a Vengeful Age.* London: Kingsley, 2015.

Caputo, John D. *What Would Jesus Deconstruct? The Good News of Postmodernism for the Church.* Grand Rapids, MI: Baker, 2008.

Catechism of the Catholic Church: With Modifications from the Editio Typica. New York: Doubleday, 1994.

Cavanaugh, William T. *The Myth of Religious Violence: Secular Ideology and the Roots of Modern Conflict.* Oxford: Oxford University Press, 2009.

Chesterton, G. K. *Orthodoxy.* New York: Hodder & Stoughton, 1996.

Chilton, Bruce, and J. I. H. MacDonald. *Jesus and the Ethics of the Kingdom.* Grand Rapids, MI: Eerdmans, 1987.

Clendenin, Daniel B. *Many Gods, Many Lords: Christianity Encounters World Religions.* Grand Rapids, MI: Baker, 1996.

Cobb, John, Jr. *Beyond Dialogue: Toward a Mutual Transformation of Christianity and Buddhism.* Philadelphia: Fortress, 1982.

———. *The Emptying God: A Buddhist-Jewish-Christian Conversation.* Maryknoll, NY: Orbis, 1990.

Collins, Francis. *The Language of God.* New York: Free, 2006.

"A Confession of Faith in a Time of Crisis." http://www.reclaimingjesus.org/.

Confucius. *The Analects of Confucius.* Translated by D. C. Lau. New York: Dorset, 1979.

Cramer, John A. "Miracles and David Hume." *Perspectives on Science and Christian Faith* 40 (1988) 131–37. https://www.asa3.org/ASA/PSCF/1988/PSCF9-88Cramer. html.

Damascene, Hieromonk. *Christ the Eternal Tao.* 4th ed. Platina, CA: Herman, 2004.

Davidson, Randall T., ed. *The Lambeth Conferences of 1867, 1878, and 1888: with the Official Reports and Resolutions, Together with the Sermons Preached at the Conferences.* London: SPCK, 1889.

Dawkins, Richard. *A Devil's Chaplain: Reflections on Hope, Lies, Science and Love.* New York: Houghton Mifflin, 2003.

———. *The God Delusion.* Wilmington, MA: Mariner, 2008.

D'Costa, Gavin. "The Impossibility of a Pluralist View of Religions." *Religious Studies* 32.2 (1996) 223–32.

de Botton, Alain. "Alain de Botton's 10 Commandments for Atheists." *Telegraph,* February 4, 2013. http://www.telegraph.co.uk/culture/9843244/Alain-de-Bottons-10-Commandments-for-Atheists.html.

———. *The Consolations of Philosophy.* New York: Vintage, 2001.

———. *Religion for Atheists: A Non-Believer's Guide to the Uses of Religion.* New York: Vintage, 2013.

Debroy, Bibek, trans. *The Valmiki Ramayana.* Volume 3. Gurgaon, India: Penguin Random House, 2017.

Derrida, Jacques. *Dissemination.* Chicago: University of Chicago Press, 1983.

———. *Margins of Philosophy.* Chicago: University of Chicago Press, 1985.

The Dhammapada. Translated by Irving Babbitt. New York: New Directions, 1965.

The Episcopal Church of America. "An Agreement of Full Communion—Called to Common Mission." https://www.episcopalchurch.org/page/agreement-full-communion-called-common-mission.

Epstein, Greg. *Good Without God: What a Billion Non-Religious People Do Believe.* New York: Morrow, 2015.

Erickson, Millard. *Christian Theology, Vol. 1.* Grand Rapids, MI: Baker, 1983.

Faith & Leadership. "Phyllis Tickle: Like An Anthill." *Faith and Leadership*, August 30, 2010. https://www.faithandleadership.com/multimedia/phyllis-tickle-anthill.

Falcon, Ted, et al. *Getting to the Heart of Interfaith: The Eye-Opening, Hope-Filled Friendship of a Pastor, a Rabbi & an Imam.* Nashville, TN: SkyLight Paths, 2009.

Felderhof, Marius C. "Evil: Theodicy or Resistance?" *Scottish Journal of Theology* 57 (2004) 397–412.

Fletcher, John. *Zelotes and Honestus Reconciled: or, The Second Part of an Equal Check to Pharisaism & Antinomianism: Being the First Part of the Scripture-Scales . . . In The Works of the Reverend John Fletcher, Vol. 2.* Salem, OH: Schmul, 1974.

"Formula of Concord—Solid Declaration." In *The Book of Concord: The Confessions of the Evangelical Lutheran Church,* edited by Theodore G. Tappert, 501–636. Philadelphia: Fortress, 1959.

Gadamer, Hans-Georg. *Truth and Method.* New York: Crossroad, 1986.

Gierach, John. *Death, Taxes, and Leaky Waders: A John Gierach Fly-Fishing Treasury.* New York: Simon & Schuster, 2001.

Gray, John. "Can Religion Tell Us More Than Science?" *BBC News Magazine*, September 16, 2011. http://www.bbc.com/news/magazine-14944470.

———. "The Child-Like Faith in Reason." *BBC News Magazine*, July 18, 2014. http://www.bbc.com/news/magazine-28341562.

———. "The Closed Mind of Richard Dawkins." *The New Republic*, October 2, 2014. http://www.newrepublic.com/article/119596/appetite-wonder-review-closed-mind-richard-dawkins.

———. *Straw Dogs: Thoughts on Humans and Other Animals.* New York: Farrar, Straus & Giroux, 2007.

———. "What Scares the New Atheists." *The Guardian*, March 3, 2015. https://www.theguardian.com/world/2015/mar/03/what-scares-the-new-atheists.

Guinness, Os. *Fools Talk: Recovering the Art of Christian Persuasion.* Downers Grove, IL: InterVarsity, 2015.

Gyatso, Kelsang. "How Do Buddhists View Other Religions?" https://www.youtube.com/watch?v=GMkeXq9IuFs.

Habermas, Jürgen. *Communication and the Evolution of Society.* Translated by Thomas McCarthy. Portsmouth, NH: Heinemann, 1979.

Harris, Sam. *The End of Faith: Religion, Terror and the Future of Reason.* New York: Norton, 2004.

———. "The Problem with Atheism." *SamHarris.org*, October 2, 2007. https://samharris.org/the-problem-with-atheism/.

Heim, S. Mark. *The Depth of the Riches: A Trinitarian Theology of Religious Ends.* Grand Rapids, MI: Eerdmans, 2001.

———. "The Pluralism of Religious Ends: Dreams Fulfilled." *Christian Century* 118 (January 17, 2001) 14–19.

————. "A Trinitarian View of Religious Pluralism." *Christian Century* 118 (January 24, 2001) 14–18.

Hick, John. "Is Christianity the Only True Religion, or One Among Others?" http://www.johnhick.org.uk/article2.html.

Himmelfarb, Gertrude. "The Christian University: A Call to Counterrevolution." *First Things* 59 (1996). https://www.firstthings.com/article/1996/01/the-christian-university-a-call-to-counterrevolution.

Hitchens, Christopher. *God is Not Great: How Religion Poisons Everything.* New York: Twelve, 2009.

Hobson, Theo. "Richard Dawkins Has Lost: Meet the New New Atheists." *The Spectator*, April 13, 2013. http://www.spectator.co.uk/features/8885481/after-the-new-atheism/.

Hodge, Geoffrey Lee. "Advancing the Atheist Movement: Dawkins, Dennett and the Second Wave." *The Humanist*, June 19, 2015. http://thehumanist.com/commentary/advancing-the-atheist-movement-dawkins-dennett-and-the-second-wave.

Hollinger, Dennis. "The Church as Apologetic: A Sociology of Knowledge Perspective." In *Christian Apologetics in the Postmodern World*, edited by Timothy R. Phillips and Dennis L. Ockholm, 192–203. Downers Grove, IL: InterVarsity, 1995.

Horkheimer, Max. *Eclipse of Reason.* Eastford, CT: Martino, 2013.

Horsch, John. *Menno Simons, His Life, Labors and Teachings.* Scottdale, PA: Mennonite, 1916.

Horst, Steven. "Miracles and Two Accounts of Scientific Laws." *Zygon* 49 (2014) 323–47.

Hume, David. *An Inquiry Concerning Human Understanding.* New York: Bobbs-Merrill, 1955.

Jaki, Stanley L. *Miracles and Physics.* Front Royal, VA: Christendom, 2004.

Jayatilleke, K. N. *The Buddhist Attitude Towards Other Religions.* Kandy, Sri Lanka: Buddhist Publication Society, 1975.

Jenkins, Philip. *The Next Christendom: The Coming of Global Christianity.* 3rd ed. Oxford: Oxford University Press, 2002.

Jenson, Robert W. "The Risen Prophet." In *God and Jesus: Theological Reflections for Christian-Muslim Dialogue*, 57–67. Minneapolis: American Lutheran Church, 1986.

————. *Systematic Theology, Volume 1: The Triune God.* Oxford: Oxford University Press, 1997.

Johnson, Allan G. *Power, Privilege, and Difference.* 2nd ed. New York: McGraw-Hill, 2005.

Jones, Gregory L. "What's the Future of Denominations?" *Faith and Leadership*, January 18, 2010. https://www.faithandleadership.com/whats-future-denominations.

Juergensmeyer, Mark. *Terror in the Mind of God: The Global Rise of Religious Violence.* 3rd ed. Los Angeles: University of California Press, 2003.

Kärkkäinen, Veli-Matti. *Trinity and Religious Pluralism: The Doctrine of the Trinity in Christian Religions.* Farnham, UK: Ashgate, 2004.

Keenan, John P. *The Meaning of Christ: A Mahayana Christology.* Maryknoll, NY: Orbis, 1989.

Kirby, Alan. *Digimodernism: How New Technologies Dismantle the Postmodern and Reconfigure the Culture.* New York: Continuum, 2009.

Knitter, Paul F. *Introducing Theologies of Religion.* Maryknoll, NY: Orbis, 2002.

———. *Without Buddha I Could Not Be a Christian.* London: Oneworld, 2009.

Kramer, Hendrik. *The Christian Message in a Non-Christian World.* Grand Rapids, MI: Kregel, 1961.

Kreeft, Peter. *Between Allah and Jesus: What Christians Can Learn From Muslims.* Downers Grove, IL: InterVarsity, 2010.

Küng, Hans. *Theology for the Third Millennium: An Ecumenical View.* Translated by Peter Heinegg. New York: Doubleday, 1988.

Levinas, Emmanuel. *Ethics and Infinity: Conversations with Philippe Nemo.* Translated by Richard A. Cohen. Pittsburgh: Duquesne University Press, 1985.

———. *Totality and Infinity: An Essay on Exteriority.* Translated by Alphonso Lingis. Pittsburgh: Duquesne University Press, 1969.

Lindbeck, George A. *The Nature of Doctrine: Religion and Theology in a Postliberal Age.* Philadelphia: Westminster, 1984.

Lipka, Michael. "A Closer Look at America's Rapidly Growing Religious 'Nones.'" *Pew Research Center,* May 13, 2015. http://www.pewresearch.org/fact-tank/2015/05/13/a-closer-look-at-americas-rapidly-growing-religious-nones/.

Louis, Ard. "Miracles and Science: The Long Shadow of David Hume." *Biologos.org,* June 1, 2010. https://biologos.org/files/modules/louis_scholarly_essay.pdf.

Luther, Martin. *Luther's Works.* Vol. 27, *Lectures on Galatians (1535) Chapters 5–6; Lectures on Galatians (1519) Chapters 1–6.* Edited by Jaroslav Pelikan. St. Louis: Concordia, 1964.

———. *Luther's Works.* Vol. 37, *Word and Sacrament III.* Edited by Robert H. Fischer. Philadelphia: Muhlenberg, 1961.

———. *Luther's Works.* Vol. 41, *Church and Ministry.* Edited by Eric Gritsch. Philadelphia: Fortress, 1966.

Lutheran World Federation and the Catholic Church. "Joint Declaration on the Doctrine of Justification." http://www.vatican.va/roman_curia/pontifical_councils/chrstuni/documents/rc_pc_chrstuni_doc_31101999_cath-luth-joint-declaration_en.html.

Lyotard, Jean Francois. *The Postmodern Condition: A Report on Knowledge.* Translated by Geoff Bennington and Brian Massumi. Minneapolis: University of Minnesota Press, 1984.

Maddox, Randy L. "Wesley and the Question of Truth or Salvation Through Other Religions." *Wesleyan Theological Journal* 27 (1992) 7–29.

Martinson, Paul Varo. *Families of Faith: An Introduction to World Religions for Christians.* Philadelphia: Fortress, 1999.

"The Martyrdom of Polycarp." In *Documents of the Christian Church,* edited by Henry Bettenson, 9–12. 2nd ed. New York: Oxford University Press, 1963.

McCabe, Herbert. *Faith Within Reason.* New York: Continuum, 2007.

McConnell, Kilian. "A Trinitarian Theology of the Holy Spirit." *Theological Studies* 46 (1985) 191–227.

McGrath, Alister E. *Why God Won't Go Away.* Nashville, TN: Nelson, 2010.

McIntyre, Alisdair. *Whose Justice? Which Rationality?* South Bend, IN: University of Notre Dame, 1988.

McLaren, Brian D. "Denominations Do Invaluable Things." *Faith and Leadership,* January 18, 2010. https://www.faithandleadership.com/brian-d-mclaren-denominations-do-invaluable-things.

————. *Naked Spirituality: A Life with God in 12 Simple Words*. New York: HarperOne, 2011.

Meadows, Philip R. "'Candidates for Heaven': Wesleyan Resources for a Theology of Religions." *Wesleyan Theological Journal* 35 (2000) 99–129.

Miller, Vincent. *Consuming Religion: Christian Faith and Practice in a Consumer Culture*. New York: Bloomsbury, 2005.

Mouw, Richard J. *Uncommon Decency: Christian Civility in an Uncivil World*. Downers Grove, IL: Intervarsity, 1992.

Moyaert, Marianne. "Postliberalism, Religious Diversity, and Interreligious Dialogue: A Critical Analysis of George Lindbeck's Fiduciary Interests." *Journal of Ecumenical Studies* 47 (2012) 64–86.

Muck, Terry. "Theology of Religions After Knitter and Hick: Beyond the Paradigm." *Interpretation* 61 (2007) 7–22.

Murashko, Alex. "EXCLUSIVE Rick Warren: 'Flat Out Wrong' That Muslims, Christians View God the Same." *Christian Post*, March 2, 2012. https://www.christianpost.com/news/exclusive-rick-warren-flat-out-wrong-that-muslims-christians-view-god-the-same.html.

Newman, John Henry. *Fifteen Sermons Preached Before the University of Oxford*. London: Longmans, Green & Co., 1918.

Olson, Roger E. *The Mosaic of Christian Belief: Twenty Centuries of Unity and Diversity*. Downers Grove, IL: InterVarsity, 2002.

————. "Reflections and Questions About the Word 'Denomination.'" *Patheos* (blog), May 22, 2016. http://www.patheos.com/blogs/rogereolson/2016/05/reflections-and-questions-about-the-word-denomination/.

————. "Why I Like Denominations." *Patheos* (blog), October 11, 2012. http://www.patheos.com/blogs/rogereolson/2012/10/why-i-like-denominations/.

Pannenberg, Wolfhart. *Jesus—God and Man*. Translated by Lewis L. Wilkins and Duane A. Priebe. Philadelphia: Westminster, 1968.

————. "The Religions from the Perspective of Christian Theology." *Modern Theology* 9 (1993) 285–97.

————. *Systematic Theology*. Translated by Geoffrey Bromiley. 3 vols. Grand Rapids, MI: Eerdmans, 1991–98.

Paul VI. "Dignitas Humanae." http://www.vatican.va/archive/hist_councils/ii_vatican_council/documents/vat-ii_decl_19651207_dignitatis-humanae_en.html.

Pew Research Center. "'Nones' on the Rise." October 12, 2012. http://www.pewforum.org/2012/10/09/nones-on-the-rise/.

Plantinga, Alvin. "What is 'Intervention'?" *Theology and Science* 6 (2008) 369–401.

Prothero, Stephen. *God is Not One: The Eight Rival Religions That Run the World— and Why Their Differences Matter*. New York: HarperOne, 2010.

————. *Religious Literacy: What Every American Needs to Know—and Doesn't*. New York: HarperOne, 2008.

Rahner, Karl. *Theological Investigations*. Vol. 6, *Concerning Vatican Council II*. Translated by Karl H. and Boniface Kruger. London: Darton, Longman, & Todd, 1969.

————. *Theological Investigations*. Vol. 10, *Writings of 1965–67 2*. Translated by David Bourke. New York: Herder & Herder, 1973.

Ricci, Matteo. *The True Meaning of the Lord of Heaven*. Translated by Douglas Lancashire and Peter Hu Kuo-chen. Chestnut Hill, MA: Jesuit Sources, 2016.

Rotman, Andy. "Buddhism and Hospitality: Expecting the Unexpected and Acting Virtuously." In *Hosting the Stranger: Between Religions*, edited by Richard Kearney and James Taylor, 115–22. New York: Continuum, 2011.

Sangharakshita. "The Buddha's Noble Eightfold Path: Lecture 48: Reason and Emotion in the Spiritual Life: Right Resolve." http://www.freebuddhistaudio.com/texts/lecturetexts/048_Right_Resolve.pdf.

Schroeder, Gerald. *The Hidden Face of God: Science Reveals the Ultimate Truth.* New York: Free, 2002.

Sennett, James F. "Bare Bones Inclusivism and the Implications of Romans 1:20." *Evangelical Quarterly* 77 (2005) 309–13.

Shermer, Michael. "How to Convince Someone When Facts Fail." *Scientific American*, January 1, 2017. https://www.scientificamerican.com/article/how-to-convince-someone-when-facts-fail/.

Smith, Huston. *The World's Religions: Our Great Wisdom Traditions.* San Francisco: HarperSanFrancisco, 1991.

Smith, James K. A. *The Fall of Interpretation: Philosophical Foundations for a Creational Hermeneutics.* Downers Grove, IL: InterVarsity, 2000.

Spener, Philip Jacob. *Pia Desideria.* Translated by Theodore G. Tappert. Philadelphia: Fortress, 1964.

Spitzer, Richard. *New Proofs for the Existence of God: Contributions of Contemporary Physics and Philosophy.* Grand Rapids, MI: Eerdmans, 2010.

Spufford, Francis. *Unapologetic: Why, Despite Everything, Christianity Can Still Make Surprising Emotional Sense.* New York: HarperOne, 2014.

Stedman, Chris. "Why This Atheist Still Needs His Former Pastor." *Huffington Post*, May 1, 2012. http://www.huffingtonpost.com/chris-stedman/why-this-atheist-still-ne_b_1308171.html.

Steiner, George. *Errata: An Examined Life.* New Haven, CT: Yale University Press, 1997.

Stetzer, Ed. "Membership Matters: 3 Reasons for Church Membership." *The Exchange with Ed Stetzer* (blog), July 7, 2015. http://www.christianitytoday.com/ed stetzer/2015/july/membership-matters-3-reasons-for-church-membership.html.

The Talmud: Selected Writings. Translated by Ben Zion Bokser. New York: Paulist, 1989.

Tennent, Timothy C. *Christianity at the Religious Roundtable: Evangelicalism in Conversation with Hinduism, Buddhism and Islam.* Grand Rapids, MI: Baker, 2002.

———. *Theology in the Context of World Christianity.* Grand Rapids, MI: Zondervan, 2007.

Tickle, Phyllis. *Emergence Christianity: What It Is, Where It Is Going, and Why It Matters.* Grand Rapids, MI: Baker, 2012.

———. *The Great Emergence: How Christianity is Changing and Why.* Grand Rapids, MI: Baker, 2012.

Torrance, T. F. *Theological Science.* Oxford: Oxford University Press, 1969.

———. *Trinitarian Faith: The Evangelical Theology of the Ancient Catholic Faith.* Edinburgh: T. & T. Clark, 1988.

Turkle, Sherry. *Reclaiming Conversation: The Power of Talk in a Digital Age.* New York: Penguin, 2015.

Volf, Miroslav. *After Our Likeness: The Church as the Image of the Trinity.* Grand Rapids, MI: Eerdmans, 1998.

———. *Allah: A Christian Response.* New York: HarperOne, 2011.

Wainwright, Geoffrey. *Doxology: The Praise of God in Worship, Doctrine and Life*. New York: Oxford University Press, 1980.

Welker, Michael. *God the Spirit*. Translated by John F. Hoffmeyer. Philadelphia: Fortress, 1994.

Wesley, John. *The Letters of the Reverend John Wesley, A.M, Vol. 3*. Edited by John Telford. London: Epworth, 1931.

———. *The Works of John Wesley*. Vol. 1, *Sermons 1*. Edited by Albert C. Outler. Bicentennial ed. Nashville, TN: Abingdon, 1984.

———. *The Works of John Wesley*. Vol. 2, *Sermons 2*. Edited by Albert C. Outler. Bicentennial ed. Nashville, TN: Abingdon, 1984.

———. *The Works of John Wesley*. Vol. 3, *Sermons 3*. Edited by Albert C. Outler. Bicentennial ed. Nashville, TN: Abingdon, 1986.

———. *The Works of John Wesley*. Vol. 4, *Sermons 4*. Edited by Albert C. Outler. Bicentennial ed. Nashville, TN: Abingdon, 1987.

———. *The Works of John Wesley*. Vol. 10, *Letters, Essays, Dialogs and Addresses*. Edited by Thomas Jackson. Grand Rapids, MI: Zondervan, 1958.

———. *The Works of John Wesley*. Vol. 11, *The Appeals to Men of Reason and Religion and Certain Related Open Letters*. Edited by Gerald B. Cragg. Oxford ed. Oxford: Clarendon, 1975.

———. *The Works of John Wesley*. Vol. 13, *Doctrinal and Controversial Treatises 2*. Edited by Paul Wesley Chilcote and Kenneth J. Collins. Bicentennial ed. Nashville, TN: Abingdon, 2013.

———. *The Works of John Wesley*. Vol. 26, *Letters 2, 1740–1755*. Edited by Frank Baker. Oxford ed. Oxford: Clarendon, 1982.

Wildman, Wesley J. "The Divine Action Project, 1988–2003." *Theology and Science* 2.1 (2004) 31–75.

World Council of Churches. *Confessing the One Faith: An Ecumenical Explication of the Apostolic Faith as it is Confessed in the Nicene-Constantinopolitan Creed (381)*. 2nd ed. Geneva: World Council of Churches, 1991.

Yong, Amos. "'As the Spirit Gives Utterance . . .'; Pentecost, Intra-Christian Ecumenism, and the Wider *Oekumene*." *International Review of Mission* 92 (2003) 299–314.

———. "A Heart Strangely Warmed on the Middle Way: The Wesleyan Witness in a Pluralistic World." *Wesleyan Theological Journal* 35 (2000) 99–129.

———. "The Holy Spirit and the World Religions: On the Christian Discernment of Spirit(s) 'After' Buddhism." *Buddhist Christian Studies* 24 (2004) 191–207.

———. "A P(new)matological Paradigm for Christian Mission in a Religiously Plural World." *Missiology: An International Review* 33.2 (2005) 175–91.

———. *Renewing Christian Theology: Systematics for a Global Christianity*. Waco, TX: Baylor University Press, 2014.

———. "The Spirit of Hospitality: Pentecostal Perspectives towards a Performative Theology of Religious Encounter." *Missiology: An International Review* 35.1 (2007) 55–73.

———. "The Turn to Pneumatology in Christian Theology of Religions: Conduit or Detour?" *Journal of Ecumenical Studies* 35 (1998) 437–54.

Yutang, Lin. *The Importance of Living*. New York: Day, 1937.

Author Index